C. Cheshire

Dec.? 1814.

THE MIRACLES OF THE
NEW TESTAMENT

WORKS BY THE SAME AUTHOR

Price 6s net
HISTORY, AUTHORITY,
THEOLOGY

Price 5s net
ST PAUL AND CHRISTIANITY

LONDON: JOHN MURRAY
ALBEMARLE STREET, W.

THE MIRACLES OF THE NEW TESTAMENT

BEING THE MOORHOUSE LECTURES FOR 1914
DELIVERED IN S. PAUL'S CATHEDRAL
MELBOURNE

BY ARTHUR C. HEADLAM, D.D.

PROFESSOR OF DOGMATIC THEOLOGY IN KING'S COLLEGE, LONDON
SOMETIME FELLOW OF ALL SOULS COLLEGE, OXFORD
AND PRINCIPAL OF KING'S COLLEGE, LONDON

LONDON
JOHN MURRAY, ALBEMARLE STREET, W.
1914

BT
97
.H43
1914

All Rights Reserved.

CONDITIONS OF THE LECTURESHIP

[Extract from the Minutes of the Chapter of S. Paul's Cathedral, Melbourne.]

MOORHOUSE LECTURESHIP

1. THIS lectureship shall be called the Moorhouse Lectureship, in memory of the Australian episcopate of the Right Rev. James Moorhouse, D.D., S. John's College, Cambridge, Bishop of Melbourne, 1876-1886.

2. The annual income of the lectureship shall be the interest upon a sum of £2000[1] held in trust by the Trusts Corporation of the Diocese of Melbourne for this purpose.

3. No lecturer shall hold the office more than twice, and at least ten years shall elapse between the first and second tenure. Any one in Holy Orders in the Church of England at home or abroad, or in a Church in communion with her, shall be eligible for election.

4. The electors shall be the Bishops of the metropolitan sees of Australia and Tasmania and the Primate of New Zealand; and the Archbishop of Melbourne shall hold the office of chairman.

5. The subjects of the lecture shall be (1) the defence and confirmation of the Christian faith as declared in the Apostles' and Nicene Creeds; (2) questions bearing upon the history and authority of the Holy Scriptures of the Old and New Testaments; and (3) the social aspects of the Christian faith in their widest application.

[1] A further sum of £1000 has been added to this endowment by Bishop Moorhouse, with a view to the occasional appointment of a distinguished English scholar, and to cover the cost of travelling to Australia.

6. The Lectures, not less than six in number, shall be delivered annually in S. Paul's Cathedral, Melbourne, on such days as the Archbishop of Melbourne may approve. Each lecturer shall be required to publish his lectures in a form approved by the electors at his charges within six months of their delivery, and shall retain any copyright in them. He shall present a copy to each of the electors, and to every Diocesan Library in Australia, Tasmania, and New Zealand.

7. It shall be lawful for a majority of the electors to decide all questions arising out of the interpretation of these conditions.

PREFACE

OF the following lectures Nos. I.-V., VIII., IX. were delivered in S. Paul's Cathedral, Melbourne, in my position as Moorhouse Lecturer. No. VI. was delivered in the chapter-house at Ballarat; No. VII. in the chapter-house at Melbourne as a special lecture to the clergy. Several of the lectures were repeated at Sydney and Brisbane, and again during my return journey in Japan, at Kyoto in the Doshisha, a university connected with the Congregational Church, at Tokyo, and at the theological college of Ikebukouro to the summer school of Catechists.

The Moorhouse Lectureship was founded by the present Archbishop of Melbourne to commemorate the episcopate in Melbourne of Dr Moorhouse, afterwards Bishop of Manchester, to whose intellectual ability and strong character the Church of England in Australia owes so much. Bishop Moorhouse himself added a further endowment, the interest of which was to accumulate so as to allow from time to time the appointment of a lecturer from England.

It is to this provision and to the kindness of
the present Archbishop of Melbourne that I
am indebted for the privilege of delivering these
lectures, and for the opportunity thus given me
of becoming acquainted with the work of the
Church in Australia, with missionary problems
in Japan and Corea, and with the magnificent
accomplishments and still greater responsibilities
of the British Empire in many parts of the
world. I hope that my journey may have been
not without profit to the Church in Australia;
it has certainly been of immense value to myself,
for it has given me an insight (which otherwise
I could never have hoped to obtain) into
problems of religion and civilization of very
varied kinds in Australasia and the Far East.
The existence of such an endowment as the
Moorhouse Lectures, and in particular the wise
provision of Bishop Moorhouse himself, are
calculated to be of great value both to the
Church in the colonies and the Church at home.

My task was set for me. I was particularly
requested to lecture on the subject of Miracles;
and that relieves me of any responsibility I might
have had in attacking so difficult and important
a problem. The problem of miracles presses
very heavily on many minds at the present day,
and presents some of the most difficult and
important questions with which theology has
to deal. I can only hope that no imperfection

of treatment on my part will weaken the strength
of the case I have to present. For I cannot
help feeling that there are many signs that old-
fashioned dogmatic beliefs are passing away.
Science is ceasing to attempt to bind us to
a hard mechanical theory of nature. It is
gradually being recognized how untenable are the
conclusions which criticism once claimed to be
assured. The mathematical conception of a
Deity whom man has created in his own image
is making way for a fuller realization of what is
implied in the idea of a Personal God. The
difference in quality between the evidence for
miracles of the New Testament and that for
other similar phenomena makes the deductions of
Comparative Religion untenable. But although
these changes are taking place in contemporary
thought, it is only slowly that this becomes
realized, and many are still hampered by old-
fashioned views of God, or Nature, or the Bible.
I can only hope once more that no imperfection
of statement on my part will prevent the importance of these changes from being realized.

After I had left England, and just about the
time that these lectures were being delivered, a
controversy broke out in the Church which
touched some of the questions raised in the
following pages. I do not think that in the
course of it any new arguments or aspects of the
subject were presented. I have not therefore

attempted, except in one or two footnotes, to
refer to it. I felt it better to leave my argument
to stand as it was originally written. Although
it does not approach the question of miracles
exactly in the same manner as it has since been
raised, I do not think that any point will be
found to have been passed over.[1]

It remains for me to express my thanks to
all those to whom I have been indebted for
help, and who have read in whole or in part
the proofs of these lectures ; especially to my
colleagues at King's College, Dr Caldecott,
Dr Nairne, Dr White, Mr Matthews, and Mr
Box ; and, on the scientific side, Professor
Jackson, Professor Halliburton, and Professor
Barkla, now Professor of Natural Philosophy
at Edinburgh. They have all been ungrudging
in the help they have given me, and have saved
me from many serious errors. I need not say
that they are not in any way responsible for
what I have said, nor does the assistance they
have given me necessarily imply adherence to my
argument. In some cases they have definitely
expressed their disagreement, and in many they
have helped me much by their friendly criticism.
I owe a special debt to my former secretary, the
Rev. Claude Jenkins, now librarian at Lambeth,
who has read the whole work in proof and

[1] I have discussed the subject in this, its latest aspect, in
the *Church Quarterly Review* for October 1914.

corrected it with the greatest care ; and to my
old friend Dr Brightman, to whom I am indebted
for similar assistance when working at the
Epistle to the Romans, who has also read all
the proofs. He is a determined foe to all sloven-
liness of expression, and has done his best to
correct my many imperfections.

A further debt of gratitude is due to the
many kind hosts and hostesses who entertained
me during my wanderings. The hospitality was
too constant and the numbers too great for me
to attempt to mention their names. I can only
assure them all of my gratitude, and of the kindly
remembrances that I have of them. These
lectures will always serve to remind me of friends
in many different parts of the world, and of
many different religious communities ; of our
fellow - countrymen in Australia with their
loyalty to the memories and religion of their
old homes; and of the keen and earnest Christians
of Japan, so eager to learn all that European
thought can give, and arduously working with
much of the old *Samurai* spirit to build up the
religion and morality of their country.

A. C. H.

Whorlton, 12th Sept. 1914.

CONTENTS

xiii

LECTURE III

MIRACLES AND GOD

LECTURE IV

THE RESULTS OF CRITICISM

LECTURE V

THE EVIDENCE FOR MIRACLES

LECTURE VI

THE RESURRECTION

LECTURE VII

THE VIRGIN BIRTH

LECTURE VIII

EXPLANATIONS OF MIRACLES

LECTURE IX

THE NATURE OF MIRACLES

THE MIRACLES OF THE NEW TESTAMENT

LECTURE I

THE HISTORY OF CRITICISM

Scope of the Problem. The Teaching of the New Testament. The Patristic Period — Origen and Celsus. Apollonius of Tyana. S. Augustine and S. Thomas Aquinas. Spinoza. The English Deists—Woolston, Middleton, Hume, Butler, Paley. German Criticism— Paulus, Schleiermacher, Strauss. Modern Treatises— 'Supernatural Religion,' Matthew Arnold, Huxley, Harnack.

It is the purpose of these lectures to investigate the questions raised in our minds by the word "miracles," and in particular the miracles of the New Testament. I do not propose to begin by defining the word—a definition should come at the end of a discussion, not at the beginning. I would prefer to state the problem in a broader way ; for in investigating miracles we are approaching what is fundamental.

The civilized world at the present time con-

A

sists of nations either nominally or really Christian, and our modern civilization may be not incorrectly called Christian. This civilization is at present confined to Christian countries, or those that have come under Christian influence; and the proposition is at any rate tenable that it is the creation of that higher ideal of life which Christianity has inspired, and that it is not improbable that civilization will be unable to endure if its source of inspiration be taken away.[1] Other religions coming into contact with Christianity either dwindle away or are transformed, with the possible exception of Mahomedanism, which appears to be the antithesis of what we call civilization. None of them have shewn any power either of creating or of maintaining such a civilization as we now enjoy, for this appeals for its existence to individual self-sacrifice.

Now this Christianity, as held and preached by the great mass of its adherents, by whatever name they call themselves—Catholic, Protestant, Orthodox—claims to be the revelation of the Son of God, who came into the world and in

---

[1] The old civilization of Japan which has now passed away must be classified with pre-Christian civilizations like those of Greece and Rome. Its new civilization is a definite imitation of Christian civilization, and it is an interesting question how far it can be maintained and preserved apart from the religious, moral, and philosophic principles that created that which it has copied.

the person of Jesus the Christ took upon Him our human nature, and thus revealed to us the true nature of God and the true destiny of man. The beginnings of this religion are described to us as a series of historical events, many of them miraculous in character. Jesus is represented as revealing Himself and the purpose of His Ministry through the miracles that He worked, and in particular we are told that after His Crucifixion He rose again from the dead, and that His Resurrection it was that finally convinced His disciples of the reality of His Mission, and inspired them to be preachers and evangelists of His Gospel.

Our problem is : Did these events happen ? Their reality has been contested. It has been maintained that they are impossible, that they are relics of a superstitious and unscientific age, and that therefore Christianity itself is either untrue or only true in a relative sense ; while the miraculous events which have been supposed to be amongst its main credentials are one of the chief reasons for disbelieving it. We have, in fact, to decide between three main propositions. It may be maintained that Christianity is not true, and that the stories attached to its origin are as valueless as the myths of the Greek, Roman, or Indian religions ; or it may be held that while Christianity presents true teaching on spiritual or moral questions, the miraculous events accompanying it are an accidental and

unfortunate addition which must be eliminated ;
or again it may be held that the Christian
religion is a true revelation of what is divine,
that the miracles accompanying it are historical,
and testify that it is in its origin not of this
world.

I propose in the present lecture to begin by
examining the teaching of the New Testament
on miracles, and then to review the history of
opinion on the subject. This historical method
of treatment will enable us to see exactly the
difficulties that have been raised, and the
questions to which we must address ourselves.

I

The New Testament teaching on miracles
may be summed up in the words of S. Peter in
the Acts: " Jesus of Nazareth, a man approved
of God unto you by mighty works and wonders
and signs, which God did by him in the midst
of you, even as ye yourselves know."[1]   This
passage contains the three words used habitually in the New Testament to describe what we
usually designate as miracles. They are, τέρατα
" wonders," σημεῖα " signs," and δυνάμεις " powers "
or " mighty works." To these we must add in
S. John's Gospel, ἔργα " works." Often two of

[1] Acts ii. 22.

these words are combined, and in some cases, as in the passage already quoted, three of them.

The term "wonders" expresses occurrences marvellous in their character such as arouse wonder in the beholder. Often we are particularly told that this was the effect of our Lord's actions. It is pointed out as characteristic of the New Testament that this term is never used alone, but only in connexion with others. We read of 'signs and powers,' of 'signs and wonders,' of 'powers and wonders,' but not of 'wonders' alone. And we may echo the remark of Archbishop Trench that it is unfortunate that the word habitually used in English "miracle," as in German "Wunder," should be one that emphasizes the abnormal character of the events without any accompanying spiritual and ethical associations such as are always present in the Gospels.

By the use of the word 'sign,' the purpose and significance of the act is insisted on. It is definitely implied that such acts are to be looked upon as the credentials of anyone who performs them. S. John for this reason habitually speaks of miracles as "signs," for they exhibited the reality of our Lord's claim on which He insisted so strongly ; and S. Paul speaks of the "signs of an Apostle wrought in him." It may be added that not all signs need be miraculous in character, and that the word alone would not necessarily imply a miracle. It may be noted also that these two words 'signs and wonders' are those regularly used in the Old Testament for miracles.

The term "powers" or "mighty works" implies that a new and unusual power is at work in the world. We find references to the 'power' which went forth from the Lord. We find used by S. Paul the paraphrase, 'in the power of the Holy Ghost.' And it is definitely implied in all cases that we have an exhibition of the power of God in the world, or, as it is put more particularly, the power of the Holy Spirit.

The term 'works' in S. John is used specifically, although not perhaps exclusively, for our Lord's miracles as witnessing to the reality of the Incarnation : " But the witness that I have is greater than that of John: for the works which the Father hath given me to accomplish, the very works that I do, bear witness of me, that the Father hath sent me." [1]

Now, still avoiding definition, and postponing for the present critical questions, we can have no

[1] S. John v. 36 ; cf. x. 25, 32, 37. For the words used describing miracles, see Trench, *Notes on the Miracles of Our Lord*, Preliminary Essay, chapter i. It may be noted that this is one of the points where the more accurate discrimination of words in the Revised Version is a great gain. A general account of the New Testament view of miracles will be found in Wendland, *Die Wunderglaube im Christenthum*, Chap. ii.

doubt that the New Testament appears to represent our Lord as performing " works " which are clearly what are commonly called miracles. They are the work of God in the world, the work of the Holy Spirit ; they are proofs and credentials of the Ministry of Jesus. He appeals to the miracles that He works. The fact of His miracles was recognized by the multitude and by His opponents. His followers were attracted by them. Similar power is represented as exercised by the Apostles, and for them also it was part of the credentials of their ministry. We may note further that while the Synoptic Gospels simply and naturally represent our Lord as working miracles and appealing to them, they do so without any special emphasis ; they have no doubt about them or their importance, but they allow them to speak for themselves. In S. John, on the other hand, the miracles are particularly emphasized ; they are spoken of as signs, and attention is drawn to them in our Lord's own speeches in a manner different from that of the other Gospels.

In the Synoptic narrative our Lord always refused the demands of the people to give a ' sign,' " An evil and adulterous generation seeketh after a sign ; and there shall no sign be given to it but the sign of Jonah the prophet." [1] Moreover, when a miracle is worked, the man

[1] S. Matt. xii. 39.

who is healed is generally bidden to conceal the fact. There is clearly a desire to emphasize that our Lord avoided anything like a thaumaturgic display. The wonders and signs were (so it is represented) a part of the real work of our Lord; they were part of His appeal, but only a part; His witness was His works as a whole, in their ethical, their spiritual, as well as their marvellous character. The conviction of His divine Mission was produced by His authority, His words, His spiritual influence, and the evidential value of His miracles is heightened by the absence of any disproportionate emphasis upon them in our records.

Finally, we have to recognize that the New Testament speaks of lying miracles as well as of true ones. Lying miracles are the sign of Antichrist. "For there shall arise false Christs, and false prophets, and shall shew great signs and wonders; so as to lead astray, if possible, even the elect." [1] "He whose coming is according to the working of Satan, with all power and signs and lying wonders, and with all deceit of unrighteousness." [2] "He doeth great signs that he should even make fire to come down out of heaven upon the earth in the sight of men." [3] Instances are given in the stories of Simon Magus and of

[1] S. Matt. xxiv. 24.   [2] 2 Thess. ii. 9.   [3] Rev. xiii. 13.

Elymas the sorcerer.[1]   We need not at present consider the significance of these texts, but we are bound to note their occurrence.

To sum up, then : *prima facie*, the New Testament represents the reality of the miraculous work of our Lord and His disciples, and emphasizes it as a part, but a part only, of the evidence of the truth of the Christian message.

II

We now pass to the judgement on these events in history.   It must be recollected that the situation with regard to miracles in the Patristic period, and from then right onwards through the Middle Ages, was very different from what it is at the present day in cultivated, scientific, or philosophical circles.   For the most part people could not conceive a world in which miracles did not happen.   The belief was natural : it accorded with people's conception of the universe and, as they believed, with their experience.   There was little or no philosophy or science such as to make acceptance difficult.   There was, of course, the incredulity and scepticism of a writer like Lucian, who treated such manifestations as in all cases the work of impostors or quacks.   But his

[1] Acts viii. 9 *et seq.* ; xiii. 8.

writings would never put any serious obstacle in the way of religious belief. The situation, in fact, which the Christian had to deal with was one in which there were too many miracles. There were miracles of the New Testament, miracles of the Church; there were miracles of Paganism, and miracles of conjurors and magicians. The Church did not disparage miracles, but had never under such circumstances laid undue stress on them. The argument from miracles was not nearly so important to the Apologists as the argument from prophecy, and to the world the great argument was the Christian life.[1]

There is indeed a regular appeal to miracles. Tertullian, for example, tells us how "Christ expelled devils from men with a word, restored vision to the blind, cleansed the lepers and reinvigorated the paralytics, raised the dead to life again, made the very elements of nature obey Him, stilling the storm and walking on the sea, thus proving that He was the Logos of God, that primordial first-begotten Word, accompanied by power and reason and based on spirit—the same who now and at all times

---

[1] The fullest account of Patristic teaching on miracles is given by Mozley, *Bampton Lectures,* Note 3, p. 195 (ed. v.). See also Wendland, *Wunderglaube,* chapter iii., p. 25; Lyttelton, *The Place of Miracles in Religion,* chapter iii., p. 81.

did all things by a word."[1] The importance
of this passage is that it not only makes an
appeal to miracles, but also gives a scientific
theory about them. Jesus was the Logos, and
the Logos was the creator and sustainer of the
Universe. To this argument we may return
in a later lecture.

Quadratus also, an early Apologist, appealed
to the evidence of those still living who had been
witnesses of the miracles of our Lord, since
they had been cured by Him:

"Our Saviour's works were always before
men's eyes, for they were true. They were the
men who were healed, the men who were raised.
And these were not only seen when they were
being healed or raised, but were continually
before men's eyes, not only while the Saviour
sojourned upon earth, but, after He had departed,
they remained a long time, so that some of
them survived even to our own days."[2]

But while Christian teachers appealed to the
miracles of our Lord, they appealed also with
equal confidence to the miracles of the Church
in their own days:

"Even now ye may learn from the things
that take place before your eyes. For many
that have been seized by daemons throughout

[1] Tertullian, *Apologeticus*, xxi.
[2] Eusebius, *H.E.* IV. iii. 2. I have ventured to use the
translation of Mr Edghill (see below).

all the world, and even in your own city, have been cured by many of our Christian folk exorcizing them in the name of Jesus Christ that was crucified under Pontius Pilate. Yea these have cured, *and even now do cure*, those whom all other exorcists and dealers in drugs have failed to cure." [1]

But the real difficulty that was experienced with regard to miracles was that miracles were performed, or claimed to be performed, by the heathen and the magicians, and many people of not very reputable character. How then was it possible to appeal to them? The situation is well represented to us in the argument of Celsus, the great opponent of Christianity in the second century, and in Origen's reply. [2] Celsus argued that no evidence could be drawn from miracles, as there was no means of discovering whether they were the work of God or of evil powers. He draws attention to the words of our Lord Himself foretelling the coming of Antichrist with signs and lying wonders, and very pertinently asks the question: If miracles can be produced alike by God and by evil powers, how can there be any evidence that the powers we are dealing

[1] Justin, *Apol.* ii. 6, trans. Edghill.
[2] On Origen and Celsus, see Trench, *On the Miracles,* p. 60. The chief passages are, *Contra Celsum,* I. lxvii., lxviii.; II. xlviii., liii.

with come from God ? There seems to be some doubt whether Celsus was really sincere in his argument, whether in fact he believed in the heathen miracles ; but that does not diminish its apparent effectiveness. In order to explain the power that Jesus had of working miracles, he says that He had hired Himself out as a servant in Egypt on account of His poverty, and having there acquired some miraculous powers, returned to His own country highly elated on account of these, and by means of them proclaimed Himself as God. It must be remembered that Egypt was looked upon as the home of magical arts, and this story was part of the legends, or rather perversions of history, invented by the Jews and other opponents of Christianity to throw discredit on its Founder.[1]

Origen meets this argument, and meets it quite effectively, by an appeal to the moral character of our Lord's works. The magicians accomplished nothing, they merely produced a thaumaturgic display ; Jesus, like Moses, had created a new nation : " Wickedness and wrong," he said, " could not have led a whole nation to rise not only above idols and images erected by men, but also above all created things, and to ascend to the uncreated ways of the God of the Universe." It is in the whole life of Jesus, and the divine works that

[1] Origen, *Contra Celsum*, I. xxviii. ; see pp. 287-289.

He accomplished, that the proof of His divine origin must be found.

" The analogy," writes Origen, " would have been a correct one if, like the jugglers, He had performed his works only for show.   But as it is, none of the jugglers uses his performances to call those who have seen them to lead a better life, nor does he instruct those who are astonished at his exhibition, in the fear of God, nor does he attempt to persuade them to live uprightly as men to be justified in the sight of God.   None of these things do the magicians, for they are not able, and have no wish or desire to work for the reformation of mankind.   Their lives, in fact, are full of most shameful and infamous sins.   But inasmuch as Jesus by the miracles that He did called those who saw them to a reformation of their moral life, was it not natural for Him to exhibit Himself as a proof of a most noble life, not only to His true disciples but to all others ? so that His disciples too might devote themselves to teaching men to live according to the will of God, and that the others being better instructed by His word and by His life and miracles, of the right way to live, might do all things with reference to pleasing God, who is over all.   If such then was the life of Jesus, how is it reasonable for anyone to compare Him to the sect of magicians, and not believe in accordance with the promises that He was God appearing in human form for the well-being of our race." [1]

[1] Origen, *Contra Celsum*, I. lxviii.

The situation is not one that concerns us directly at the present time, although as a matter of fact it touches on an important side of the problem. But the soundness of Origen's argument must be emphasized ; it was believed that miracles occurred : it was believed that they might be the work either of a divine or of a demoniacal agency. To decide between these two Origen appeals, and appeals with complete success, to the moral character of our Lord's life and teaching, and to the beneficial and far-reaching effects of His work upon the world. This argument might be used with even greater effect at the present day.[1]

Some eighteenth century and other writers were accustomed to lay considerable stress on the life of Apollonius of Tyana by Philostratus. It was supposed to represent a rival to the life

---

[1] There is a brilliant discussion on the evidential use of miracles in the second century in Edghill, *Revelation of the Son of God*, by a theologian and evangelist whose early death has been one of the greatest losses the Church has in recent years sustained. Mr Edghill's contention that the appeal to miracles is not made apart from other arguments, and that greater stress is laid on prophecy, on the life and teaching of the Lord, and on the power of the Gospel as shewn by its influence on character, is substantially true ; but I cannot but think that he underestimates the extent of the appeal, and that there is a certain amount of confusion of thought and of the overstatement natural in one who had so great oratorical gifts.

of Christ, and it was argued that there was just
as much evidence for the one as for the other.
Such a position cannot now be maintained.
In fact, the contrast of the two might be
emphasized very much in favour of the historical
character of the Gospels. Apollonius lived in
the time of Domitian ; the Life was not written
until the beginning of the third century. It
was the product of the courtly, religious movement organized under the imperial ladies of the
Syrian emperors who took such an interest in the
ecclesiastical problems of the day. There may
have been some historical basis, but a large
portion of the Life is clearly as apocryphal as
the Apocryphal Gospels, with which it should
be compared. It contains obvious and frequent
anachronisms and contradictions ; the hero, for
instance, manages to reach the Indies by way of
the Caucasus. Some part of it seems definitely
moulded on the Gospels, not so much, apparently,
as a rival, but rather in the interest of religious
syncretism. It was not until the time of
Diocletian that Hierocles attempted to make
use of it as a rival to the Gospels. It is chiefly
remarkable as a monument of the superstitious
religious movement of the third century which
formed both the opportunity and the danger
of Christianity. It shewed what need there
was for a reconstruction of faith. It might
tempt the Church to conciliate the popular

mind by descending from its lofty ethical and
intellectual position.

III

The first beginnings of a philosophical consideration of miracles may be found in S. Augustine, and his discussion of the subject demands
our attention. He shares in the normal position
of his time and appeals unhesitatingly not only to
the miracles of the Bible, but also to the current
ecclesiastical miracles. He demands, however,
and finds evidence for the latter, and the record
that he gives is of considerable interest. What,
however, is of importance in his writings is that
for the first time we find a discussion on the
subject in the light of a philosophy of nature.[1]

S. Augustine had clearly to meet some form
of scientific criticism; there were people who
refused to believe in miracles, or who asked how
things so contrary to nature could happen. He
first of all draws attention to the fact that many
things are reported and believed in the world
which are very marvellous. If these things
happen, why should it not be believed that other
marvellous things happen? You cannot, he
argues, explain them to me, and yet you believe;

[1] The chief passages in S. Augustine dealing with
miracles are *De Civitate Dei*, xxi. 4-8; xxii. 8-10; *Contra
Faustum*, xxvi. (*Opera*, tom. ix., x.).

B

why cannot you believe in these other wonders ?
Some of the instances he cites represent legendary stories of travellers, others are instances of
known phenomena, such as magnetism, which
the science of that day could not explain.   To
these instances the answer that was made was :
It is quite true that these things cannot be
understood, but there is no reason for thinking
that they are against nature.   " Our adversaries,"
says S. Augustine, " are in the habit of reply-
ing, ' This is their natural property, their nature,
these are the powers naturally belonging to
them,' " and he admits that the reply is an
adequate one.   But he proceeds : " if you believe
in acts which are so abnormal and unusual
merely because you say it is natural to them,
although you have no means of proving that it
is so ; why refuse to believe extraordinary events
when they are well attested and can be ascribed
to the work of God—Almighty, as you yourselves admit, and therefore able to do all things
—Himself the author of nature."   But it is
argued against him : " These events you want
us to believe in are contrary to the natural
property of things."   His reply is that we know
the nature of things may change ; " the nature
of things is one at one time, another at another—
why then should not God also be able to
change the nature of things ? "   And then he
goes on to a more profound thought.   It has

been said that portents are contrary to nature,
but that is not really the case. Nothing can
happen contrary to nature. " How can anything
be contrary to nature which happens by the
will of God, since the will of such a Creator is
the nature of each thing. A miracle then is
not contrary to nature, but contrary to nature
as it is known."[1] And this thought is worked
out in another treatise more fully.

" But as to what is according to nature and
what against nature, men who err as you do
cannot know. According to the ordinary habit
of speech, that is said to be contrary to nature
which is contrary to nature as men know it.
. . . But God, who is the Creator and Founder
of all natural things, does nothing contrary to
nature ; for that will be natural to anything
which He may have done, from whom comes
every mode and number and order of nature.
And man himself does nothing against nature
except when he sins, and then he is recalled to
the order of nature by punishment. . . . But
we say not unsuitably that God does a thing
contrary to nature, which He does against what
we know in nature. For we give the name of
nature to the customary and well-known course
of nature. And when God does anything contrary to this we speak of mighty works or

[1] *De Civitate Dei*, XXI. viii. 2. Quomodo est enim contra
naturam, quod Dei fit voluntate, cum voluntas tanti utique
Conditoris conditae rei cuiusque natura fit ? Portentum ergo
fit non contra naturam, sed contra quam nota est natura.

miracles.   But against the highest law of nature
which is far removed from the knowledge of
those who are irreligious or still weak, God does
nothing, inasmuch as He cannot do anything
against Himself." [1]

The full value of this argument will be
brought out later when we discuss generally
the relation of miracles to ' nature ;' but we may
note now that it represents an interesting historical position. ' Nature' is the Platonic method
of stating what we call 'Natural Law.' This
Platonic conception of Uniformity was partly
based on experience, partly the result of an
a priori philosophical conception. Against these
current Uniformitarian theories S. Augustine

---

[1] *Contra Faustum*, xxvi. Quid sit autem secundum naturam,
quid contra naturam, homines qui sicut vos errant, nosse non
possunt. Dici autem humano more contra naturam esse, quod
est contra naturae usum mortalibus notum nec nos negamus.
. . . Deus autem Creator et Conditor omnium naturarum, nihil
contra naturam facit: id enim erit cuique rei naturale, quod
ille fecerit, a quo est omnis modus, numerus, ordo naturae.
Sed nec ipse homo contra naturam quidquam facit, nisi cum
peccat, qui tamen supplicio redigitur ad naturam. . . . Sed
contra naturam non incongrue dicimus aliquid Deum facere,
quod facit contra id quod novimus in natura. Hanc enim
etiam appellamus naturam, cognitum nobis cursum solitumque
naturae, contra quem Deus cum aliquid facit, magnalia vel
mirabilia nominantur. Contra illam vero summam naturae
legem, a notitia remotam, sive impiorum, sive adhuc infirm-
orum, tam Deus nullo modo facit, quam contra se ipsum
non facit.

argues that because a thing is strange and
wonderful that is no reason for disbelieving it;
that there are good grounds for accepting the
faith and record of the Gospel; that to anyone
who believes in God, the will or power of God
will seem an adequate cause; that such a cause
is not contrary to nature, for nature is God's
will; it is only contrary to nature as we know it,
and our knowledge is, and always must be,
incomplete.

The influence of S. Augustine's teaching
lived on, and formed the basis of the scholastic
doctrine of miracles. We may take as a typical
mediaeval philosopher S. Thomas Aquinas, and
we shall find that he sees far deeper into the
conditions under which it is reasonable to believe
miracles than many modern writers. Probably
in what we may call academic circles, there was
during the Middle Ages a considerable amount
of free thought. Anselm, for example, when
discussing the Atonement, refers definitely to
what unbelievers think and say. Mediaeval
philosophy was largely derived from Aristotle and
the Arabians, some of whom, such as Averroes,
had at any rate Pantheistic tendencies, even if
there was no more definite free thought. It was
thus necessary that an adequate philosophical
explanation should be found for miracles.

The Schoolmen believed in the Uniformity
of Nature, but not as modern science professes

to do, as the result of observation, but on *a priori* grounds.   Nature is what it is because God has made it so, and having been made as it is by God, that is what it must be.   That certain "natures" were produced by God was voluntary on His part; but, once having been created with the properties He has assigned them, it is a matter of necessity that certain effects should proceed from them.   That which belongs to a thing by reason of its essential principles must obtain by absolute necessity always.   It is important for us to remember that this doctrine of the Uniformity of Nature is not a discovery of modern science; rather it was deduced on *a priori* grounds from the conception of the Divine nature, and thus preceded and assisted the later development of Natural Science.

Can God then change or interfere with this order of nature?   The answer, according to S. Thomas, is that He can.[1]   God has brought all things into being, and therefore He who created all things can produce directly the effects of things which He has created.   If we examine nature we see that nothing invariably

---

[1] The chief passages in S. Thomas Aquinas on miracles are, *Summa Theologiae*, I. cv.; CX. iv.; *Summa Contra Gentiles*, III. xcix.-cvii.   Of the latter I have used the translation by Rev. J. Rickaby, S.J., published under the title, *Of God and His Creatures*.

produces its proper effect ; it is prevented either through lack of power or some more superior power intervening.

" If, therefore, by the action of some created power the natural course of events may be altered from the usual to the unusual, and that without any alteration of divine providence, much more may the divine power sometimes do a thing, without prejudice to its own providence, beyond the course assigned to natural events by God. This God does at times to manifest His power : for there is no better way of manifesting the subjection of all nature to the divine will than by something being done at times beyond the course of nature ; for thereby it appears that the course of events proceeds from Him, and is not of necessity of nature, but through free will. Nor should this be accounted a frivolous reason to allege, that God works some effects in nature to the end of manifesting Himself to human minds, since it has been shewn that all the material creation is subordinated to serve the end of intellectual nature, while the end of intellectual nature itself is the knowledge of God. No wonder then if some change is wrought in corporeal substance to afford intelligent nature a knowledge of God."[1]

Following the teaching of S. Augustine, and making use of the passage we have already quoted, S. Thomas goes on to shew that the things which God does beyond the order of

[1] *God and His Creatures* (*Contra Gentiles*), III. xcix.

nature are not contrary to nature, for that cannot be contrary to nature which comes from God, who is the author of nature. While it is thus laid down that God can directly interfere with the order of nature as we know it, and the possibility of miracles is admitted, the extent to which this is possible is limited. "So far as the order of nature depends on the first cause, God cannot act contrary to it: He can only interfere with secondary causes."[1] He cannot alter that which depends on the first cause or essential nature of things, because that is Himself, and He cannot act against Himself. But he can produce secondary causes Himself, for they are not part of Himself but the result of His actions.

A miracle is defined as follows :—

"Things that are done occasionally beyond the usual established order of events are commonly called miracles. . . . An event is wonderful relatively to one man and not to another. The absolutely wonderful is that which has a cause absolutely hidden. This then is the meaning of the word 'miracle,' an event of itself full of wonder, not to *this* man or *that* man only. Now the cause absolutely hidden to every man is God, inasmuch as no man in this life can mentally grasp the essence of God. Those

[1] *Summa Theologiae*, I. cv. vi. Prout ordo rerum dependet a prima causa, non potest Deus contra ordinem rerum facere : prout vero dependet a qualibet secundarum causarum, praeter ordinem rerum facere potest.

events then are properly to be styled miracles, which happen by divine power beyond the order commonly observed in nature."[1]

It is interesting to hear that Coleridge used to contrast the greatness of Aquinas' teaching on miracles with the inadequacy of many modern thinkers. And it is interesting to note further that neither Aquinas nor Augustine would have anything to say to such a definition as that miracles are a violation of the order of nature. They recognize that, properly speaking, no variation from the law of nature is possible—for nature is what is, whether we look upon it as the sum of observed things or as the Will of God. Looking upon law as derived from God, they do not speak of any violation of law, but they observe in nature that, as it seems, one law interferes with the working of another law, and therefore, they argue, there is no reason why that which is the highest law of all, the ultimate nature of things unknown to us, the Will of God Himself, should not be more powerful in itself than secondary manifestations of law. In this there is nothing derogatory to the dignity of God if He seems to interfere with the laws which He has made, for He does it that intelligent beings may learn about Him. We shall have later to examine this conception

[1] *God and His Creatures*, III. ci.

of law, and to see within what limitations a scheme like this of the universe may be held; but it must be recognized that from the point of view of religion—and it is, of course, from that point of view that Aquinas approaches the question—he brushes away many cobwebs which have been created by later and less capable thinkers.

IV

The first writer who definitely and deliberately attacked belief in miracles was Spinoza. He was born in 1634, and his *Tractatus Theologico-Politicus*—the work of his which chiefly concerns us—was published anonymously in 1670; he died in 1677.

"The masses," he tells us, "think that the power and providence of God are most clearly displayed by events that are extraordinary and contrary to the conception they have formed of nature, especially if such events bring them any profit or convenience; they think that the clearest possible proof of God's existence is afforded when nature, as they suppose, breaks her accustomed order; and consequently they believe that those who explain or endeavour to understand phenomena or miracles through their natural senses are doing away with God and His providence." [1]

[1] Spinoza's *Works*, translated by Elwes, i., p. 81.

People imagine two powers, God and Nature. God they think is like a royal potentate ; Nature consists of force and energy. Men imagine that God has arranged everything for their sole benefit, and

"this idea is so pleasing to humanity that men go on to this day imagining miracles, so that they may believe themselves God's favourites, and the final cause for which God created and directs all things." [1]

He then goes on to lay down the following propositions :—

" 1. That nature cannot be contravened, but that she preserves a fixed and immutable order. 2. That God's nature and existence, and consequently His providence, cannot be known from miracles, but that they can all be much better perceived from the fixed and immutable order of nature. 3. That by the decrees and volitions, and consequently the providence of God, Scripture means nothing but nature's order following necessarily from her eternal laws." [2]

These propositions Spinoza seeks to prove by deductive reasoning based on the nature of God.

" Nothing is necessarily true, save only by divine decree. . . . The universal laws of nature, therefore, are decrees of God, following from

---

[1] Spinoza's *Works*, translated by Elwes, i., p. 82.
[2] *Ibid.*, i., p. 82.

the necessity and perfection of the divine nature. Hence any event happening in nature which contravenes nature's universal laws would necessarily also contravene the Divine decree, nature, and understanding ; or if anyone asserted that God acts in contravention to the laws of nature, he, *ipso facto*, would be compelled to assert that God acted against His own nature— an evident absurdity. . . . Nothing, then, comes to pass in nature in contravention to her universal laws, . . . whatsoever comes to pass, comes to pass according to laws and rules which involve eternal necessity and truth, although they may not all be known to us, and therefore she keeps a fixed and immutable order."

For these reasons

"miracles are only intelligible as in relation to human opinions, and merely mean events of which the natural cause cannot be explained by a reference to any ordinary occurrence, either by us, or, at any rate, by the writer and narrator of the miracle." [1]

Miracles, then, give us no knowledge of God, for God is really only law.

"Miracles in the sense of events contrary to the laws of nature, so far from demonstrating to us the existence of God, would, on the contrary, lead us to doubt it, where, otherwise, we might have been absolutely certain of it, as

[1] Spinoza's *Works,* translated by Elwes, i., pp. 83, 84.

knowing that nature follows a fixed and immutable order." [1]

The conception that Spinoza formed of God
is further worked out in his *Ethics*, and a
good deal more will be found about miracles in
his Correspondence with Oldenburg. 'God'
he defines as a Being absolutely infinite—that
is, "a substance consisting in infinite attributes
of which each expresses eternal and infinite
essentiality." [2]   "Besides God no substance can
be granted or conceived." [3]   "Whatever is is
in God, and without God nothing can be or be
conceived." [4]   "God acts solely by the laws of
His own nature, and is not constrained by anyone." [5]   And Spinoza goes on to say that in the
ultimate end of things, everything must be as
it is, for everything is in God, and nothing can
exist in any way but as it does exist. He
therefore shews in his view the impossibility of
freedom in the world.

For the present we may confine ourselves to
certain preliminary observations on this system.
It is obvious that the whole force of Spinoza's
argument depends upon the conception or
definition of God with which he starts. He

---

[1] Spinoza's *Works*, translated by Elwes, i., p. 85.
[2] *Ibid.*, ii., p. 45, definition vi.
[3] *Ibid.*, ii., p. 54, prop. xiv.
[4] *Ibid.*, ii., p. 55, prop. xv.
[5] *Ibid.*, ii., p. 59, prop. xvii.

assumes that God is everything, and everything
is God. And then he proceeds to prove that
nothing can be except through God. He
assumes that God must be as He is, and then
proceeds to prove that nothing can be except
as it is; he assumes that all things are God,
and that God cannot change, and then proves
that there can be nothing which does not
proceed by the laws of things which are the
Laws of God. It is a criticism which has been
made against any form of deductive reasoning,
that it can never prove anything but what is
already contained in the premisses. This seems
to be obviously true with regard to all Spinoza's
deductions as to the character of nature.
He assumes everything he wishes to prove.
His whole argument depends upon an *a priori*
conception which he has formed as to what
Nature and God are. All this seems to him to
be in accordance with reason, but he does not,
and cannot give, any reason for this belief. His
so-called arguments are purely tautological.
Moreover, this conception of his—which may
without injustice be described as Pantheistic
—involves certain very definite consequences.
If it takes away the possibility of miracles
happening, it also takes away the possibility of
freedom existing in any form. This must be
recognized as a necessary deduction from the
premisses, and must be accepted by those who

are attracted by the apparent certainty of
Spinoza's methods. For Spinoza's conclusions
are the inevitable result of his premisses. In
fact, they are but the repetition of them in
a different language; but the premisses themselves are assumed, and no reason for their
truth is ever given except the fact that they
are so.

And the source of this *a priori* conception
of God and Nature is not far to seek. The
early triumphs of science were made in
the regions of Mathematics, Mechanics, and
Astronomy. Mathematics appeared to give an
example of rapid, accurate, and certain reasoning,
and naturally directed men's minds to a particular
method of thought. Mathematical science,
therefore, was supposed to be a true representation of things as they are. Hence the construction of the universe was conceived on a
mathematical and mechanical basis, and this
origin of his views is recognized by Spinoza
himself. He discusses various reasons that have
led men to form different conceptions of the
universe, and then proceeds as follows :—

"Men laid down as an axiom that God's
judgements far transcend human understanding. Such a doctrine might well have sufficed
to conceal the truth from the human race from
all eternity, if mathematics had not furnished
another standard of verity in considering solely

the essence and properties of figures without
regard to their final causes."[1]

It was, then, on a mathematical basis that this
hard, rigid system was built up, and we have
not yet realized the immense difference in our
conception of God and Nature that has been
produced by the very different aspects of
Nature which later scientific discovery and
research has placed before us.

But Spinoza's system is of the greatest
importance, for it is the most perfect and
complete representation of these attempts to
explain things by a spiritual monistic principle.
So Dr A. S. Farrar writes :—

"The central principle of his philosophy,
the pantheistic disbelief of miraculous interposition, which has subsequently entered into so
many systems, was first clearly applied to
theology by him. Wherever the disbelief in
the supernatural has arisen from *a priori*
considerations, and expressed itself, not with
allegations of conscious fraud against the
devotees of religion, nor with attempts to
explain it away as merely mental realism, but
with assertions that miracles are impossible,
and nature an unchanging whole ; this disbelief,
whether insinuating itself into the defence of
Christianity, or marking the attack on it, has
been a reproduction of Spinoza."[2]

[1] Spinoza's *Works*, translated by Elwes, ii., p. 77.
[2] A. S. Farrar, *Bampton Lectures*, p. 160.

But not only is this the case with regard to pantheistic philosophy ; it is true also of more modern systems. Here at the very beginning of the modern era of scientific discovery, we find the absolute uniformity of nature asserted, not as the result of scientific investigation but as something known on *a priori* grounds and proved by methods which, as we shall see, the later philosophy of nature looks upon as entirely unsubstantial. Nothing can shew us more clearly how this conception of the uniformity of nature was not the creation of Natural Science, but has been throughout assumed. It was the inspiration of Natural Science, not its result ; it goes back to the Stoic and the Platonist. It has its starting-point in the nature of things, or the being of God. We shall have eventually to investigate the statement made in the name of science that no violation of natural law is possible. To help us in our investigation we must realize that such a dictum is not a conclusion of science, which has in fact no method of arriving at any such conclusion at all, but an assumption built up on certain *a priori* methods of thought which are entirely inconsistent with the true methods of science.

c

V

We now come to that movement of free-thought which prevailed in England in the seventeenth and eighteenth centuries, and is generally called Deism. Nominally it maintained a belief in God as a Creator and First Cause, of whom we might learn by means of reason and natural religion ; but it denied divine providence, and in particular denied the possibility of a revealed religion. Really the tendency was, under the name of Natural Religion, to develop into almost complete scepticism and materialism. If the rise of the movement may be traced originally at any rate to political events, its form was undoubtedly the outcome of that conception of nature which the science of the time had created. This conception had a twofold origin. We have already described the development of that *a priori* method of thought which was due originally to Descartes, which proceeded by deductive methods and was carried to a logical conclusion by Spinoza with his conception of rigid law and uniformity. On the other side were the new-born scientific studies of which Bacon was the prophet if not the father, which led to the foundation of the Royal Society, which were typified by the astronomical theories of Kepler and culminated in the natural philosophy of Isaac Newton. These earliest scientific investigations were, it may be remarked, mathematical, astronomical, and mechanical. They all seemed to corroborate that theory of the universe which described nature in the terms of rigid law and harmonized with the *a priori* speculations of the philosophers. Thus arose that conception of rigid mechanical law which has formed such a dominant feature in the thought about Nature during the last two hundred years.

A rigid separation between the ideas of God and of Nature arose. The science of that day had nothing to tell of origins, or of development, it had no conception of a world that had slowly grown into being; its ideas were purely static. So it needed a beginning. God, therefore, was represented as having created the world and given it laws. Once created, Nature pursued its way without God. That theory of law which seemed to have been found in the fields of Astronomy was transferred gradually to other departments of nature. Law prevailed likewise in human life and in the human mind. Man must guide himself by the laws of nature; God had made the world, which was governed by the laws He had made, and in these laws, and these laws only, could we learn about Him. He could not have revealed Himself, and there was no reason that He should do so; revealed religion, it was generally argued, was the invention of priests and prelates in their own interest.

The religious movement began on *a priori* grounds, just as the science from which it started was *a priori;* but in the realms both of science and of religion it tended more and more to become inductive. As Sir Leslie Stephen says, the tendency of the discussion was to pass to historical criticism. A movement which had begun by asserting that there was no possibility of revelation, failed when it attempted to prove that there had not been a revelation. The science which had started on an *a priori* basis produced an empirical science of the human mind which went far to overthrow its foundations. The philosophy of Hume when once understood destroyed the supposed scientific basis of the philosophy of Spinoza, and the whole conception of natural law.

There are three works which particularly demand our notice : Woolston's *Discourses on Miracles,* Conyers Middleton's *Free Enquiry into the Miraculous Powers which are supposed to have subsisted in the Christian Church,* and Hume's *Essay on Miracles.*

Woolston's six discussions were published in 1727 and the two following years. They contained the bitterest attack which had yet appeared on the Christian religion, and were remarkable for their humour and for a most

mordant power of satire. Each discussion was
dedicated to a bishop, and there is hardly
anything in the English language more biting,
more subtle, or more impudent in its irony
than these dedications. Their sale was immense
—Voltaire was in England when they were first
published, and informs us that it reached 30,000
copies. Other evidence shews that this statement was certainly not exaggerated ; and it was
from them as also from Middleton that the great
French infidel learnt much of the manner and
method of his attack upon Christianity. Woolston was fined and imprisoned for the publica-
tion, and died in prison.

Woolston's thesis was that the miracles were
not to be taken as history, but were only
allegories to be understood in a spiritual sense.
Our Lord's "whole life in the flesh is but Type,
Figure and Parable of His mystic and spiritual
life and operations in mankind." "Neither the
Fathers, nor the Apostles, nor even Jesus Himself meant that the miracles, as recorded in the
Evangelists, should be taken in a literal sense,
but in a mystic, figurative, and parabolic one."
Whether or no he really held this belief may
be doubted. Probably it was originally sincere,
but by the time he came to write these discussions all genuine religious belief had been
overwhelmed by the bitterness which misfortune
and perhaps ill-treatment had aroused. At any

rate under the cloak of this theory he delivered a violent attack upon the historical character of miracles, which he described as "full of Absurdities, Improbabilities, and Incredibilities." No doubt his criticism in some cases seems effective, but it must be remembered that a sufficiently unsympathetic critic is able to make any story or history that has ever appeared seem ridiculous and absurd. Woolston found it necessary to ascribe the origin of miracles to direct imposture. The raising of Lazarus, for example, was "a monstrous imposture," and "this piece of fraud" was an article in the indictment against our Lord.

As an illustration of his style and methods, may be taken his account of the Resurrection. This is put into the mouth of a Jewish rabbi, who describes it as the "most notorious and monstrous imposture that ever was put upon mankind." It was a fraud that was arranged by Jesus and carried out by His disciples. He had prophesied that He would rise again on the third day, but the fulfilment was frustrated by the sealing of the tomb, and the knowledge that the chief priests would come to see the expected resurrection. "But notwithstanding this precaution in sealing the stone—the best that can be taken against fraud—Jesus' body was privately slipped off early in the morning of the day before, and the Resurrection pretended by His disciples." The guards were bribed or intoxicated, and the deceit acquiesced in by Pilate. The stories of the appearances, it was quite easy to invent. As for the acceptance of the belief, that is quite natural. "Why it has been believed through these latter ages of the Church is no wonder at all. The priests had their interest in it; the ignorant and superstitious had their comfort in it; and the wise and considerate, for fear of persecution, dared not enquire into the grounds of it."

The whole thing was a fraud kept up to start and establish the priesthood. The writer was determined to insult and defy the bishops to do their worst.

"My heart aches a little for our divines," he says, ". . . what must they then do? Why, they must give up their religion along with their Church, and go with me to the Fathers with their mystical interpretation of the whole story of Jesus' Resurrection."

Middleton's *Free Enquiry* was published in 1747. It was an attack on the miracles of the first three centuries, mainly in the interests of Protestantism. Anglican divines had appealed to these centuries in corroboration of their doctrinal position, and there was a tendency to accept and defend the existence of miracles in the Early Church for a certain time.

Middleton is severe on the difficulty of drawing a line as some do in the third, others in the fourth or fifth century, and would solve this problem by denying all ecclesiastical miracles. Their growth is explained by a general attack on the credulity and want of intelligence of the Fathers who supported them. The effect of the work was first of all to make Gibbon join the Roman Church on the ground that there was as good evidence for later miracles as for earlier, and ultimately to become a freethinker on the ground that the same arguments might be used against Scripture as had been used against the Fathers. How far Middleton himself had drawn these conclusions we do not know, but he is considered by Leslie Stephens to be one of the few divines who can fairly be accused of conscious insincerity. Like Woolston he ascribes the testimony of miracles to direct imposture. "The sole inference," he says, "which reason would teach us to draw from an attestation of miracles so conspicuously fabulous, is that the same witnesses are not to be trusted in any, as being either incapable from a weakness of judgement of discerning the truth and proba-bility of things, or determined by craft and fraud to defend anything that was useful to them." [1] Men of sense know, "on subjects of a miraculous kind, how forcibly the prejudices

[1] Middleton, *Free Enquiry*, p. 187.

of education, a superstitious turn of mind, the interests of party, or the views of ambition are apt to operate on a defender of these miracles, which the government and religion of his country are engaged to support." [1]

Whilst the works of Middleton and Woolston are forgotten or almost forgotten, the name of Hume has survived as that of the most acute and most famous of all sceptics. His *Enquiry concerning the Human Understanding*, which contained an essay on Miracles, was published in 1748. Its argument consists of two main divisions : First, he argues that "a miracle is a violation of the laws of nature," and as the evidence in favour of the laws of nature is greater than that in favour of any miracle, there never has been (he first wrote 'there never can be') any testimony sufficient to establish the reality of one.

"A miracle is a violation of the laws of nature ; and as a firm and unalterable experience has established these laws, the proof against a miracle, from the very nature of the fact, is as entire as any argument from experience can possibly be imagined. . . . There must, therefore, be a uniform experience against every miraculous event, otherwise the event would not merit that appellation. And as a uniform experience amounts to a proof, there is here a direct and full 'proof,' from the nature of the fact,

[1] Middleton, *Free Enquiry*, p. 229.

against the existence of any miracle ; nor can
such a proof be destroyed, or the miracle rendered
credible, but by an opposite proof, which is
superior." [1]

The plain consequence is (and it is a maxim
worthy of our attention), " That no testimony is
sufficient to establish a miracle, unless the
testimony be of such a kind that its falsehood
would be more miraculous than the fact which
it endeavours to establish." [2]

In the second part he proceeds to examine
the character of the evidence for miracles, and
shews that as a matter of fact none of the
alleged evidence is such that it is possible to
rely upon it.

" As the violations of truth are more common
in the testimony concerning religious miracles
than in that concerning any other matter of
fact, this must diminish very much the authority
of the former testimony, and make us form a
general resolution never to lend any attention
to it, with whatever specious pretence it may be
covered." [3]

The examination of Hume's position must
be reserved for a later lecture. It is sufficient
at present to remind ourselves that Hume's
general philosophy had entirely destroyed that

---

[1] Hume, *Enquiries*, ed. Selby-Bigge, p. 114.
[2] *Ibid.*, p. 115.   [3] *Ibid.*, p. 129.

conception of the law of nature which he describes miracles as violating. He aimed at making his reasoning demonstrative and epigrammatic, and by that attempt he made it less strong than otherwise it might appear to be. The real point of his argument is that we should not believe such things as miracles unless we have good evidence ; that in many cases evidence for miracles connected with religion is avowedly untrue ; and that therefore we should hesitate before we are prepared to accept any miracles. Stated in that form it becomes a wise caution, and reminds us that clearly we should not accept testimony until we have thoroughly tested it.

The eighteenth century produced two of the best-known English Apologists—Butler and Paley. Bishop Butler published his *Analogy* in 1736, Archdeacon Paley his *Evidences* in 1794. The former deals with the Deist controversy in its earlier *a priori* period, the latter sums up the Christian apologetic literature in relation to the question of testimony which marked the latter development of the movement.

Butler is spoken of with respect, even by those who are least inclined to accept his teaching. It is generally admitted that as against the Deists his arguments were singularly effective; but it is asserted that he only succeeds inasmuch as he shews that it is no more difficult to believe a revealed religion than a natural religion. And

it has been argued that the logical conclusion
would be that it is equally difficult to believe
either. This sometimes seems to suggest that
those who argue in this manner have not read
the *Analogy*. The above description does not
in the least represent the main point of the
argument. Butler's argument is not confined
to the proposition quoted above; what he does
argue is that there is no pre-supposition from
the analogy of nature itself against the Christian
scheme of things. The argument of the Deists
had been: If you study nature—by which they
meant the sum of existing things—you will see
that it makes Christianity absurd or impossible.
The point of Butler's argument is to prove that
that is not so. So with regard to miracles he
argues that, considering the vastness of nature,
considering the wide extent of what we do not
know, considering the value and power of the
Christian religion, we cannot say on *a priori*
grounds that there is any reason for not accepting them. Again, with regard to evidence, all
human testimony may be vitiated by fraud or
credulity, but that does not prevent us from
guiding our life upon testimony. Because some
miracles are based upon fraud and credulity, we
cannot argue that all miracles are; we must
examine in each particular case. He seems
almost to have discounted, before it appeared,
Hume's celebrated argument.

Neither the philosophy nor the apologetics of Paley are in good repute at the present time, and probably the retention of his *Evidences* as a text-book when his whole scheme of things is so little in accordance with present methods of thought is unfortunate ; but it must be recognized that his arguments were singularly conclusive for the time when he wrote. Stripped of all adventitious additions, the final argument then used against miracles always ultimately reduced them to fraud. None of the later or more refined forms of criticism had arisen, and against the contemporary methods of arguing Paley's *Evidences* were entirely sound. Certainly few people at the present day would feel it possible to accept the eighteenth-century position. Both Butler and Paley put the argument from miracles and from prophecy in the forefront. Paley seeks to give a demonstrative character to his reasoning, which is really never possible when dealing with subject-matter such as we are considering. No logical demonstration seems quite convincing when we are dealing with the realities of life. At the present time the spiritual and moral arguments would be put first. But that must not blind us to the fact that the English Church came out of the long controversy with the Deism and Scepticism of the eighteenth century triumphant, and that the sober, if limited, theology of that period prepared the way for wider spiritual revivals.

VI

We now pass to Germany. Whilst in the eighteenth century England was in the van of destructive criticism and free-thought, that position passed to others towards the end of that century, partly, perhaps, owing to the rise of personal religion with the series of great religious movements which began with Wesley, partly owing to the revulsion of feeling aroused by the excesses of the French Revolution, which on the intellectual side was largely the result of the destructive philosophy of the English Deists, popularized and internationalized by the brilliance of the great French sceptics. During the nineteenth century all the developments of rationalism had their origin in Germany, and the English liberal theologians have confined themselves to the task of copying German criticism—generally just about the time when its inadequacy has been discovered.

It would be impossible to range over the whole field, and for the particular purpose of dealing with the question of miracles in Germany, as opposed to the more general question of biblical and historical criticism, it will be convenient for us to confine ourselves to three names—Paulus, Schleiermacher, and Strauss.

Paulus we can take as a typical rationalist.[1] For forty years he was Professor of Theology at Heidelberg, where he died in 1851 at the age of ninety. His commentary on the Gospels was published in 1800, and his Life of Christ in 1828. His philosophical inspiration was due to Spinoza, whom he interpreted as a Deist rather than a Pantheist. He was a believer in Christianity, and the problem before him was to reconcile the historical truth of the life of Jesus with the denial of the miracles. From Spinoza he had learned two points which were to him of primary importance. One—" that unexplained alterations of the course of nature can neither overthrow nor attest a spiritual truth "; the other, "that everything that happens in nature emanates from the omnipotence of God."[2]

We notice at once a fundamental difference of atmosphere from that of the English controversy. It was assumed in England that miracles were the best method of proving a revelation, and it was considered necessary to disprove the miracles in order to disprove the revelation.

---

[1] I have unfortunately not had access to Paulus' own works. The following account is based on Schweitzer, *The Quest of the Historical Jesus*, chapter v. See also Trench, *On the Miracles*, pp. 74-78.

[2] Schweitzer, *op. cit.*, p. 51.

Paulus, however, was of opinion that miracles were of no value as a proof, that they were in fact a detriment to the Gospel narrative, and it was necessary in the cause of truth to eliminate them.

He recognizes as an incontrovertible fact that the writers of the Gospel narratives believed in miracles. That was natural, he held, to their stage of culture; but it simply arose through their ignorance of secondary causes, where our superior knowledge and insight can shew how they made their mistake. And it is our duty to explain the miracles, for we know the real causes of things. Miracles of healing were worked by the influence of spiritual power on the nervous system, or by medicine and other secret remedies which our Lord was acquainted with, and others did not know. When the Twelve were sent forth they healed the sick by the use of oil—a well-known remedy. Demoniacs were dealt with by sedatives. The stilling of the waves arose from the fact that just at that moment the boat came under the shelter of a hill. As regards the feeding of the five thousand, "when Jesus saw the multitude an hungered, He said to His disciples, 'We will set the rich people among them a good example that they may share their supplies with the others, and He began to distribute His own provisions, and those of the disciples, to the

people who were sitting near them. The
example had its effect, and soon there was
plenty for everyone."[1] The raisings from the
dead were deliverances from premature burial.
The explanation of the Resurrection was that
our Lord was not really dead. He revived in
the tomb, an earthquake rolled away the stone,
He escaped and put on the clothes of a gardener.
The following is the explanation of the words
of Thomas :—

"Thomas was not present at this first
appearance, and at a later interview was suffered
to put his hands into the marks of the wounds.
It is a misunderstanding to see a reproach in
the words that Jesus addresses to him. What,
then, is the meaning of 'Blessed are they that
have not seen and have believed'? It is a
benediction on Thomas for what he has done
in the interests of later generations. 'Now,'
Jesus says, 'thou, Thomas, art convinced
because thou hast so unmistakably seen Me.
It is well for those who now or in the future
shall not see Me; for after this they can feel
a firm conviction, because thou hast convinced
thyself so completely that to thee, whose hands
have touched Me, no possible doubt can remain
of My corporeal reanimation.' Had it not
been for Thomas' peculiar mental constitution,
we should not have known whether what was
seen was a phantom or a real appearance of
the reanimated Jesus."[2]

[1] Schweitzer, *op. cit.*, p. 52.   [2] *Op. cit.*, pp. 54, 55.

Strangely enough the only miracle that Paulus retains is the miraculous birth.

"It is true that there is one miracle which Paulus retains—the miracle of the birth, or at least, the possibility of it; in the sense that it is through holy inspiration that Mary receives the hope and the power of conceiving her exalted Son, in whom the spirit of the Messiah takes up its dwelling. Here he indirectly denies the natural generation, and regards the conception as an act of the self-consciousness of the mother." [1]

It may be noted how remarkable is the contrast presented by different points of view. To the normal religious mind the miraculous is natural, to many it seems the only means of authenticating a revelation. To Paulus, on the other hand, and to those who are influenced by the same mental conception, miracles are considered as impossible and inconsistent with the religious idea. It is necessary, therefore, as we have seen, to eliminate them in the cause of religion. We shall examine later Paulus' premises; it is at any rate almost universally admitted that however plausible in one or two cases his explanation may appear, the attempt that he has made to carry out his rationalistic explanation consistently throughout has demonstrated its falseness. We have always a natural

[1] Schweitzer, *op. cit.*, pp. 51, 52.

feeling of respect for anyone, even if we think him wrong-headed, who has had courage to work out his theory consistently; for this, Paulus must have our respect and our thanks. He has steadily and systematically attempted to explain away the miracles of the New Testament while retaining his belief in its general historical character. Take one or two isolated miracles and it is possible to rationalize them, but attempt to apply such a system to the whole number, and the result is a picture which, to any person of literary insight or intelligence, becomes impossible.

Schleiermacher represented the constructive religious speculation of Germany as against the rationalist movement, and from his chair at Berlin he dominated the religious thought of the time.[1] The problem he always had before him was to reconcile the claims of religion with the dominant philosophical system of the day. To those inspired by Spinoza and by Hegel, there was no place for any form of supernaturalism in their philosophical system. He therefore built up his religion primarily on the basis of feeling. He looked upon the whole of nature as representing the will of God, and the problem

[1] On Schleiermacher, see Wendland, *Der Wunderglaube im Christenthum*, p. 39 ff.; Trench, p. 70; Schweitzer, p. 62. The most important place where he treats the subject is in *Die Christliche Glaube*, sect. 47.

before him was to harmonize the idea of religious revelation with the conception of a fixed and determined order of nature. He asks what is a miracle, and says that its only meaning is that of a sign or intimation. It is an intimation of immediate relationship to what is infinite and universal.

What we have to realize then about a miracle is that it need be a miracle only as regards the religious sense. Enough that some event has happened of such a character as to be a sign to the person of religious instincts that he is brought in relation to the infinite God. That may be quite possible without any infringement of the order of nature. All that is necessary is that the cause of the miracle should be something with which we are unacquainted, some deeper unknown cause which makes the event have the appearance of being a violation of that order. The whole of nature is inspired and represents the work of God. Therefore nature could be so arranged that when and how it was necessary the religious sense should be stirred up by a miraculous event. Thus from the side of religion, a miracle is a miracle or sign ; from the side of nature, there is no breach in order and uniformity.

That being the point of view from which Schleiermacher approaches history, we need not be particularly concerned with the manner in which he deals with the miracles, and the more so because Schleiermacher had little or no historical sense. He was a philosopher and a theologian who approached the study of the Gospels as much from the definitely theological point of view as any mediaeval Schoolman. Moreover, his *Life of Christ* was not published until 1864, although the lectures were delivered more than thirty years before, and was then clearly out of touch with the development of criticism.

There are just one or two points of interest to notice. Throughout his writings Schleiermacher, as a philosopher, preferred the Gospel of S. John to the others. It was more in accordance with his theological conception, and he assumed that what seemed to him sound as theology was equally sound as history. He therefore is prepared to accept any miracle that occurs in that Gospel, while for those in the Synoptists he can always assume that the narrators have made some mistake. He is, still, to a certain extent, under the influence of rationalism; some miracles he explains away. As it did not matter from his particular point of view whether a miracle really happened or how it happened, he is quite prepared to believe that the Resurrection may have been either a return to consciousness from a trance state, or a supernatural restoration to life. On the other hand, the important point for him is that, however it happened, Christ in a bodily form appeared to His disciples. There must be no sign of docetism, nothing unreal in the bodily appearance.

The name of David Friedrich Strauss is known as that of the first modern critic who attacked the life of our Lord in a spirit of complete disbelief. So far rationalism had been content to accept the life as a whole, but to eliminate any particular incident that seemed displeasing from its particular point of view. Strauss turned upon the life of Christ the same spirit of historical criticism which was being applied to the early histories of most nations of antiquity, and no longer content with merely eliminating the marvellous, resolved the narrative as a whole into poetry and myth. To him it was not merely the supernatural which was mythical, it was the life of Jesus as a whole ; for it was the translation into story of the Messianic idea.

He published his first Life of Jesus in 1835. It was received, as is well known, with indignation, and he found himself banned by all the theologians of the time. His second Life, addressed to the public, and not to theologians, appeared in 1864. His object was to do for Germans what Renan had done for Frenchmen. He has not changed his point of view ; he has merely strengthened it, and put it in a new

form. The main point for us is his relation to
the miraculous, and he is perfectly frank as
to his attitude. His aim is to destroy the
miraculous. Our sole consideration must be
that 'in the person and acts of Jesus no supernaturalism shall be suffered to remain.'[1] 'He
who would banish priests from the Church must
first banish miracles from religion.'[2] "If we
enquire how such heterogeneous elements could
have mingled with the religion of Jesus, and
have been retained in it, we shall find the cause
to be the very same as that which to us con-
stitutes the chief offence of all ancient religion,
namely, belief in the miraculous."[3] "And
clearly, so soon as Christianity ceases to be
thought miraculous, the clergy must cease to
seem the miraculously gifted persons they have
hitherto represented themselves."[4] With this
avowed and definite purpose in view he is
particularly severe on all those who say that
their aim in investigating the life of Christ is a
purely historical one. He does not claim that
he is a person inspired only by the spirit of
unbiassed research. "Christianity is so living
a power, and the problem as to its origin so
rife in important consequences to the immediate
present, that the student must be literally stupid
whose interest in the determination of such

[1] Strauss, *New Life of Jesus*, I. xii. [2] *Op. cit.*, p. xvi.
[3] *Op. cit.*, p. xv. [4] *Op. cit.*, p. viii.

a question can be strictly confined to the historical."[1]   And again, "Our great and common aim is not so much to resuscitate an obliterated history, as to assist the human mind in emancipating itself from the oppressive thraldom of creeds; and I fully coincide in thinking historical enquiry, together with general philosophical education, to be the best means of effecting this object."[2]

If such was Strauss' point of view at starting, it is obvious that he would succeed in attaining his end; and this frank confession of a clear-headed thinker is important enough for our purpose.   There is a conception abroad that theologians and investigators of the early history of the Church are to be divided into two classes : those who are free and unbiassed in their investigation, and those who are trammelled and bound by the necessity of supporting the existing state of belief.   Such a picture is an incorrect one. Of course, it is true that in normal times the great body of persons accept the beliefs in which they are brought up, and the natural tendency of the ordinary theologian is to accept the traditional theology.   But even this is not an entirely true picture; even in times when there is little general controversy, every able man who studies theological questions studies them in a spirit of research as well as of belief.   He

[1] Strauss, *op. cit.*, p. x.   [2] *Op. cit.*, pp. x., xi.

is always anxious to find out more exactly what is true, and there is a continuous transformation or development of belief going on. There was just as much unbiassed historical research in Newman as there was in Baur.

It is, however, a fundamental mistake to imagine that there is any less degree of bias in the spirit of revolt than in the spirit of acquiescence. Strauss did not disbelieve in miracles and therefore disbelieve in priests; but he was carried away by what seemed to be a liberal movement of the time, and he disbelieved in miracles because he wanted to get rid of priests.

It must be recognized, then, that negative criticism has no particular claims upon us as representing an unbiassed spirit of research in contrast with more orthodox tradition. It has its pre-suppositions just as much as orthodox belief has its pre-suppositions. In fact, many orthodox theologians probably represent more than any other people the spirit of fair research. Many of them have passed through a period of disbelief, some of them have been converted even against their will, all of them have felt that in a matter of such importance they must be true to their rational convictions. Sometimes one side, sometimes another may be biassed. It will be better for us at the beginning of our investigation to assume the genuineness of all alike, to realize that pre-suppositions may influence all men equally, and to try to solve our problems on the merits of the arguments rather than in the spirit of controversy.

It may be remarked in conclusion about Strauss that his mythical theory of the Gospels has not prevailed in the world of scholarship. Later critical and historical research has undermined his foundations, and however the problems he touched may be solved, his own solutions have passed away.

VII

Since the time of Strauss the principal discussions on the origins of Christianity have centred in the long succession of critical studies, which go back for their inspiration to the writings of Ferdinand Christian Baur, and have been the product either of his example or of opposition to him. In these discussions miracles have played a part of secondary importance. The tendency has been to be more and more historical, and to aim at greater soundness and objectivity of method. The results we will consider later. At present, in order to complete our historical survey, we shall consider briefly four writers who represent different points of view from which miracles have been examined during the last half century.

The work entitled *Supernatural Religion*:

an Enquiry into the Reality of Divine Revelation,
was first published in 1874. The preface to
the sixth edition is dated 16th March 1875,
and the complete edition which, we may presume,
represents the author's final conclusions, is dated
1879. It is the most complete and thorough
attack on the reality of the Christian revelation
which has appeared in recent years ; it is written
with a considerable appearance of learning, and
covers the whole field of enquiry. Its scope
may be realized from its author's conclusions. A
divine revelation could only be necessary for the
purpose of communicating knowledge otherwise
undiscoverable, and such knowledge can only be
attested by miraculous signs : "by no rational
being could a just and benevolent life be accepted
as proof of such astonishing announcements."
But as a matter of fact, miracles are of little
value as evidence for divine revelation, as it is
equally possible they may be due to Satanic
agency. When either ignorance or superstition
has prevailed, miracles have always existed, and
therefore must in all cases be due to the same
causes. An attempt has been made to justify
them on the assumption of a belief in "an
Infinite Personal God," and "a Divine design
of revelation." There are no adequate reasons
for believing in either. Whatever definition
be given to miracles, such phenomena are as a
matter of fact incredible. The evidence for the

uniformity of nature must be infinitely greater
than can be the testimony of any alleged exception to it.

When we turn to the Gospel narratives and
examine them, we find no reason for making
any exception to this general statement. Our
four Gospels are strictly anonymous works : we
do not know who wrote them, we have very
little evidence for their existence until far into
the second century. Neither external nor
internal evidence gives us any adequate grounds
for accepting them as sound historical documents.

"We were compelled," he says, "to pro-
nounce the evidence for the Resurrection and
Ascension absolutely and hopelessly inadequate
to prove the reality of such stupendous miracles,
which must consequently be unhesitatingly
rejected. There is no reason given, or even
conceivable, why allegations such as these, and
dogmas affecting the religion and even the
salvation of the human race, should be accepted
upon evidence which would be declared totally
insufficient in the case of any common question
of property or title before a legal tribunal."[1]

The work was remarkably clear and trenchant
in its style, and created at the time when it
was published considerable sensation. That
part of it that was concerned with historical
investigation was severely criticized by Light-

[1] *Supernatural Religion*, vol. iii., p. 578

foot and Westcott, and the subsequent course of investigation has made it of little value. Moreover the writer weakens his case by the extreme confidence he has in the correctness of his views, and the determination he shews to prove his case so many times over. If, as he states, miracles are incredible, there is no need for all these elaborate investigations, and the ordinary reader cannot help having a feeling of suspicion at investigations undertaken on the assumption that they can only have one conclusion. The author is clearly prejudiced before he begins to prove his statement, if he has already said that under no circumstance could a miracle be possible. His investigations, therefore, would seem otiose and hardly likely to be of value. As a matter of fact it has become apparent that that is the case.

A writer of a different and more attractive character is Matthew Arnold. *Literature and Dogma: An Essay towards a Better Apprehension of the Bible*, was published first in 1873. The aim was throughout to make the Bible the vehicle of culture. Philistinism, against which Matthew Arnold carried on such a determined crusade, might be represented equally by popular Protestantism, by uneducated science, or by an uncouth and rationalistic criticism. While he does not feel able to accept the normal religious teaching of the Bible, while he thinks much

of it erroneous, and some of it harmful, the
Bible itself, if we will only treat it as literature,
has a high vocation to fulfil, and for that it
must be reserved. As for miracles, we disbelieve them, not from any argument, not
because their historical character can be dis-
proved, but because we know how they come
into existence. They naturally attract the human
mind.

"It is almost impossible to exaggerate the
proneness of the human mind to take miracles
as evidence, and to seek for miracles as evidence ;
or the extent to which religion, and religion of
a true and admirable kind, has been, and is
still held in connexion with a reliance upon
miracles. . . . To pick scripture-miracles one
by one to pieces is an odious and repulsive
task ; it is also an unprofitable one, for whatever we may think of the affirmative demonstration of them, a negative demonstration of
them is, from the circumstances of the case,
impossible. . . . It is what we call the
Time Spirit which is sapping the proof from
miracles—it is the *Zeit-Geist* itself. Whether
we attack them or whether we defend them,
does not much matter. The human mind, as
its experience widens, is turning away from
them. And for this reason : *it sees as its
experience widens, how they arise.* It sees that
under certain circumstances they always do
arise, and that they have not more solidity
in one case than another. . . . Imposture is
so far from being the general rule in these cases,

that it is the rare exception. Signs and wonders
men's minds will have, and they create them
honestly and naturally ; yet not so but that
we can see *how* they create them." [1]

There is no doubt that no one of culture or
historical insight could, in the present day,
accept either the criticism of Woolston and
Voltaire or the rationalism of Paulus. But is
this position of simply saying that we cannot
believe a thing, whether it be demonstrated or
whether it be not, really a defensible one?
What it means is that we have certain
pre-suppositions in our minds ; that a certain
scheme of history, of human nature, and of the
universe, has grown up, and that that makes
our belief impossible. But are these pre-suppositions really true and sound? Have they
creative value? A man of strong religious
temperament finds it equally easy to believe
in miracles. Does not the creative and constructive genius of S. Paul appear to be nearer
the truth than the cultivated literary criticism
even of a Matthew Arnold?

The third writer we may select as bringing
some originality into the study of miracles is
Huxley. He deals with the subject first in
his *Essay on Hume* published in 1879, and
then in a number of controversial essays

[1] Matthew Arnold, *Literature and Dogma*, pp. 132-134.

which were republished together as " Science
and Christian Tradition." His attitude is of
interest, because of the definite and decisive
manner in which he denies the scientific character
of the conception of "the laws of nature," and
condemns the pseudo-realism which he finds so
often, both in those who defend and those who
attack the belief in the supernatural. On the
other hand, he is equally emphatic that the fact
that makes us disbelieve miracles is the absence
of evidence. While it is unscientific to say that
miracles are incredible or impossible, it is
imperative that for events so contrary to
ordinary experience we must have strong and
conclusive evidence if we are to believe them.
To him the evidence was clearly inadequate.
It must be noticed, however, that in his
controversy with Dr Wace, he, with great
ingenuity, confines the whole question at issue
to one single miracle, isolated from the rest,
which undoubtedly presents considerable difficulty—the story of the Gadarene Swine. It may
be suggested that in a scientific investigation,
the attempt to settle a large and fundamental
question on one instance is entirely unsound.
If we are to arrive at any degree of truth about
the miracles of the Gospels, it must be the
miracles as a whole that we must consider, and
not a particular incident selected because it
happens to suit our controversial purpose.

As a typical instance of the attitude of what we may call the mediating theologian of the present day towards miracles, we may turn to Professor Harnack and his lectures, delivered in 1899-1900, and published in England under the title *What is Christianity?* "Historical science," he tells us, "has taken a great step in advance by learning to pass a more intelligent and benevolent judgement on the narratives of the miracles." We must recognize to begin with that "the Gospels come from a time when the marvellous may be said to have been something of almost daily occurrence. . . . No one can feel anything to be an interruption of the order of nature who does not yet know what the order of nature is. Miracles, then, could not possess the significance for that age which, if they existed, they would possess for ours." To condemn a narrative because it contains stories of miracles is mere prejudice. On the other hand, "we are firmly convinced," he assures us, "that what happens in space and time is subject to the general laws of motion, and that in this sense, as an interruption of the order of nature, there can be no such things as 'miracles.'" Yet, "although the order of nature be inviolable, we are not yet by any means acquainted with all the forces working in it and acting reciprocally with other forces. Our acquaintance even with the forces inherent

E

in matter, and with the field of their action, is incomplete ; while of psychic forces we know very much less. We see that a strong will and a firm faith exert an influence upon the life of the body, and produce phenomena which strike us as marvellous." [1]

He would classify miracles as follows :—

1. " Stories which had their origin in an exaggerated view of natural events of an impressive character."

2. " Stories which had their origin in sayings or parables, or in the projection of inner experiences on to the external world."

3. " Stories such as arose in the interests of the fulfilment of Old Testament sayings."

4. " Stories of surprising cures effected by Jesus' spiritual force."

5. " Stories of which we cannot fathom the secret." [2]

He notices that our Lord did not lay undue stress upon the miracles. He bids us study the narrative without being deterred by the miracle. " The question of miracles," he concludes, " is of relative indifference in comparison with everything else which is to be found in the Gospels. It is not miracles which matter ; the question on which everything turns is whether we are helplessly yoked to an inexorable necessity, or whether a God exists who rules and governs,

---

[1] Harnack, *What is Christianity*, pp. 24-27.
[2] *Op. cit.*, p. 28.

and whose power to compel nature we can move by prayer and make part of our experience."[1]

I do not know that Professor Harnack's position is a very logical one, or one that shews great depth of either philosophical or scientific thought, but it is a very fair representation of the point of view adopted by cultivated people at the present time, and may be for us a fitting conclusion of this historical survey.

Looking back on this record of some 1900 years of criticism, the following appear to be the main questions that have been raised. It is asserted :

1. That miracles are impossible because they are violations of the laws of nature.

2. That miracles are inconsistent with the nature and character of God.

3. That no evidence for miracles can be sufficient—not because miracles are impossible in themselves, but because it is more likely that a witness should be mistaken than that such events should have happened.

4. That whether or no adequate evidence could exist, it is clear that the evidence for belief in Christian miracles is not sufficient.

5. That we cannot believe in miracles because we know how they arise. The belief in them is a natural accompaniment of all great religious

[1] Harnack, *op. cit.*, pp. 29, 30.

movements, and there is no reason for accepting
the miracles of Christianity any more than those
of other religions.

It is with these questions that we propose to
deal in the remaining lectures.

And now, in conclusion, looking back over
this long historical survey, one leading fact will
become apparent to our minds, and that is how
very speedily negative criticism goes out of
date. In each successive age of the Church
the Christian apologist and theologian seems to
have been equal to the work before him—or
if not that, at any rate the progress of thought
and development has proved that the rationalistic
philosophy which in each age seemed so formid-
able and terrible, has been a mere reflection of
the spirit of the time—the *Zeit-Geist* of Matthew
Arnold—and has passed away with the rise of
a new generation. We are not inclined at
the present time to accept the views of Celsus,
and the answer of Origen to his arguments would
seem to be quite conclusive. When Butler
wrote he tells us with grave sarcasm how in the
opinion of many people Christianity was done
for, yet Butler's Analogy is remembered when
the work of Collins or Tindall is almost
forgotten. Paley we cannot think of so highly
as of Butler, but no one would doubt that
Paley made out his case against Woolston's
attacks. Hume lives as no other philosopher

of his time, but it is significant that by his very philosophy he destroyed the main point of his argument against miracles. Who would care to subscribe nowadays to Paulus or even to Strauss? Matthew Arnold does not believe in miracles himself, but he is more scornful of the rationalistic explanation than of the miracles themselves. The critical attitude on which the author of *Supernatural Religion* prided himself would be accepted by few even of the most extreme rationalists of the present day. Huxley is a little out of date; and we have already begun to recognize that even Harnack's reconstruction of Christianity was but its translation into a guise that might make it palatable to the particular form of academic Liberalism which prevailed while he gave his lectures. The problems which we have before us are difficult; we cannot expect or hope that this age any more than other ages can provide the final solution; but at any rate we must realize as part of the argument which we have to consider, that, while the main outline of the Gospel narrative would be accepted now frankly and fully by the religious instinct of the day as true to religion and true to human nature, the many rival systems and creeds which have played their part on the stage of human thought have one and all passed away, and would be as much condemned by the philosopher or historian as by the simple Christian.

LECTURE II

MIRACLES AND THE ORDER OF NATURE

Hume's Definition of a Miracle. Huxley's Criticism of
Hume. Laws of Nature as conceived by Hooker and
by Modern Science. The Uniformity of Nature. The
Mechanical Interpretation of Nature. Are Miracles
improbable on the Analogy of the Development of the
World? The Modification of the Scientific Attitude.
Relation of Science to Theology.

I SUPPOSE that the commonest definition of
miracles is that they are violations of the laws
of nature, and the equally common deduction
from that definition is that they are therefore
impossible. For instance, the author of *Supernatural Religion* writes: "There is absolutely
nothing in the constitution of nature . . .
which does not prove the incredibility of a
divine suspension of physical laws, and does
not create a presumption against it. There is
no instance producible, or even logically conceivable, of any power whose effects are opposed
to the ultimate ruling of the laws of nature.
The occurrence of anything opposed to these

laws is incredible."[1] Hume had previously
defined a miracle as "a violation of the laws
of nature"[2] or as "a transgression of a law of
nature by a particular volition of the deity, or
by the interposition of some invisible agent."[3]
Nor is this definition confined to those who
disbelieve in miracles. I suppose the commonest
definition of a miracle on the part of those who
believe in them would be that they are violations of the laws of nature and that that is just
the reason why they are of such value as
evidence. It is obvious, therefore, that a part
of our enquiry must be into this expression
'the laws of nature.' We must ask what it
means, whether it is a term correctly employed,
what is the validity of these laws, and whether
there is anything in them of such a character
as to make the violation of them impossible.

I

It will, I think, be our best introduction to
this branch of our subject if we begin with an
examination of Huxley's criticism of Hume.
Huxley was not only a great exponent in his
own day of natural science, but also one of

[1] *Supernatural Religion*, vol. i. p. 44.
[2] Hume, *Enquiry, etc.*, ed. Selby-Bigge, p. 114.
[3] *Ibid.*, p. 115 note.

the most definite defenders of an Agnostic
position. He did not believe in miracles, and
therefore if we make use of his criticism it is
with full knowledge of the fact that he is not
really our ally.

We have just given Hume's definition of a
miracle. Every term in that definition, says
Huxley, is open to objection. A miracle really
means something wonderful, something wonderful because it transcends or is inconsistent with
ordinary experience. The definition of a
miracle as a 'violation of the laws of nature'
cannot be justified, "for nature means neither
more nor less than that which is : the sum of
phenomena presented to our experience ; the
totality of events past, present, and to come.
Every event must be taken to be a part of
nature, until proof to the contrary is supplied,
and such proof is from the nature of the case
impossible." [1]

It is interesting to pause here and remind
ourselves of the similarity of Huxley's language
to that of Augustine and Aquinas. Neither
of these will allow us to speak of a miracle
as *contra naturam*, for to them nature is the
totality of God's action, and nothing that God
can do can be contrary to His action. Nor is
this merely a matter of words. The error in

[1] *Hume,* 'English Men of Letters,' by Professor Huxley,
p. 130.

language arises, as will be ultimately apparent, from an error of philosophy.

At any rate we have to realize that whether we look at nature from an empirical point of view as the sum of phenomena or consider it from a theological point of view as the sum of God's actions, in neither case can we make any such distinction as to say that some things are a part of nature and some things are not. God's action is one, whatever different aspects it may have to our minds, and the sum of phenomena is one, however much we may, to suit our own investigations, divide it up and give it different appellations and different names.

Now Hume has, it will be remembered, gone on to argue :

" There must be a uniform experience against every miraculous event, otherwise the event would not merit that appellation. And as a uniform experience amounts to a proof, there is here a direct and full *proof*, from the nature of the fact, against the existence of any miracle ; nor can such a proof be destroyed, or the miracle rendered credible, but by an opposite proof which is superior." [1] " Why is it," he asks, " more than probable that all men must die ; that lead cannot of itself remain suspended in the air ; that fire consumes wood and is extinguished by water ; unless it be that these events are found

[1] Hume, *Enquiry*, p. 115.

agreeable to the laws of nature, and there is required a violation of these laws, or in other words, a miracle, to prevent them ? " [1]

To this Huxley answers :

" The reply is obvious ; not one of these events is ' more than probable ' ; though the probability may reach such a very high degree that, in ordinary language, we are justified in saying that the opposite events are impossible. Calling our often verified experience ' a law of nature ' adds nothing to its value, nor in the slightest degree increases any probability that it will be verified again, which may arise out of the fact of its frequent verification." [2]

But Hume himself may be quoted against his own argument. In his *Sceptical Doubts* he had written : " Whatever is intelligible, and can be distinctly conceived, implies no contradiction, and can never be proved false by any demonstrative argument or abstract reasoning *a priori*." [3]

Now Huxley points out that " a miracle in the sense of a sudden and complete change in the customary order of nature, is intelligible, can be distinctly conceived, implies no contradiction and therefore, according to Hume's own shewing, cannot be found false by any demonstrative argument." And then he goes on to

[1] Hume, *op. cit.*, p. 114.   [2] Huxley, *op. cit.*, p. 130.
[3] Hume, *Enquiry, etc.*, p. 35.

shew how Hume " in diametrical contradiction of his own principles," says, " it is a miracle that a dead man should come to life : because that has never been observed in any age or country."

But language like this must ultimately lead to a position which is absurd : There is a uniform experience against an event ; therefore if it occurs it is a violation of the laws of nature.

" Or to put the argument in its naked absurdity, that which never has happened, never can happen, without a violation of the laws of nature. In truth, if a dead man did come to life, the fact would be evidence, not that any law of nature had been violated, but that these laws, even when they expressed the result of a very long and uniform experience, are necessarily based on incomplete knowledge, and are to be held only as grounds of more or less justifiable expectations."

And he sums up his discussion as follows :—

" The definition of a miracle as a suspension or contradiction of the order of nature is self-contradictory, because all we know of the order of nature is derived from our observation of the course of events of which the so-called miracle is a part. On the other hand, no event is too extraordinary to be possible ; and therefore if the term miracle means only ' extremely wonderful events,' there can be no just ground for denying the possibility of the occurrence." [1]

[1] Huxley, *op. cit.*, p. 133.

The real fact of the matter is that Hume was using the term 'law of nature' in a manner inconsistent with his own philosophy or with its current use at the present day in physical science. Unfortunately his fallacious method of argument is still widely prevalent. People still talk of miracles as violations of the laws of nature, still think that the laws of nature have a real existence, still think that they imply the ideas of necessity and cause, and still say that violations of the laws of nature are impossible. It will be remembered, for example, that in a passage quoted in our first chapter, that was the statement of Professor Harnack. It will be necessary, therefore, to examine more particularly this phrase, "the laws of nature."

II

As an illustration of the term 'laws of nature' as it was understood in the pre-scientific days, and as it is still conceived at the present time by a vast number of people, we may turn to the magnificent exposition of law in the first book of Hooker's *Ecclesiastical Polity*. Nature is there of course represented as created by God and ordered by the law that He has imposed upon it.

"That law which, as it is laid up in the

bosom of God, they call Eternal, receiveth according unto the different kinds of things which are subject unto it different and sundry kinds of names. That part of it which ordereth natural agents we call usually Nature's law ; . . . Wherefore to come to the law of nature : albeit thereby we sometimes mean that manner of working which God hath set for each created thing to keep ; yet forasmuch as those things are termed most properly natural agents, which keep the law of their kind un- wittingly, as the heavens and elements of the world, which can do no otherwise than they do ; and forasmuch as we give unto intellectual natures the name of Voluntary agents, that so we may distinguish them from the other ; expedient it will be, that we sever the law of nature observed by the one from that which the other is tied unto."

And then he goes on to describe this natural law :

"God did then institute a law natural to be observed by creatures, and therefore according to the manner of laws, the institution thereof is described, as being established by solemn in- junction. His commanding those things to be which are, and to be in such sort as they are, to keep that tenure and course which they do, importeth the establishment of nature's law. . . . And as it cometh to pass in a kingdom rightly ordered, that after a law is once published, it presently takes effect far and wide, all states framing themselves thereunto ; even so let us think it fareth in the natural course of the world : since the time that God did first proclaim the edicts of His law upon it, heaven and earth have hearkened unto His voice, and their labour has been to do His will." [1]

Now with such a conception of the universe the use of the term 'laws of nature' is quite legitimate. Hooker conceives the universe as ruled by the laws and commands of God. The orderly procession of events in the world is due to His will. " He hath given them a law which shall not be broken." If we explain natural phenomena by such an ideal reconstruction, then the conception of miracles as in a sense violations of law is also justified, and such a violation by the direct will of God who suspends His own laws is conceivable. Although I should still myself prefer to say that it was not a violation of law but rather the emergence of one more fundamental. At any rate the conception implied in such a term as 'laws of nature' can only really be justified on a theistic basis, and on that basis the interference with or suspension or neutralization of natural laws is not an impossible, or even necessarily an improbable, contingency. The laws of nature are but the will of God, their universality and necessity depend upon His will, and if it be His will to suspend any law He

[1] Hooker, *Ecclesiastical Polity*, book i. chapter iii. 1, 2 [pp. 205-207, ed. 1845].

can do so. From such a point of view a miracle is neither improbable nor incredible.

Now let us turn to the modern teaching of physical science and find out in what sense and with what meaning the term 'law of nature' is there used. And here again we may ask in the first place for the assistance of Huxley. The following is his definition :—

"A law of nature, in the scientific sense, is the product of a mental operation upon the facts of nature which come under our observation, and has no more existence outside the mind than colour has. The law of gravitation is a statement of the manner in which experience shews that bodies, which are free to move, do, in fact, move towards one another. But the other facts of observation, that bodies are not always moving in this fashion, and sometimes move in a contrary direction, are implied in the words, 'free to move.' If it is a law of nature that bodies tend to move towards one another in a certain way, it is another and no less true law of nature that if bodies are not free to move as they tend to do, either in consequence of an obstacle or of a contrary impulse from other source of energy than that to which we give the name of gravitation, they either stop still or go another way.[1] . . . The tenacity of the wonderful fallacy that the laws of nature are agents, instead of being as they really are, a mere record of experience upon which we base

---

[1] Huxley, *Science and Christian Tradition*, p. 76.

our interpretations of that which does happen
and our anticipation of that which will happen,
is an interesting psychological fact; and would
be unintelligible if the tendency of the human
mind towards realism were less strong." [1]

Another and similar definition is given us
by Mr Whetham in his book on the *Recent
Development of Physical Science*:

"Many brave things have been written, and
many capital letters expended in describing the
Reign of Law. The laws of Nature, however,
when the mode of their discovery is analysed,
are seen to be merely the most convenient way
of stating the results of experience in a form
suitable for future reference. The word 'law'
used in this connexion has had an unfortunate
effect. It has imparted a kind of idea of moral
obligation, which bids the phenomena 'obey
the law,' and leads to the notion that, when we
have traced a law, we have discovered the
ultimate cause of a series of phenomena." [2]

And again,

"We must thus look on natural laws merely
as convenient shorthand statements of the
organized information that at present is at
our disposal." [3]

And to take a third instance, a very full

---

[1] Huxley, *op. cit.*, p. 77.
[2] Whetham, *Recent Development of Physical Science*, p. 31.
[3] *Op. cit.*, p. 37.

and elaborate discussion on the meaning of the term 'laws of nature' and of all the ideas implied in Cause will be found in Professor Karl Pearson's *Grammar of Science*. While his metaphysical or quasi-metaphysical reasoning will be found on an examination to be entirely unsatisfactory and incapable of giving a logical basis to the science which he is constructing, that makes for us his testimony as to the real meaning of 'law' as applied to nature all the more valuable.

"The discussion," he writes, "of the previous chapter has led us to see that law in the scientific sense only describes in mental shorthand the sequences of our perceptions. It does not explain *why* those perceptions have a certain order, nor *why* that order repeats itself; the law discovered by science introduces no element of necessity into the sequence of our sense-impressions; it merely gives a concise statement of *how* changes are taking place. That a certain sequence has occurred and recurred in the past is a matter of experience to which we give expression in the concept *causation ;* that it will continue to recur in the future is a matter of belief to which we give expression in the concept *probability.* Science in no case can demonstrate any inherent necessity in a sequence, nor prove with absolute certainty that it must be repeated. Science for the past is a description, for the future a belief; it is not, and never has been, an explana-

F

tion, if by this word is meant that science shews the *necessity* of any sequence of perceptions."[1]

Let us then be quite clear. The term 'law of nature' is used scientifically to describe those generalizations in which we sum up the at present exceedingly imperfect knowledge that we have of natural things. And if this be the scientific definition of a law, and if this is the character of the knowledge that science gives us of nature—that it is the sum total of our collective and systematized experience— two deductions will follow.

Our first deduction is that to say of something which happens that it is a violation of a law of nature, and, therefore, impossible, is absurd. What are called laws of nature are being violated every day. Supposing that thirty years ago anyone had asserted that a bone in a man's body was broken because he had seen photographs which shewed a fracture, he would probably have been told that he was a liar or talking nonsense, because it was impossible to take a photograph of the interior of the human body. It is quite conceivable that some of the half-informed people who write on scientific subjects would have said that such a feat was contrary to the laws of nature ; and yet now, owing to our further knowledge of what nature means, such

[1] Karl Pearson, *The Grammar of Science*, p. 113.

photographs are taken every day. It used to be looked upon as a 'law of nature' that the mass of all bodies was constant. Now we know that the greater the velocity the greater is the mass of an electron and probably of all matter. When Darwin's *Origin of Species* was first published, it seemed to many scientific men to be overthrowing the whole order of nature. They had learned to look upon species as fixed. The fixity of species was one of the 'laws of nature.' And they did not see how such a law could be interfered with. I have no doubt that there are still many people who would laugh at the attempts of the alchemist to turn lead into gold, and would say that the experiments that they made merely shewed the folly of the Middle Ages. They might even drag in a little out-of-date science and tell us that in accordance with the discoveries of the chemists, the atoms of lead and gold are different units of matter, that they are indestructible, indivisible, and unchangeable ; that therefore, according to the laws of nature, such a change was impossible. I do not know whether such a change may ever be accomplished : if it were possible to do it with any great degree of facility it would be most confusing to society ; but there is nothing in the nature of things impossible in it. The only reason for believing it impossible would be that we held a certain theory about atoms, and that theory now is to say the least profoundly modified. When people say that anything is contrary to the laws of nature, they mean really either that it is contrary to the particular form of scientific opinion prevailing at the time, or that it is contrary to experience; and the most complete human experience is very limited.

The second deduction is that as far as science goes, the idea of necessity in nature is neither proved nor proveable. Let us take an example. There is probably no event for which we have stronger grounds of belief than the rising of the sun every morning. So far as human records go, the sun has always risen every morning at its expected time, and a study of the life-history of the world would probably enable us to conclude, with something like certainty, that it had so risen for some millions of years in the past. Yet, as a matter of fact, there is no necessity that it will so rise to-morrow. In fact, we know that the whole of the Solar System depends for its cohesion upon a nice adjustment of forces which might be varied at any moment. Neither experience nor science, which is systematized experience, can tell us anything certain about the future.

We are, it must be remembered, discussing this question from the point of view of science. There is no doubt that most people would think that the progress of scientific discovery would

justify us in holding that events contrary to
a law of nature are impossible, and they do not
realize that they are confusing in their minds two
entirely different things.   On the one side, there
are the generalizations of modern science which
for convenience we call laws, but which are not
laws, are not certain, fixed, or definite, which
vary continuously as science progresses, and
have no immutability about them.   On the other
hand, there are certain metaphysical reconstructions in accordance with which people were in
the habit of explaining nature, for which there
was no scientific proof, and which might or might
not be true.   These two conceptions of the
laws of nature have been, and continually are,
confused together, and as a result of that confusion, on the one side the ideal reconstruction
is supposed to be proved by the discoveries of
science, and on the other hand, the generalizations
of science which are in reality a purely mental
construction are supposed to have some element
of fixity about them.

The belief then that miracles can on *a priori*
grounds be proved to be impossible, and that the
progress of science makes it more difficult to
believe in them, appears as a result of this discussion to be due to the confusion together of
two different conceptions of natural law—the
one scientific, the other in its ultimate origin
theological.

III

It may, however, be objected that in thus explaining away the significance of the expression 'laws of nature,' we have really been guilty of evading the point at issue. All this discussion about laws is largely one of words. What we must recognize is the fact of the uniformity of nature. The result of all experience and the postulate of all science is, it may be asserted, that nature is uniform.

The adoption of this postulate has been one of the great results of the intellectual development of the race. The original attitude of primitive man to the order of nature was, on the one side, a mythological explanation of all the phenomena with which he was surrounded, on the other such an instinctive perception of uniformity as enabled him to regulate his conduct. The movement of the sea, the flow of the river, the eruption of a volcano, the produce of the earth—all these were the work of beings, beneficent or malignant, whose actions were supposed to be as incalculable as those of mankind. It was necessary, therefore, that they should be appeased ; their friendliness must be secured by gifts and sacrifices, or their actions neutralized by magic. But while this was the intellectual attitude of the savage, his natural instincts, sharpened by the struggle with the conditions by which he was surrounded, and by the need for self-preservation, had taught him how to regulate his actions in accordance with his environment. This instinctive expectation of a uniformity in nature he shared with the higher animals who, equally with man, regulate their conduct on the assumption that things may happen as they expect. The orderly succession of darkness and light, of summer and winter, the regular provision of the fruits of the earth, the alternation of seed - time and harvest, the trustworthiness of things he came in contact with—all these were part of his mental equipment, and helped to build up this expectation of uniformity quite independently of his intellectual conceptions. It may be noticed as an interesting change of attitude, that while the intellectual conception of the present day is that of the uniformity and order of nature, it is primarily our instinctive beliefs that bear witness to the spiritual basis of life.

The growth of science has been the gradual realization of this uniformity of nature which lies at the basis of our conduct in the world. We have generalized from our experience, and laid down a fundamental principle which we call the uniformity of nature. We must be quite clear, however, as to exactly what it means.

Here is Mr Whetham's description of it which will serve us as well as any other :

"Physical Science," he writes, "seeks to establish general rules which describe the sequence of phenomena in all cases. Underlying all such attempts is the belief that such an orderly sequence is invariably present, could it only be traced. This belief, which is the result of constant experience, is known as the principle of the Uniformity of Nature. In its absence no organized knowledge could be obtained, and any attempt to investigate phenomena would be perfectly useless. Unless, to use the conventional language justified above as a matter of convenience, like causes always produce like effects in like circumstances, science, and indeed all organized knowledge, would be impossible." [1]

In popular language, then, the Uniformity of Nature means to us that the same cause or causes produce the same effect ; or dropping this word 'cause,' which is really metaphysical and not scientific, it means that the sequence of events is uniform. Where the antecedents are the same or approximately the same, the consequences will be the same. If we know as a result of observation that the antecedents abc are in one case followed by x, they will always be so followed ; but if some new circumstance

[1] Whetham, *op. cit.*, p. 30.

were added and the antecedents were *abcd*, the
result would be *y*.

The point which I wish to emphasize is
this : that this doctrine is entirely limited to
the same sequences of events.   There is no
certainty that any particular event will happen
in the world ; there is only the certainty that
that particular event will happen in the same
circumstances.   It is not in the least certain
that the sun will rise to-morrow ; it is certain
that it will do so so long as the circumstances
remain the same.

Let us take some instances which will
shew the limitations of this idea of uniformity.
Apply a magnet to some powdered haematite :
it has no effect ; but apply this same to
magnetite and it will bring away a cluster of
grains.   Now both of these substances are
compounds of iron and oxygen.   The one is
described chemically as Fe_2O_3, the other as
Fe_3O_4 ; that is to say, in the one there are
2 atoms of iron and 3 of oxygen in each
molecule, and in the other there are 3 of iron
and 4 of oxygen.   Here the property of each
compound is, of course, uniform, but a very
slight change in the composition produces a
complete change in the properties.   Gold is
flexible, but drop a pellet of lead weighing
only the thousandth part of its weight into
the mass and it becomes brittle.   Or take the

case of molten iron. A trace of phosphorus makes it hard; more makes it more flexible; still more tends to harden it again.[1]

Or let us take another and more important instance. Here, as it is difficult for the non-scientific person to be accurate, I will quote Mr Whetham's own language:

"In the year 1895, Professor Röntgen of Munich made the first of the sensational discoveries in physical science for which the last few years have been remarkable. Many other recent investigations have been as interesting, and several have more profoundly modified our outlook on nature, but few have struck so readily the imagination of the plain man as the revelation of the skeleton within the living flesh. The origin of this discovery may be said to have been almost accidental. Röntgen noticed that photographic plates, kept under cover in the neighbourhood of a highly exhausted tube through which electric discharges were passing, became fogged, as though they had been exposed to light. He investigated this effect, and found that, when cathode rays impinged either on the glass of the tube, or on the anode, or on any metallic plate within the tube, a type of radiation was produced which would penetrate many substances opaque to ordinary light. Dense bodies, like metal or bone, absorbed the rays more fully than did lighter materials, such as

[1] For these instances I am indebted to Professor Bonney's work on *The Present Relations of Science and Religion*, pp. 139, 141.

leather or flesh, and Röntgen, at once putting
this discovery to some purpose, was able to
photograph the coins in his purse and the bones
in his hand." [1]

What this means is as follows : Supposing
that I have some photographic plates and I
keep them properly covered, I find that they
are not injured in any way. Now I know by
experience that nature is uniform ; therefore, if
I keep my plates covered as they ought to
be, I shall always expect within a reasonable
length of time to find them ready for use
at all times. If I do not I shall probably say
that the plates are bad. But nature is only
uniform if the conditions remain the same.
Here an absolutely new condition is introduced,
quite unexpectedly, and what might be thought,
on *a priori* grounds, to be entirely impossible,
has happened. We believe in the uniformity
of nature, but that will never justify us in
saying that there is anything that cannot
happen.
If we turn to living things the absence
of uniformity is even more marked. No two
individuals of the same species are ever exactly
alike, no individual is exactly the same from
moment to moment : therefore no conclusions
can ever be drawn about living beings which

[1] Whetham, *op. cit.*, pp. 163, 164.

are more than approximate, and it is impossible
to say that any event with regard to them will
necessarily happen. All idea of necessity must
then be eliminated from nature, although we
may believe in the uniformity of nature.

An illustration may help to show how
uniformity in each part is consistent with
freedom in the whole. So long as a motor
car is in good order each separate part must
necessarily do what it is made for ; if you press
the accelerator the engine will work more rapidly,
if you reverse you will inevitably go backwards,
if you put on the brake you will check the
speed. In all these separate cases the action
is necessary ; but it is just because each of these
things is necessary and can be relied upon, that
the whole car is responsive to the will of the
driver. The inevitableness of each separate
movement when isolated is what conduces to
the freedom of the whole.

We may now apply these conclusions in
relation to miracles. It has been argued that
because nature is uniform, therefore a miracle
cannot happen. A miracle is an event contrary
to ordinary experience, of which the cause is
not known. Now there is nothing in the
uniformity of nature as explained above to
prevent anything happening which is contrary
to ordinary experience, and as a matter of
fact things do constantly so happen, and at

different periods in the history of the world
they have done so, in a very remarkable manner ;
nor does any conception of uniformity take
away the possibility of some unknown cause
operating in the world. Supposing we were to
compare the conception of the world as it
was held by men of science a hundred years
ago with the conception in man's mind now ; we
should be astonished at the number and variety
of new aspects of nature which have been
presented. The curious deduction seems to
have been made from this that it is less easy to
believe in the reality of miracles now than
it was. The real fact is that all these discoveries only shew us how inadequate our
previous conceptions of nature were, and they
further suggest to us as a corollary from a
hundred years' experience, how inadequate our
present scientific ideas must be as a true interpretation of reality.

IV

There is still another point of view from
which people feel the difficulties of miracles.
They have formed a conception or plan of the
universe, originally drawn from the idea of
mechanical construction in which there seems
no place for any anomaly. They have pictured
to themselves a uniform development of the

whole of nature; everything is linked with what has preceded it in one great far-reaching scheme. There has been no break in the continuity, no departure or change from the order of things arranged in accordance with laws which, if not known, yet may very possibly be known in the future. This uninterrupted process of nature has gone on. Here clearly is no place for miracles. They mar the symmetry of the whole conception, and it becomes impossible for any man whose mind is possessed with such a scheme to believe in them.

The following extracts, which I owe to Bergson's *Creative Evolution*,[1] will represent this point of view.

"'An intellect,' says Laplace, 'which at a given instant knew all the forces with which nature is animated, and the respective situations of the beings that compose nature—supposing the said intellect were vast enough to subject these data to analysis—would embrace in the same formula the motions of the greatest bodies in the universe, and those of the slightest atom : nothing would be uncertain for it, and the future, like the past, would be present to its eyes.'"

And so also Du Bois-Reymond:

"' We can imagine the knowledge of nature arrived at a point where the universal process

[1] See Bergson, *Creative Evolution*, E.T., p. 40.

of the world might be represented by a single mathematical formula, by one immense system of simultaneous differential equations, from which could be deduced for each moment, the position, direction, and velocity of every atom in the world.' "

It is somewhat surprising to find Huxley in the same company, for it is difficult to harmonize the following extract with the empirical view of the world which he has suggested in his other writings.

" If," he says, " the fundamental proposition of evolution is true, that the entire world, living and not living, is the result of the mutual inter-action, according to definite laws, of the forces possessed by the molecules of which the primitive nebulosity of the universe was composed, it is no less certain that the existing world lay, potentially, in the cosmic vapour, and that a sufficient intellect could, from a knowledge of the properties of the molecules of that vapour, have predicted, say the state of the Fauna of Great Britain in 1869, with as much certainty as one can say what will happen to the vapour of the breath on a cold winter's day."

Now I have no doubt that a position such as this represents a widely diffused conception of the universe, which has really been inherited from the early days of science. The first point to remember about it is that it is clearly not anything which science has proved. The grounds on which we believe it are not proofs that this must be the case, but a deduction built in our minds on the basis of some acquaintance with some operations of the universe.

Nor must it for a moment be supposed that a conception of the universe, as developed according to a single plan such as might have been grasped in the mind of God, is inconsistent with theistic belief or belief in miracles. Those miracles might have been quite easily part of the original scheme conceived of from the beginning and, so to speak, arranged for.

The real question at issue is whether we have adequate grounds for believing that such a scheme is mechanistic, and that a sufficiently good mathematician could create the world from a knowledge of the original atoms or molecules out of which it is composed. I do not think that we should be overstating the fact if we were to say that there is neither evidence for such a theory, nor is it consistent with the progress which science has made.[1] The earliest discoveries of science were mechanical, and were capable of being easily expressed by

[1] See Whetham, *op. cit.*, pp. 19-20, quoting Mach: 'Now, after a century has elapsed, after our judgement has grown more sober, the world-conception of the encyclopaedists appears to us as a mechanical mythology in contrast with the animistic mythology of the old religions. Both views contain undue and fantastical exaggerations of an incomplete perception.'

mathematical formulae.   In this way a mental prejudice or expectation was built up which has profoundly influenced the later development of science.   In some cases it has led to new discoveries being made, and it has only gradually broken down as a principle of universal application.   To the English Deists or the French Encyclopaedists working under the influence of Descartes, such a theory seemed to present the fulness and completeness of knowledge. The actual discoveries that had been made, as is always the case when a great body of new knowledge has been built up, so overpowered people's minds that they neglected other phenomena.   Since then it has been realized that the universe which science has to interpret is far too complex to be comprehended in any single conception.

Mechanical principles, of course, are found everywhere.   Not only are the relations of plants regulated by mechanical principles, but, in so far as they are characterized by mass and energy, the tissues of the human body ; presumably also the physical machinery of the brain is subject to, though not wholly dominated by, the laws of mechanics.   But after all these laws are themselves only mental abstractions.   No phenomena in nature are really regulated by them exclusively.   It is because they are not real that they seem so inevitable.   If we work out a problem of mechanics correctly in our study, quite clearly only one result is possible. If we create a machine on mechanical principles, we are able to eliminate very largely other factors, and the result is again inevitable. But what happens in nature is never the result of mechanics alone, and no result in nature is, from the mathematical point of view, inevitable.[1] Supposing an artist paints a picture, mechanical laws, if we may call them so, are obeyed in all his mechanical contrivances, in the poise of the brush and the palette; chemical laws are obeyed, if we may use the expression, in his mixture of colours; and if he disregards either the laws of physics or the laws of chemistry he cannot produce the picture. But the picture itself is *prima facie* not produced by laws of physics, and no evidence has ever been produced which would suggest that it is. The fact, therefore, that mechanical principles prevail everywhere does not prove that the development of the world has been determined in any such way.

No doubt this appearance of inevitableness comes largely from our use of mathematics;

---

[1] *Cf.* Bergson, *Creative Evolution*, E.T., p. 230. "It is this merely negative tendency that the particular laws of the physical world express. None of them taken separately has objective reality; each is the work of an investigator who has regarded things from a certain bias, isolated certain variables, applied certain conventional units of measurement.

but the apparent inevitableness of everything connected with mathematics is not due to any inevitableness in real things. Mathematics is simply a conceptual science; it is a convenient method of summing up a deductive argument, a form of symbolical logic. The inevitableness of the result simply arises from the fact that we are dealing, not with things, not with phenomena, but with ideas—ideas which we have formed by a process of abstraction as a convenient means of dealing with certain aspects of natural things, and of forming our own rules for guidance in the future. Mathematics is of the highest value, but it does not give us any complete insight into things as they happen; and it is because our minds have been filled with the mathematical idea, that we have such a tendency to form a one-sided and imperfect view of what the universe is like. [1]

As a matter of fact we do not and cannot use mathematics for a large part of science. Of course, in chemistry, so long as we are dealing with quantity or with size, mathematics

[1] Bergson, *op. cit.*, p. 230. "We cannot insist too strongly that there is something artificial in the mathematical power of a physical law, and consequently in our scientific knowledge of things. Our standards of measurement are conventional, and, so to say, foreign to the intentions of nature : can we suppose that nature has related all the modalities of heat to the expansion of the same mass of mercury, or to the change of pressure of the same mass of air kept at a constant volume?"

will come in. Atoms and molecules are things
that can be measured, at any rate, in theory,
and we can conceive that the properties of these
somewhat minute and hypothetical particles
may be treated, as they are treated, by
mathematical methods. A large part of the
developments of modern physics have been
arrived at by mathematical calculations, that
enable us with some measure of probability to
discuss the movements of particles, which bear
the same relation in magnitude to an atom as a
speck of dust does to the dome of S. Paul's.
But are there any grounds for saying that we
can by mathematics, or any form of foresight
possible to an intelligence of the same nature
as the human intelligence, conceive what would
be the properties of chemical things? Can we
on *a priori* grounds conceive that the combination of two gases, oxygen and hydrogen, could
produce a substance with the exceedingly different
characters which water possesses?[1]

---

[1] I have put this in the form of a question, as I find that
opinions are not fixed on the point. The physicist believes
that all the characteristics of chemical compounds might
be deduced from our knowledge of the characteristics of
electrons: he has, of course, made no steps as yet towards
justifying this belief. That there is a different conception in
the minds of many men of science may be seen from Dr
Haldane's book referred to below. "The main outstanding
fact is that the mechanistic account of the universe breaks
down completely in connexion with the phenomena of life.

When the principles of Evolution were first discovered, it was argued that this meant the application to living things of the same mechanistic principles which were supposed to prevail elsewhere, and the whole of Herbert Spencer's philosophy was built up on this supposition. It is, of course, true that the evolutionist philosophy tells us how things have come to be as they are, and it describes in convenient language the process which has been followed. But nothing that has been discovered yet, or is mentally conceivable in relation to what has been discovered, would have enabled anyone to predict that the world of living things now would be what it is. It is quite true that in a sense the primitive amoeba, or whatever the most primitive form of life may be, has developed into living things as they are; but it is using a language which is unreal to say that the whole of living things are present

Whether it is not also insufficient in connexion with phenomena outside what we at present regard as life is a further question which need not be discussed at present. . . . It may be that the practical failure of vitalism has depended on the fact that vitalists have accepted without criticism the physico-chemical account of an experience, and have thus placed themselves in a position in which they are powerless to help biological investigation " (*Mechanism, Life, and Personality*, pp. 64, 65). "The ultimate ideal of biology is to bring within the scope of biological conceptions even the phenomena which we at present interpret as inorganic " (*ibid.*, p. 138).

potentially in that amoeba. There is really no justification for such a statement on any scientific grounds. That amoeba has had the power of reproducing itself. Each separate offspring has varied somewhat from every other, why and how we do not know. Probably they have been influenced by their environment, but that we cannot assert. In this way living things have developed, but no formula can embrace the manner in which they have done so.[1]

More different still are the phenomena which are introduced by the development of the human race and of the human mind. A

[1] The whole question of the mechanical theory of life is discussed in *Mechanism, Life, and Personality : An Examination of the Mechanistic Theory of Life and Mind,* by J. S. Haldane, F.R.S., Fellow of New College and Reader in Physiology, University of Oxford. " As a physiologist I can see no use for the hypothesis that life as a whole is a mechanical process. This theory does not help me in my work ; and, indeed, I think it now hinders very seriously the progress of physiology. I should as soon go back to the mythology of our Saxon forefathers as to the mechanistic physiology" (pp. 60, 61). He could conceive each living thing to be an organism—an organism and not a mere machine. It builds up its body and develops all its living processes as the 'expression of organic activity.' It does unconsciously what we as personalities do consciously. " The apparent physical and chemical changes are the signs of sensuous data which point to the underlying living activity" (p. 82). It is not, in fact, certain molecules which come together to constitute the organism, but the organism which uses the molecules to express its nature or purpose.

very perceptible change has been made in the earth's surface by the construction of the Panama Canal. Have we any scientific proof that that was the inevitable result of the arrangement and form of the primitive molecule? It has been the result not merely of the development of the mechanical power of the human mind, but of a long series of political events: of the discovery of America, of the populating of the northern portion by the Anglo-Saxon race, of the American Civil War; and these both in their causes and in their results are dependent on the idiosyncrasy of individuals, on the influence, extending far beyond mechanical possibilities, of great minds.[1]

It is hardly necessary to discuss these matters further. The point that I wish to

[1] I have to thank Professor Barkla for the following note: "What it appears to me is here logically necessary is some sort of proof that processes of mind are not simply the *result* of mechanical processes, but may *direct* mechanical processes. An illustration that occurs to me is this: Two sentences differing only slightly may affect a person in quite opposite ways. They result in quite different trains of action. Yet the only physical difference between these two sentences is a slight difference in the form of the wave train falling upon the ear. These sentences may neither have been heard before by either the individual or any ancestor, so that there can be no connexion between a particular sequence of sound waves and pain or pleasure. To my mind it is inconceivable that any purely mechanical explanations can be given of this."

emphasize is this: that for a mechanistic explanation of the plan and development of the universe we have no evidence at all; that the formation of such a view has arisen only from the fact that the early development of science was on mechanistic lines, and that men have approached later problems imbued with mechanical theories. What is really true is that in order to study the universe at all we have to take particular groups of phenomena by themselves. We study them in isolation, and the science we create is only true of these particular phenomena as separated from others. We have many separate lines on which we investigate — Mechanics, Physics, Chemistry, Biology, and so on; but neither their isolated nor even their combined testimony enables us to form a complete idea of the total sum of phenomena.

We are not indeed yet in a position to do anything towards constructing a scheme of the universe. Rather our position is this: we are like explorers tracking in an only partially known country; in various directions tracks have been made into the interior. Each of them gives us a more or less imperfect view of the whole; we attempt to construct a picture of the country from our imperfect knowledge, but we must recognize that it is and must, so far as we can see, always be more or less incomplete. And if this incompleteness and imperfection of our knowledge is a fact, the conclusion that we must arrive at is that it is not scientifically or logically legitimate to say on *a priori* grounds that anything is possible or not possible.

V

We have now examined from different points of view the various scientific grounds which have made people think that miracles must be ruled out of court as things that are impossible. We have seen that you cannot say that they are contrary to the laws of nature and therefore cannot have happened, because the laws of nature are simply constructions of the human mind representing the somewhat imperfect knowledge that we happen to possess at the moment. We have seen that you cannot say that they are ruled out by the uniformity of nature, for the uniformity of nature merely means that like causes produce like effects, and no one would conceive that a miracle would happen unless some new cause were operative ; only it is believed that that cause is one remote from ordinary human experience. We cannot say that nature, and everything that happens in nature, is inevitable, because we have no proof that it is so. The idea of inevitableness has arisen through the influence on our minds of mathematical and mechanical science, and these sciences deal not with things as we know them, but with abstractions that our mind makes. Nor are we justified in saying that miracles are inconsistent with any theory of the universe we may have formed, for science is quite incapable of forming a theory of the universe. All its knowledge is partial and incomplete.

But now there is a further point which may be urged. It may be said : ' We quite agree that you cannot say that miracles are impossible, but at any rate science shews that they are so improbable, that for all practical purposes we may consider them impossible.'

Let us consider for a moment how we should describe the beginnings of Christianity. We believe that the introduction of Christianity into the world was accompanied by two great miracles—the Incarnation or appearance of the Divine on earth in human form, and the Resurrection ; that it meant giving new powers and thoughts to mankind, and that certain events happened which were inconsistent with ordinary experience. It meant, in fact, a new starting-point in the world. Now does the history of the world as conceived by science at the present time suggest that such a new departure is impossible ?

Supposing that there had existed a being with a mind of limited, but at the same time of very great intelligence observing this earth from the time of its first formation, and that he had been able to study the history of each successive epoch. We can conceive him observing it during the time when it was still a molten mass or its outer crust was cooling; he might form a very adequate idea of its structure, and the order by which it was regulated, and the materials out of which it seemed to be composed. He would amongst other things see no sign upon it of life at all. Supposing that some millions of years later, he again were to study it, he would find a completely new series of phenomena upon it—phenomena which we should call life. They would have entirely transformed the whole appearance of things. They represent something inconsistent with his previous experience, and so far as we can see, incalculable. How this changed aspect of the world came into existence is not known, and it does not matter for our argument. The point is that a series of events happened entirely contrary to experience. Our observer may go forward again some millions of years, and again he will examine the world and he will find that a race of beings has arisen quite different in character and power from all those that preceded them; they are what we call men, and they are able to accomplish and to do

things quite contrary to any experience there
may have been previously.

Now if that be the scientific picture of the
history of the world, and I believe it to be
so, does it not suggest that there is nothing
inconsistent with the teaching of science in the
coming into the world of new forces and powers
contrary to experience?

It must be pointed out that the value of this
argument is quite independent of any particular
theory that we may hold either of the origin of life
or of the origin of the self-consciousness of man.
As a matter of fact we know nothing as to how
life came into being. It may demand, some
people would hold, an act of special creation;
it may be the natural development of inorganic matter at a particular period in the
world's history, and amid particular circumstances: at any rate we know that at some period
or other, living beings, in enormous masses and
quantities, must have appeared in the world.
The conditions of things were quite different
from what they are now. Even if we were able
in an imperfect way to create in a laboratory
something which seemed to resemble the living
organism, it would still mean that quite un-
paralleled circumstances existed in the world at a
certain epoch. The same thing is true within
certain limits of another characteristic of the
world—the existence of water. Now here, of

course, we have more knowledge; we know exactly what water is, and we are able, to a certain extent, to produce it; it is probably produced in limited quantities in the world at the present time. But quite certainly there was once a time when no such thing as water in any form existed, or could exist, in the world. The original gases of which it is composed were there in enormous quantities. Owing to certain conditions that prevailed at one period, and one period only, water in enormous quantities was produced, and the amount of water in the world has probably remained constant, or approximately constant, since that time.

We do not know, and we are not likely to know, how what we call a man came into being. We recognize that there was a long period of preparation for man's coming into existence; but there must have been a particular period in the world's history when the special characteristic which we call self-consciousness, for lack of a better term, first became developed, in however rudimentary a form. That probably happened once, and once only; it is not, as far as we can see, likely to occur again, and it produced changes of which there could have been no experience.

Now, broadly speaking, the claim of Christianity is much the same as this. It is that at a particular time in human history, a time for

which preparation had been made, there occurred
something of which there had been no experience,
and could be no experience; that there came a
change in the aspects and powers and capacities
of human nature, and that this change was
accompanied by certain events contrary to all
ordinary human experience. The point that I
would urge is this: that science does not give
us any grounds for thinking that such a change
is improbable, and that it is quite untrue to say
that events do not happen contrary to experience; that the whole history and development
and evolution of the world shews that things do
happen quite contrary to any finite experience;
that the world changes, and that the uniformity,
which as a matter of fact we observe, is only
limited and conditional in character. Judged
by the analogy of nature, there is a reasonable
ground for believing in the occurrence of events
of a remarkable character at a particular time in
the history of the human race.

VI

The purpose of this chapter has been to
discuss the question of the *a priori* possibility
or impossibility of miracles from a scientific
point of view; and I would venture to suggest
as a conclusion that science has transgressed its

bounds so far as it has attempted to say in an
authoritative way that anything can or can
not happen. The whole dispute has arisen
from a confusion between scientific investigation,
properly so called, and the ideal reconstruction,
often more or less metaphysical in character,
which people have created on the basis of a
more or less imperfect scientific knowledge.
The object and duty of science is the investigation of all phenomena, past and present, so far as
it is able, by methods which experience has shewn
to be fruitful.   And recent years have shewn that
science itself is learning to recognize more fully
both the extent and the limitations of its domain.
Anyone acquainted with recent scientific literature or with the official expositions of scientific
progress put forth at meetings of the British
Association, will realize that a great change has
come over its spirit.

These changes may, I think, be summed up
as follows.   In the first place, science has learned
the limitations of the generalizations on which it
has lived in the past.   The whole tendency of
the most recent investigations has been to suggest
to us the incompleteness of former theories.   It
must cause somewhat of a shock to the ordinary
mind when we find a meeting of the British
Association quietly discussing whether Newton's
laws of Motion are really true, and we are told
that if Kepler had only known the imperfection

and the inadequacy of his theories, he would have hesitated to publish them. Only a few years ago we were listening to Lord Kelvin arguing, with what seemed to be sound, logical arguments, that the world could have existed for only eight million years while the geologists were demanding a thousand million. Now we are told that all his calculations are vitiated by the probability that there is stored up in atoms an enormous amount of energy which may be set free by the resolution of these atoms; and the possibility of nature, when necessary, having recourse to this storehouse, must make every form of calculation doubtful. When Evolution was first discovered, the brilliancy of the new light thrown on the life-history of the world hid from us its limitations; but suddenly some one asked the question : How do we account for variation? And how do we account for correlative variations? And we realize how imperfect our knowledge is.

The second result is a changed attitude in the minds of many scientific men. They are far less confident and far less inclined to press their conclusions to a point further than these will go. They realize that each line of investigation which they undertake is one-sided and imperfect; they realize the tentative character of their results and the limitations of their knowledge and of the scope of their investigation.

Then thirdly, science has realized how far wider are the phenomena which should be studied than was once conceived. It is right that the facts of human thought and society should be studied scientifically as much as any other facts, but the scientific methods of doing so would not be those of Herbert Spencer, who, whatever service he may have rendered as a pioneer by the collection of facts, having conceived certain formulae, proceeded to rank the facts of the universe and of human life into a systematic philosophy which harmonized with those limited pre-conceptions. Rather we should recognize that all phenomena must be investigated so far as is possible without the prejudice of *a priori* theories. For example, it is realized now that religious phenomena demand special investigation, and Professor William James' book on the *Varieties of Religious Experience* suggests that the actual phenomena of the religious life when carefully explored will not fit into any ordinary scientific reconstruction.

I would venture, therefore, to suggest that our right attitude with regard to miracles is to banish clearly from our minds any *a priori* conception of their impossibility, and to ask whether these things did happen, and if they did happen what did they mean. The problems of life and existence are infinitely larger than any one branch of science or one branch of

H

knowledge—whether Science or Metaphysics or Theology — can solve by itself. We should recognize that if each method of approaching truth keeps to its own sphere and does its work properly it will help towards a more perfect solution of the problems of life for mankind, but if it encroaches on and interferes with other methods progress will be checked. So long as theology put any bar on the progress of science, so long scientific men had a legitimate ground of complaint; so long as science, making exceedingly imperfect deductions on very inadequate knowledge, tried to claim on any scientific grounds that what theology taught was impossible, theologians had equal right to complain. If each works on its own lines, studying human experience in different ways, we may hope to make some small steps forward in solving the many problems that beset our human life.

LECTURE III

MIRACLES AND GOD

Metaphysical Explanations of the Universe. Sensationalism, Materialism, Pantheism. The Philosophy of the Absolute. Mr Moberly in *Foundations*. Bradley. Bergson. Theism. Grounds of our Belief. Anthropomorphism. God not Law but Wisdom, Freedom, Purpose. Revelation. The Purpose of Miracles. Miracles shewn by Experience to be necessary for a Revelation.

So far we have confined ourselves to considering the world of nature as revealed to us by the researches of Physical Science, and the conclusion at which we arrived was that scientific investigation is not properly able to say that anything is possible or impossible on *a priori* grounds. It investigates phenomena as they are presented to it, and it makes generalizations summing up its present knowledge; but that knowledge is always varying, and new possibilities are continuously presenting themselves to its notice. Moreover, we noticed that the past history of the earth shews that although its development has been, in a sense, continuous, at certain

115

epochs new and striking phenomena have
appeared; while the whole process described as
Evolution implies that the unprecedented continually occurs.

It is not, indeed, Natural Science that can
say anything against miracles. It is rather those
systems of philosophy which have claimed to
be based on or to explain the results of scientific
investigation, and it is to these that we must
now turn. While the greater part of this lecture
will be devoted to considering miracles in
relation to Theism, it will be necessary first to
examine certain other explanations of things
which have been put forward. We must ask
whether they have any particular grounds for
denying the possibility of miracles, and what
claim they may have to speak with any authority.
Though we may not be prepared in any way
to accept these systems, it is still necessary to
say something about them, because at different
times they have had a considerable influence
on thought, and a good many difficulties which
have been raised with regard to the miraculous
have resulted from the confusion of Science with
Metaphysics. Metaphysical explanations have
been supposed to represent the results of
scientific teaching.

Now science clearly is not metaphysics, but
it provides some of the problems that metaphysics has to solve, and certain data which

will help towards the solution. Science seems
to assume and to prove that the universe is
rational. The fact that we can with some
considerable accuracy predict and calculate what
will happen in the future implies a system and
reason in things, and also implies the adequacy
of the human mind, at any rate up to that
point. Science too seems to imply that the
universe as we perceive it and know it only
exists as such in relation to the human mind,
and that things in their own nature, even so
far as we can believe they exist, must be very
different from what they appear to be. Science,
in fact, starts from the examination of our
sensations, and it is the main problem of metaphysics to decide what may be the ultimate
cause of these sensations.

I

But we have had enough of preface The
first system I would touch on is the purely
empirical philosophy of the Sensationalist. He
would have us accept a position in which we
acquiesce in knowing nothing outside our
sensational experience. We must put aside, he
would urge, any belief in matter or in God,
even in things in themselves. We must be
content with accepting the fact that we have

certain sensations ; we must study these and
thus discover for ourselves the best method of
arranging what we call our life. Such a system
does not recognize the existence of any rational
order in the universe. Science is purely the
creation of the human mind, and what is
rational in science comes not from the object
of study, but from the mind that studies. It
follows that if such a system be adopted there
is no particular reason why a miracle should
not happen; only it is difficult to see exactly
how it would be a miracle; nor would it have
any meaning did it occur. According to such
a system our only ground of prediction lies in
probabilities, and it is argued that the improba-
bility of an event occurring which is unprecedented or contrary to ordinary experience, is so
great that we may assume that it cannot happen.
Quite a sufficient number of instances might
be given of entirely unprecedented events
happening, and the attempts to bring mathematical processes into these calculations might,
if pressed, lead to very strange conclusions.
But, as a matter of fact, the whole of this theory
of the universe is untenable. If the laws of
nature are only the creations of the human mind
without any relation to objective phenomena,
nothing can explain how it is that we can, within
reasonable limits, predict future events. The
existence of Physical Science implies a rational

order in the universe, corresponding to the reason in the human mind. Moreover, this philosophy does not explain in any way what mind is, or how it can be such as to create the world in which we live. If the mind is enabled to create the fabric of material things, what creates the mind?[1]

Equally unsatisfactory is the explanation of things on the basis of pure Materialism. We are indebted, indeed, to writers of the purely

[1] A system such as is here described seems to be that taught by Karl Pearson in his *Grammar of Science*, which represents the most thorough-going Empiricism with which I am acquainted. His views of miracles are given on p. 142 of the second edition. "The odds against a miracle occurring are so great, the percentage of permanently diseased or temporarily disordered perceptive faculties so large, as compared with the percentage of asserted breaches of routine, and the advantage to mankind of evolving an absolutely certain basis of knowledge so great, that we are justified in saying miracles have been proved incredible."

Similarly, a photograph of the interior of a closed box was entirely contrary to routine, and by this method of argument would be proved incredible. According to Karl Pearson the only standard of truth is routine. "Man in the course of evolution has attained a perceptive faculty which in the normal condition can only present sequences of perception in the form of routine. Such routine, being as we have seen the whole basis of knowledge, is of enormous advantage to man" (p. 143 note).

A very satisfactory refutation of any such position as that described in this last sentence seems to be given in Bradley, *Essays on Truth and Reality*, chapter iv., pp. 75 *seq*.

Sensational School for reminding us that we
have no more direct knowledge of matter than
we have of any other ideal reconstruction of
nature—than we have, shall we say, of God;
that matter is only a creation of the human
mind to explain and unify our sensations. The
progress of science also has largely tended to
undermine any crude Materialism, and it would
be difficult to construct a tenable materialistic
theory of the universe at the present day which
would differ much from Pantheism.

The claim of Materialism would be this:
that all the phenomena of life and mind are
purely functions of what we, for convenience,
call matter; that granted certain initial principles,
the universe has been self-evolved. It is the
result of chance. Neither purpose nor cause
exists for anything. Life has no existence apart
from the material body; nor mind apart from
the material brain. Both alike vanish on the
death of the natural body. Now the relation of
any such theory to miracles is quite clear—if it
be true, miracles cannot happen, and conversely,
if miracles do happen, it cannot be true. Moreover if such a theory be true nothing much else
can be true. It is inconsistent with any belief
in freedom or morality, or God or immortality,
and it banishes all idealism from life.

Nor can we say that there are any
adequate reasons for believing that such a theory

is true.   A theory of the universe will be adequate in so far as it gives an explanation of the
facts of experience.   Now a purely materialistic
theory gives no real explanation; it does not
explain how a universe has been evolved; it
rules out in fact every possible explanation.
The result has been simply due to chance.
Why the original particles of matter originally
existed, how they came there, how they came
to act as they do, how they came to combine
with one another: none of these things are
explained, they are simply assumed.   Further
than that, it attempts to explain mind by
matter.   But matter we only know through
mind.   How then can it explain the existence
of that which for us exists before matter?   No
explanation of the universe will be tenable
which does not explain the whole of experience,
and all experience must start with my
experience of my own mind.   Materialism
denies the existence of that which is the
necessary condition of the experience and
therefore of the existence of matter.

II

There is a natural tendency of the human
mind (under certain conditions, at any rate) to
desire unity, and the systems of thought that

are probably most in vogue at the present day
are those which appear to satisfy this demand.
Such are Pantheism, and the Philosophies of
the Absolute. The one represents a monistic
system expressed in religious phraseology, the
other is the more philosophical exposition of
the same point of view. It is, I believe,
largely the influence of this type of thought,
whether conscious or unconscious, that makes
miracles for many so difficult to believe.

Pantheism means the belief in one impersonal
spiritual principle, of which all phenomena in
the universe are manifestations. It is seen working in the world around us, in the organic and in
the inorganic alike. The laws or forces of nature
represent it. It is working in all the activities of
the human mind, and the Polytheist may believe
that all the various superhuman beings that his
mythology describes may be different forms of
its activity. What is meant by a spiritual
principle like this may be somewhat difficult to
define. Some might believe in it as force or
will, or law or reason, but the fundamental
characteristic which all would demand would
be uniformity. The manifestations may be
varied, but there must be no break in
continuity.

Pantheism claims to postulate a spiritual
principle, but it is somewhat difficult to say
how or in what points it differs from Materialism,

at least from any form of Materialism that is
philosophically tenable. Spirit we only know
as that which 'knows,' 'wills,' 'feels,' and thus
apart from these attributes of personality it is a
misleading phrase. It really makes very little
difference whether we say that all spirit is matter
or all matter spirit. But there is no doubt that
on the whole a spiritual Monism appears much
more satisfactory to the human mind ; it seems
to admit the use of such terms as God ;
it appears to give a satisfactory account of
the relation of the human mind to nature, and
the reason in us and the reason in things. It
presents a conception of a continuous, unbroken,
harmonious development which would seem a
satisfactory account of the universe.

It may be admitted that in such a conception of the universe miracles have no place—
that is, miracles in any sense in which the word
can have a meaning for us. It is, of course,
true that the different manifestations of this
spiritual force may be very varied, that strange
new forms of it may arise and thus produce
novel and unlooked-for events. In that sense
indeed miracles might occur, but they could
not be miracles in the sense in which we
look upon them as signs of the action of a
personal God. For clearly the God of Pantheism
is not personal, and the religious satisfaction that
is gained by the use of the word God in such

a connexion is delusive. Nor can Pantheism be considered to offer an adequate explanation of our experience. It cannot account for personality, nor for the distinction between good and evil. But if we only know things through our own personality, and if a fundamental fact of our own personality is the distinction of good and evil and the capacity of forming moral concepts, no theory of the universe will be ultimately tenable which will not account for these facts of our experience.

There is always some difficulty in knowing exactly what is meant by a Philosophy of the Absolute, and the meaning is not always made clearer by a careful study of the writings of its exponents. To an outsider a good deal of modern philosophy undoubtedly raises the question whether there is any clearness of thought behind the very obscure language in which it is presented, or whether the obscurity of the language does not really imply obscurity of thought. The particular point, however, of any such philosophy may be taken to be that it is an explanation of things in terms of pure thought. It is arrived at by a logical process, by an examination of the contents of the human mind, and it would represent that all our experience is the result of thought. Now the particular point of importance for us is that underlying all the speculations about the

"Absolute" is the idea of logical necessity. Nature and thought are alike the unfolding of the Absolute. Thought takes the form of the dialectical method, and therefore all thought is necessary; and the counterpart of thought in nature is the unfolding of reason in the world of nature, and that too is necessary. All such philosophical speculation then as would depict the world as the unfolding or development of absolute thought brings in the idea of necessity. It therefore harmonizes with that conception of the laws of nature as necessary and inevitable which we have shewn that science itself repudiates. It sees in mathematical reasoning the real way in which things happen, and it has thus helped to build up that conception of the universe which makes a conception of miracles an impossibility to human minds.

One of the most sincere attempts that has been made to find in a philosophy of the Absolute a basis for Christian Theism is that made by Mr Moberly in *Foundations*, but I do not think that it has been generally accepted as successful. He certainly does not seem to succeed in explaining how it is possible to admit the existence of miracles in his system, or of any discontinuity in the necessary unfolding of things; and this difficulty, it must be recognized, means not merely the absence of a place for what we may describe as the ordinary miracles of the

Gospels, but also for that which, from this point
of view, is as much a miracle as any others, and
from the Christian point of view is so fundamental—the miracle of the Incarnation. How
can the God who is absolute become incarnate?
Here is a question which must inevitably be put,
to which he does not, as far as I can see, give an
answer.

"Religion," he tells us, "it may be said,
does not demand a God who is the same everywhere, who is never here and not there, who
never does anything in particular, never inter-
poses at the difficult minute. It demands
miracle and intervention in the older sense;
in fact, what William James distinguishes as
'crass' from 'refined' supernaturalism. Theology may make too great sacrifices, in order to
achieve philosophical 'respectability.'"[1]

Our criticism may be confined to two
points. In the first place, from the Christian
point of view no system can be satisfactory
which does not explain and admit a real Incarnation, and surely any incarnation must be a
miracle, and must be an intervention, and can
hardly be included under the term 'refined
supernaturalism' — whatever that somewhat
peculiar expression may mean. It is difficult,
in fact, to see how anything like an incarnation
is possible from the point of view of any

[1] *Foundations*, p. 492.

consistent philosophy of the Absolute. And secondly it may perhaps be legitimate to express a doubt as to the claims which any form of Monism can make to philosophic respectability. No such system it may be said, and we believe correctly, can account for all the facts of experience, for our conception of personality, for our sense of moral obligation, and for the more specifically religious conception of God as our Father.

I do not believe that we shall ever ultimately be satisfied with any such systems as these. The important point, however, for us to emphasize is that the fundamental difficulty of believing in miracles has not arisen from any necessary logical deduction from the discoveries of Natural Science, but has arisen from *a priori* conceptions of the universe which have started with the idea of law—whether as a logical or as a physical necessity—and have demanded that the universe should be fitted in to that conception.

I do not think that the preceding exposition or criticism of the doctrine of the Absolute as it is often held is unfair. None of it, however, would be justified in any way in relation to any such philosophy as that expounded by Mr Bradley. He seems, in fact, definitely to condemn such theories.

"Everywhere on behalf of the real Absolute I have been warning the reader against that

128 MIRACLES AND GOD

false absolutism which in philosophy is to me
another name for error. And it is an error
which results in a twofold mistake. It takes
some distinction within the whole, and asserts it
as being real by itself and unconditionally ; and
then from this misconceived ground it goes on
to decry or to belittle other complementary
aspects of the same whole. But as against such
absolutism, the very soul of the Absolute which
I defend is its insistence and emphasis on an
all-pervasive relativism. . . . The absolute right
owned by every side of life is, in other words,
conditional on its service, and on its acceptance
of limited value and reality. . . . And this principle throughout conflicts with what we have
condemned as the vice of abstractionism and
absolutism." [1]

Further on he writes :

"One main work of philosophy is to shew
that, where there is isolation and abstraction,
there is everywhere, so far as this abstraction
forgets itself, unreality and error." [2]

I do not suppose that Mr Bradley would
agree with the argument of these lectures ; but I
am quite sure that his principles would condemn
all those theories—whether scientific, pseudo-
scientific, or metaphysical—which would assert
on *a priori* grounds that miracles are impossible.
To me it is just because I try to look at things

[1] *Essays on Truth and Reality,* p. 470.
[2] *Op. cit.,* p. 473.

as a whole, and to avoid constructing any theory
of the universe, either theistic or scientific, by
abstracting and isolating certain aspects ; because
I try to judge truth by the standard of coher-
ence and comprehension ; that I feel that room
must be found for the possibility, even the
probability, of what is called miraculous. I
think even thus much might be considered as a
legitimate application of Mr Bradley's principles.

The philosophy of Bergson is too recent, too
original, and too incomplete, to make it possible
to see its bearings either on religious thought
as a whole or on our own particular subject.
What, however, is important for us to note is
the support that it gives to the critical position
which we have been aiming throughout at estab-
lishing, that our intellectual conceptions of nature
do not constitute or correspond with the whole
of reality, but only formulate a particular knowledge which we can grasp at the moment, or the
particular aspect that we may require for our
practical purpose. Our *a priori* difficulties have
arisen not from the reality of nature, but from
the intellectual conceptions which we have
substituted and confused with this reality.
The unreality of our mental constructions is
what Bergson seems never tired of emphasizing.[1]

---

[1] Bergson, *Creative Evolution*, E.T., p. 230. " We cannot
insist too strongly that there is something artificial in the
mathematical power of a physical law, and consequently in

As for his own conception of an evolution which is itself creative and is undetermined, it is quite incompatible with any of the *a priori* conceptions of God which we have considered; it is not in itself perhaps incompatible with God as He is revealed to us in Christian thought; but it is probable that before Professor Bergson has completed his book he will be compelled to modify his extreme hostility to any form of finalism.

But it is time that we pass to consider miracles from the point of view of Christian Theism.

III

By Theism we mean the belief in creation, the sustaining, and the government of the world by a Personal God. Whatever intuitions of such belief there may have been at times in the world's history, it seems to have come to

our scientific knowledge of things. Our standards of measurement are conventional, and, so to say, foreign to the intentions of nature: can we suppose that nature has velated all the modalities of heat to the expansion of the same mass of mercury, or to the change of pressure of the same mass of air kept at a constant volume?" Or again, "None of these (laws of the physical world) has objective reality; each is the work of an investigator who has regarded things from a certain bias, isolated certain variables, applied certain conventional units of measurement."

us in any definite form only through revelation ;
but if that be the origin of the belief, we may also
look upon it as the hypothesis which is the best
capable of explaining to us the universe of our
experience. It is not necessary to say now that
proofs of the existence of God of a demonstrative character are not possible. We have no
reason for thinking that we can prove in a
demonstrative fashion anything outside the
limits of human experience or that our mental
powers are adequate to say what must be the
nature of things. What we can, I think, say is
that if we take the whole of our experience, the
hypothesis of God as revealed by Christianity
is the most adequate explanation that we can
give of it. It starts from a recognition of human
personality, it explains the moral facts of life,
it helps us to understand the purpose and aim
of the universe.[1] The problem before us now is
—granting the existence of such a God, how
far does it allow and justify a belief in miracles.

In what sense, and how far, can we know
the nature of God ? Let us turn back first of

[1] An able exposition of the argument for the belief in
a Personal God will be found in Illingworth, " Personality
Human and Divine," *Bampton Lectures*, lecture iv. I do not
see that his statement is anyway open to the criticisms
made in *Foundations*, p. 432. See also Lotze, *Microcosmus*,
bk. ix., chap. iv. A long extract on the 'Personality of
God' is given in Caldecott and Mackintosh, *Selections from
the Literature of Theism*, p. 368.

all for two or three minutes to that conception which comes to us from Spinoza, the outline of which has already been sketched. It was there stated that Spinoza's system was really pantheistic, and as such it might have been treated so as to illustrate what was said above about the influence of pantheistic conceptions upon our beliefs. But as it has been looked upon as theistic, and as his philosophy has been accepted as an adequate representation of what we might conceive God to be, it will be useful for us to examine it in this connexion. It represents, as we have already noticed, the philosophy which inspired the Rationalism of Paulus and other theologians, especially in the early nineteenth century. And like all other such conceptions, it still lives on and influences religious thought. Now to Spinoza, and to those who think like him, God is represented as Law and Necessity. By a process which has the appearance of a demonstrative argument, an attempt is made to prove this; but any cogency in the argument only comes from the fact that it assumes the conclusion that it wishes to arrive at. His conception of God is mathematical and mechanistic. We have noticed how, in the early days of science, mathematical and mechanistic systems of thought were a natural development, and how these early speculations have impressed themselves upon our study of nature. But it is equally true to say that similar conceptions have been read into our idea of God, and that He too has been made a machine. It is a good illustration of that tendency which seems to be inherent in mankind to create God in its own image, and must make us hesitate and examine most critically our own speculations.

It is obvious, indeed, that any attempt that we can make to conceive God must be imperfect, that we cannot know Him as He is. We can only approach Him by the analogy of human nature; but if we are to approach God from what we know of man, we must be careful that we take this human nature in its highest form, and then we must realize how imperfect and limited our conception must be. In a sense, in fact, we must be anthropomorphic. When we say that God is Personal, we recognize that we only know personality through ourselves. When we say that God is good, we recognize that we argue from moral ideals as we know them amongst men. When we say that He is reason, we argue from the reason which we know as a characteristic of the human mind, and which we think is exhibited in the nature around us. But having made use of these epithets we recognize that they are but an imperfect expression of what must transcend all experience. Above all, we recognize that we cannot limit the power of God by any limitations that our own limited intellects create.

For example, we may quite rightly speak of the laws of nature as God's laws, expressing the fact that what is to us the beauty and order of nature is the result of God's work ; but that does not mean either that our generalizations as to the world around us are the same as God's laws, or that law represents the aspect of nature from the point of view of God.

Many years ago Archbishop Trench wrote of the laws of God and of nature in a far more adequate manner than was usual in his day.

" To speak," he says, " of 'laws of God,' 'laws of nature,' may become to us a language altogether deceptive, and hiding the deeper reality from our eyes. *Laws* of God exist only for us. It is a *will* of God for Himself. That will, indeed, being the will of highest wisdom and love, excludes all wilfulness—is a will upon which we can securely count ; from the past expressions of it we can presume its future, and so we rightfully call it a law. But still from moment to moment it is a will ; each law, as we term it, of nature is only that which we have learned concerning this will in that particular region of its activity. To say then that there is more of the will of God in a miracle than in any other work of His, is insufficient. Such an affirmation grows out of that lifeless scheme of the world, of which we should ever be seeking to rid ourselves, but which such a theory will only help to confirm and to uphold."[1]

In the same way it is not necessary to think of miracles from the point of view of God as contrary to law, that is to say, as a breach of divine consistency; for our knowledge of the divine government of the world must obviously be imperfect, just as our knowledge of nature is; and it is obvious that both the Incarnation itself and all its attendant circumstances, and those means by which it was made known to man, must all have been part of divine fore-knowledge, the work of divine wisdom in dealing with mankind.

And this word 'wisdom' probably provides us with the least inadequate manner of describing our conception of God in His dealings with man. At the end of his great argument in the Epistle to the Romans, justifying so far as he could see the ways of God to man, the Apostle ends with the following great ascription of praise :—

"O the depth of the riches both of the wisdom and the knowledge of God! how un-searchable are his judgements, and his ways past tracing out! For who hath known the mind of the Lord? or who hath been his coun-sellor? or who hath first given to him, and it shall be recompensed unto him again? For

[1] Trench, *Miracles*, p. 10.

of him, and through him, and unto him, are all things." [1]

If then we want a word which may best express in the highest manner possible for us what we think of God, it is Wisdom, as that idea was developed in the Wisdom literature of the Jews. The term 'wisdom' seems to have denoted all that was implied in the divine Logos of the Greeks; but wisdom has a personal connotation, while the Logos primarily was impersonal. The word 'wisdom' includes within itself all those lesser qualities which go to make up our conception of intellectual power. It includes the idea of skill, of knowledge, of reason; it includes the idea of moral restraint; it means a character which is trustworthy. Wisdom in fact represents our highest conception of what is possible for man, and therefore may, to the exclusion of all other and lesser ideals, be our starting-point in thinking what God may be. For it includes the conception of consistency, order, freedom, goodness, purpose; it excludes all idea of rigid law and determinism or impulse and caprice. It represents the highest point attainable by man, the least inadequate conception of what God may be.

God we may look upon then as wisdom, goodness, love. And that means for us certain

[1] Rom. xi. 33-36.

conceptions which may help us in understanding the world.

It means in the first place the freedom of God, and through God freedom for man. The idea that God's works were mechanical, and that He was limited in His power by His own mechanism was really ascribing to Him less power than man enjoys in relation to his own machines. It looked upon God as a superior artisan who, having constructed the world, was not in a position to alter or change his model. Apart from other ideas, the idea of Evolution, which has more and more given a better grasp of the nature of things, has profoundly changed our conception of God's work. We no longer look upon it as something static, we see in it a power and growth, we recognize development not only in human life, but in the whole universe. God has created the universe, which has the power of developing freely, because God is free; and man is free because God has created him to be free. Abstract difficulties which have been raised in people's minds as to the freedom of man have really arisen from an inadequate conception of what we mean when we say that God is almighty. We have formed a conception of God, as explained above, as a very clever artisan, and we can conceive Him making a machine which we call man. Supposing that machine had the power of voluntary action, of acting independently,

we think that it is inconsistent with our belief
in God as almighty, we think that we are
limiting His power. The reverse is really true.
We limit His power by our own human conception of what we can conceive He would
be capable of. If God were only a very superior
man, then He might make a man who was not
free ; but if God is, as we believe, almighty, if
His power and wisdom transcend that of man,
not only in degree but in kind, then because
He is almighty He can make man free. The
God who cannot make man free is a God created
after our own image.

And then such a conception of God means
purpose in the world. How far we can argue
from the apparent purpose in the world to
God may be doubtful : that we can argue from
a belief in God to a purpose in the world
seems to me undoubted. If we believe in God
as a Personal God, and that He made the world,
it follows as a corollary that there must have
been a purpose in the making of the world.
If then we find, as we fancy we do, signs of
purpose everywhere, however that purpose may
have been worked out, we may reasonably
believe that we have some indications of what
the divine purpose is. And as we believe that
God's wisdom far transcends anything that we
can conceive, when we cannot understand that
purpose we may realize that it is our limitations

and not the failure of God that cause our ignorance. If we believe in God, if we know enough to see some signs of God's will working in the world, it is a reasonable work of faith to believe that His will and purpose is working where we cannot follow. God's ways are unsearchable.

Nor again have we any difficulty in believing that God's purpose might culminate in a divine revelation. If God made man, or to put it perhaps more correctly, if He made the world so that it should issue in man, then in the time and way that His wisdom would suggest, it is natural that He should reveal Himself to mankind. And when we look at the history of the world so far as we can trace it, we can see it developing gradually up to the revelation of God in Christ. In our last lecture we depicted the progress of the universe from the point of view of science. We did not attempt to argue from that progress of the universe, except so far as to point out that it suggested that it was not improbable that wonderful and unexampled things should happen in the world. Now we may look at it from the point of view of a divine purpose of which we think we can trace the outline, although we may recognize that our insight into it is still faint and uncertain.

Out of the undifferentiated nucleus of what we may still for convenience call matter, the

world developed and it reached a stage when
life appeared upon it. It has sometimes been
supposed that a belief in God would demand
or require some special creation of life; it has
always seemed to me that such a conception is
unnecessary. It is equally marvellous to believe
that the undifferentiated atoms and molecules
should have the power to be transformed into
living things, as it is to believe that some act
of divine interference was necessary. What is
important for us is to recognize that in whatever way it happened, a completely new force
appeared in the world—a new force which we
call life, and that it entirely transformed the
whole of the nature of things.

Then comes the strange and wonderful
development of living things upon the world,
leading up ultimately to the development of
man with his power and reason and self-
consciousness. Again we do not know how
the change happened. How was it possible
that molecules of matter could learn to think?
But we know that they did—and again we see
another stage in the fulfilment of the divine
purpose. And then comes the long history of
the development of human society through
which we can see a purpose working, until in
the fullness of time God sent forth His Son.
The great fact of the Incarnation was, in a way
which nothing else could be, a miracle. A new

fact had come into the world, not indeed out of organic relation with existing thought, but still a new and stupendous fact in the fulfilment of the purpose of God—that purpose which was conceived of God, as S. Paul tells us, before the creation of the world, and revealed in these last days in His Church.

And if God thus gave a revelation to the world, which meant, of course, the union of the world which He had created — the offspring of His wisdom—with His wisdom itself, then it is not unreasonable to think that He would give an adequate and sufficient sign of that revelation, and that that sign would consist of events which would make those that saw them say, Here certainly is the power of God.

IV

It has been argued that whether miracles are possible or not, they are so improbable that it comes to the same thing as if they were impossible ; that it is far more likely that men should be deceived, or deceive, than that events of such a nature should occur. I would venture to suggest in answer to this that a reasonable probability has been established that events such as are called miracles are not in

themselves unreasonable or unlikely to occur.
If we look at the Christian miracles from the
point of view of the progress of the world, we
find that it is not unreasonable to expect that
at a definite stage in the development of the
universe events of an extremely wonderful
character should take place. We know that
they have in the past. If, on the other hand,
we look at it from the point of view of religion, it seems reasonable to believe both
that God should reveal Himself to mankind,
and that He should give those men to whom
He revealed Himself adequate proof of His
presence.

Now it has been argued that the only
possible proof of a revelation is miracles, that
nothing else can give sufficiently authoritative
testimony. [1] There are many who would be
inclined to question such a position nowadays.
It would certainly be claimed that miracles alone
are not sufficient; some would go so far as to
say they are not adequate. Now an *a priori*
point of view such as the above, whether in
favour of or against miracles, I am not personally
prepared to defend. I have the greatest
suspicion of that type of argument which
undertakes to prove in a deductive manner that
things could only possibly happen in one

[1] See, for example, Mozley, *Bampton Lectures*, lecture i.,
" Miracles necessary for a Revelation."

particular way. All such arguments are most precarious. I would, however, suggest that there is another and less uncertain way in which we can approach things. It is quite easy for one person to assert that miracles must happen, if we want evidence; it is quite easy for another person to assert that miracles are not evidence. It would be better for us to consider how things actually happen in the world.

Now in the first place we must remember that it is one thing to accept Christianity now, it is another thing to have accepted it when it was first preached. We have now the authority of centuries of Christian life, we have the fact of the progress and power of Christianity, we can trace the growing development of a new conception of life which arose owing to the influence of Christian teaching. We have a very large part of mankind on our side, we can form a conception of what Christianity has meant for the world, we can see things with a certain amount of perspective. If we ask a man now to become a Christian, we ask him to join what is, at any rate, a large existing society. But none of these things existed in the first days of the Church; there was no external authority behind Christian teaching; it came from a body of poor uneducated men; it had neither wealth nor wisdom, nor power nor prestige to back it up. It came making enormous claims upon the credence of mankind. Surely people might say some clear indication of God's purpose was necessary.

Then, secondly, whatever may be the *a priori* judgement of philosophers or theologians, the popular mind has always held that it is a miracle that witnesses to the immediate presence and work of God. We shall have, at a later stage of our investigations, to consider the difficulties which have been raised as to the credibility of evidence as to miracles owing to the wide-spread existence of miraculous stories. At present all I wish to do is to point to the existence of these as a proof that according to the universal expectation of mankind, miracles are looked upon as the natural way in which God might be expected to witness to His presence. It was necessary that the first followers and preachers of our Lord should have sufficient means for knowing who He was and what claims He could make. There is no doubt that some expectation of miracles existed among people. Would it have been possible for Jesus to reveal Himself to His disciples as the Christ unless He had given evidence of Himself in ways which would appeal to them and which they would expect.

And then, thirdly, whether we believe that miracles really happened or not, it is quite

certain that the progress of Christianity from
the beginning was, as a matter of fact, helped
by belief in miracles. It was so believed by
the disciples, by the people, by the Early Church,
and the records of early Christianity told people
that miracles had been worked : S. Paul claimed
himself to have worked miracles. More important still, as we must emphasize later, the
belief in the Resurrection was the belief in a
miracle. It was through events that they
looked upon as miracles that people believed
in it. Now if we believe that Christianity is
in any way true, and accept the fact of God's
revelation through Christ, can we really believe
that God would allow the belief in Christianity
to grow up based on what were illusions. It
is surely more difficult to believe this than to
believe that miracles would happen. At any rate
it is quite clear as a matter of fact and from
the point of view of human nature that miracles
were neither unnecessary, nor useless, nor ineffective.

We are now in a position to sum up our
argument so far as it has proceeded. In our
second lecture we examined the teaching of
science, and asked, Can science give any reason
a priori for not believing in miracles ? and we
gave to that question a negative answer. We
then saw that the prejudice against miracles
came from the influence of various hypothetical

reconstructions of nature which were supposed to represent the result of scientific investigation, but were really based on a most imperfect view of what science had taught, and could not put forth on their behalf any scientific authority.[1]

We then further asked the question, If there be a God is it likely that miracles would occur? and we shewed that if we attempt to interpret the world from the point of view of divine purpose, it was clear that at certain stages in the development of the world striking and marvellous changes had taken place, and that it was not unnatural that God should reveal Himself to mankind, or that He should reveal Himself in a manner that was marvellous, looked at from the point of view of ordinary experience. We then asked what would be the natural incidents of a revelation, and we saw that whatever *a priori* view people nowadays may form of what a revelation should be, there was a natural instinct of humanity which looked upon a miracle as a sign of God's activity in the world, that some strange and distinct event was needed to bring home to man the truth of Christian revelation, and that as a matter of

[1] On the whole question of *a priori* presumptions against miracles, see Butler, *Analogy,* part ii., chapter ii., "Of the supposed presumption against a revelation, considered as miraculous."

fact Christianity was undoubtedly based upon
a belief in miracles.

So far we have been dealing with certain
a priori difficulties that have been raised; we
have now to turn to the question of the
evidence for Christian miracles.

LECTURE IV

THE RESULTS OF CRITICISM

Recent Tendencies of Criticism.   The Tübingen School.
    Schweitzer ; The Quest of the Historical Jesus.   Result
    of New Discoveries.   Constructive Criticism.   The
    Synoptic Gospels.   Their Sources.   S. Mark.   "Q."
    Their Dates.   Their Text.   Their Trustworthiness.   The
    Fourth Gospel.   The Epistles of S. Paul.

I PROPOSE in the present lecture to begin the
examination of the evidence.   That is mainly
contained in the books of the New Testament,
and a preliminary question arises as to the degree
of authority that can be ascribed to them.   It is
widely if vaguely known that a large amount
of criticism has been directed against these
works, that their authority, their authenticity,
and their historical character have been much
depreciated.   It will therefore be necessary to
make some preliminary observations on the
general question of the character and results of
this criticism.   The subject is too large to be
treated at all completely, and I propose to

confine myself first of all to considering how far, generally speaking, it has been successful ; and secondly to ascertaining what results, if any, have been arrived at as to the date and historical character of the New Testament books. So much is necessary for our purpose.

I

How far has the negative criticism of the New Testament justified itself? When a devout Christian is told that in obedience to the voice of criticism he must give up much that he has believed all his life, that has been associated with his deepest religious feelings, much that he considers to lie at the foundations of his creed, he is naturally somewhat slow to listen to its voice. He demands that its methods should be sound, that some general agreement should be arrived at by its advocates, and that it should shew some authority to compel its acceptance. He considers that the teaching of the Christian Church is not only of vital importance to every individual, but also to the well-being of mankind. The records of early Christianity seem to give adequate proof of the events recorded. He is conscious of his own religious experience. He naturally asks : Are the results of criticism strong enough to overturn this chain of evidence on which my beliefs are supported ?

The so-called scientific criticism of the New Testament has now prevailed for somewhere about one hundred years, and we are able to find some test of its claims by examining its history. Does it shew the characteristics of being a progressive science ? Is there that certainty in its conclusions that would justify the demands it makes upon us ?

It is natural to turn first of all to the Tübingen School of Theology. This was not the first beginning of New Testament criticism, but it was the first great school of German theology of a critical character to impress itself strongly on the world. It had all the appearance of approaching its problem by way of careful historical research. Most of us can remember how some thirty years ago a novel, which obtained some considerable notoriety at the time, presented to us the picture of an earnest and devout clergyman who felt himself compelled by the claims of the teaching of this school to start a new organization for preaching a non-miraculous Christianity. What has the last twenty years done with regard to the teaching of the Tübingen School ? It is a remarkable fact that it is now entirely discredited. If you look through the pages of Baur's *Church History* you will find a series of

second-century dates ascribed to the books of the
New Testament which would not be accepted by
any serious scholar at the present time. Baur
explained the development of Christianity by
the antagonism of Jewish and Gentile Christianity gradually merging into Catholicism.
With the exception of some lingering echoes
of its phraseology, the whole theory has passed
away. Baur's historical investigations were
originally based on a study of the Church
parties in Corinth described in S. Paul's epistles.
Mr Kirsopp Lake, to take an example, himself
an admirer of Continental theology, has in his
book on the early epistles of S. Paul, following
up the work of other investigators, destroyed
the last remnants of the tradition that Baur
created. I only quote that work as an illustration of what almost any scholar of the day
would say.[1] There is, in fact, nothing more
remarkable in the history of literary criticism
than the way in which a theory like this which
everyone who prided himself on being in touch

[1] Kirsopp Lake, *The Earlier Epistles of S. Paul,* chapter
iv. See especially p. 116. It is unfortunate that Mr
Lake should speak in a way which is too common of
those who refuse to submit to all the claims of criticism.
It is not the case that those who venture to dissent from an
excessive admiration for the Tübingen School "have usually
never read their books." It is this attitude of those who
claim to be critics which does so much to increase the
irritation felt for their often somewhat arrogant demands.

with modern thought proclaimed to be the last great discovery of research, a final blow to traditional Christianity, to which allegiance was demanded from anyone who would preserve his reputation as an intelligent thinker, has been entirely given up. And this, not only as regards its general claim on history, but also as to most of its details.

It is pointed out by those who defend criticism, that after all Baur was a great man. That may be true. It may be true that he gave an impulse to the historical studies because he seems to go behind the scenes and reconstruct events as they really happened. If we were only concerned with the literary study of the New Testament, we should be prepared to give Baur the credit due to him ; but we are dealing with something much more serious than that ; we are concerned with the claims made by a critical movement to overthrow the whole of traditional Christianity. And the result of our experience in this one case ought certainly to give us pause whenever we are brought in contact with what often are described as "the assured results of criticism." The writings Baur produced may be interesting, he may have given a stimulus to historical research ; but we are concerned with things that are deeper and more vital, and we should certainly hesitate to give them up in response to the demands

of criticism simply because of its intellectual
pretensions.

A similar conclusion is suggested by a
remarkable work published some few years ago
of Dr Albert Schweitzer under the name of
Von Reimarus zu Wrede, and translated under
the title *The Quest of the Historical Jesus*.
Here we have put before us in a vivid and
interesting style an account of the various
attempts that have been made during the last
one hundred and fifty years in Germany to
write a life of the Founder of Christianity.
The intellectual effort, the industry, the mental
power implied by much of the work is pro-
digious; but when we have finished our study
of this long list of critical investigators we
naturally ask the question, "Where does this
lead us?" Is there any unity of method or
of result running through this long array of
remarkable writers? The answer must be
emphatically, "There is not." As Bacon says
of the earlier schools of science *Variantur non
augentur*. There is variation, there is no progress.
And the reason is, that the method is wrong.
Most of these writers do not construct the life
out of the material before them, they attempt
to fit the material into an *a priori* conception.
Some of these lives were written under the
influence of Hegelian philosophy—a philosophy
which sought to represent the whole of history

as the result of an uninterrupted process of development, and could not therefore admit the idea of miracle or of the supernatural. Others were written under the influence of that dogmatic scientific determinism which has characterized the development of the study of Natural Science. Others again under the influence of that intense hatred of organized Christianity which was one feature of the intellectual and political revolt of the French Revolution and subsequent movements. The general impression left is that the material has been fitted into the theory, not the theory developed out of the material. The criticism has been used to justify conclusions already formed.

Now we do not wish to maintain that all this remarkable effort has been wasted. Much of it if misguided was thoroughly honest, and it has played its part in helping us to reconstruct our picture of the historical Christ; but if we are asked whether it shews evidence of sound method or of trustworthy conclusions, we must answer emphatically that it does not. Criticism in this instance also gives us no reason for giving up our traditional theological ideas.

A third method of testing the comparative value of the destructive and apologetic criticism of the Gospels is the bearing of new discoveries. Have they on the whole strengthened our belief in the early date of the books of the New Testament or have they corroborated the traditional view? Let us take one instance— the *Diatessaron* of Tatian. This was a work incidentally referred to in various places by early Fathers about which we had no certain knowledge. Its name, however, and such indications as we had of its methods, implied that it was a harmony of the four Gospels, and Westcott, for example, wrote of it as follows: "Not only then was the *Diatessaron* grounded on the four canonical Gospels, but in its general form it was so orthodox as to enjoy a wide ecclesiastical popularity."[1] The author of *Supernatural Religion*, however, refuses to admit these conclusions and proceeds to explain away all the evidence. "No one," he writes, "seems to have seen Tatian's Harmony, probably for the very simple reason that there is no such work."[2] Again, "As we have clearly seen there is not up to the time of Tatian any evidence of the existence of three of our Gospels, and much less of the four, in collected form."[3] Since then the work of Tatian has been recovered, and Westcott's view is justified in

[1] Westcott, *On the Canon of the New Testaments* [ed. 3], p. 281.

[2] *Supernatural Religion*, ii. 155.

[3] *Op. cit.*, p. 156. The whole discussion in *Supernatural Religion* is both in character and result most illuminating.

every detail. It is, in fact, accepted. For
instance, Dr Moffat in his *Introduction* tells
us that Tatian compiled his *Diatessaron* during
the last quarter of the second century, and that
it was a harmony based on the four canonical
Gospels.[1]

Now this is not an isolated instance. The
author of *Supernatural Religion* makes great
play of his critical examination of the external
evidence of the New Testament and especially
of the Gospels. It was examined at the time
by Bishop Lightfoot; since then there has been
a considerable amount of literary discovery, and
on almost all points on which definite results
have been arrived at, the opinion of Bishop
Lightfoot has been established. The establishment of the genuineness of the Ignatian letters
alone has swept away a great collection of
cobwebs which had accumulated round the
literary history of the New Testament.

During the last one hundred and fifty years
there has been a continued succession of attacks
on the historical character of the New Testament. They have often attracted the world by
their brilliance, they have for a time carried
away a large number of scholars, but one after
another they have been found unsubstantial.
There has not been behind them really sound
critical principles. Each wave of theory may

[1] Moffat, *Introduction*, p. 183.

have contributed some little permanent result to the historical study of the New Testament, but their conclusions as a whole have not been established; and the reason is that their methods have not been sound. They have not been built up on a sound induction. They have largely assumed what they desired to prove. There are still theories of similar character more or less in possession. They are forced on us by a wave of intellectual acceptance. They have a certain brilliancy that makes them dazzling, but our experience in the past ought to make us hesitate in accepting these newer claimants for destroying the authority of the Gospels and the traditional character of Christian teaching.

II

So far we have dealt with the negative results of criticism. But it may well be that some one will say: You ask us to believe certain remarkable events which you call miracles; you put forward in their support the authority of certain documents; you say that these were written at a certain date. Can you give us any good grounds for believing that what you say is true?

Side by side with the more obtrusive forms of criticism which have attracted public atten-

tion and have been so largely negative in
character, there has been silently developing
another school which has sought to bring to the
study of the New Testament a more objective
and critical method. It is represented in
Germany by Zahn and Schürer and to a
certain extent by Harnack, and has been largely
developed in England. Zahn's work on the
history of the Canon, Schürer's *History of New
Testament Times*, Westcott and Hort's *Greek
Testament*, Lightfoot's *Ignatius,* the recent
work done at Oxford on the Synoptic Gospels,
especially that by Sir John Hawkins, all these
seek to arrive at results regarding the date,
composition, and history of the New Testament
books by methods which are independent of
the particular opinions of the investigator. To
a certain extent, sufficient I believe for the
purpose of our investigation, results which may
be considered assured have been arrived at, and
may shortly be summed up.

On the general question of the history of
the Canon and the use of New Testament
writings—that is to say, the external evidence—
a position has been attained which makes the
extravagant dates of the older literary school of
criticism impossible. The whole contention,
for example, elaborated by the author of
Supernatural Religion with so much vigour and
dogmatism, to which we have already referred,

has become impossible. With regard to the greater number of New Testament writings, the judgement of Harnack may be quoted, who in his history of Christian literature assigns to them approximately the traditional dates. With the possible exceptions of Jude, 2 Peter, and James, all the writings of the New Testament must have been produced not later than the beginning of the second century.[1]

Passing to the separate writings it will be convenient to start with the first three Gospels, usually called the Synoptic Gospels, and in close association with them the Acts of the Apostles. On the problems connected with these books considerable progress has been made in recent years. There is far greater agreement, and results appear to have been obtained which are objective and scientific in character. The opinions widely held at the present day are as follows.

It is recognized that the amount of resemblance between the three Gospels cannot be explained without presupposing sources in Greek and those written. The resemblance not only in language, but in order and arrangement, is too great to be accounted for on any

---

[1] Harnack, *Die Chronologie der Altchristlichen Litteratur bis Eusebius*, I. viii. ' Die älteste Litteratur der Kirche ist in den Hauptpunkten und in den meisten Einzelheiten, litterar-historisch betrachtet, wahrhaftig und zuverlässig.'

theory of oral tradition. Of course there was a period when the Gospel story was told in Aramaic and when oral tradition helped to establish it, but that was very early, and the sources out of which at least two of the Gospels were composed must have been written, and written in Greek.

The only method we have of arriving at any knowledge of these sources is to compare the Gospels with one another, and the result of this comparison is as follows. It is agreed that the First and the Third Gospels are not dependent upon one another to any considerable extent; on the other hand, it is agreed that the common source of the narrative which is common to all three Gospels is the Gospel of S. Mark, or a document very closely resembling it. But besides those episodes common to the three Gospels there are a large number of others common to S. Matthew and S. Luke only, and it is recognized that for these there must be a second common written source. The ultimate result of these investigations is that the greater part of the subject-matter of the Synoptic Gospels is derived from two sources, one of which is S. Mark's Gospel, while the other, more hypothetical in character, is generally known as " Q."

As regards the first, it was long customary to consider that the S. Mark used by S. Luke, and also perhaps that used by S. Matthew, were not identical with the one we possess, but were an earlier edition or editions. Some writers speak of a " Proto-Marcus," and a " Deutero-Marcus," some even of a " Trito-Marcus "; others were satisfied with an " Ur-Marcus." The progress of investigation has relieved us from the strain of believing in all these documents. The minor differences may be explained by the ordinary methods of literary composition, whilst the investigations of Sir John Hawkins shew us that what is called the "great omission" of S. Luke—that is to say, the omission of the matter contained in S. Mark vi. 45-viii. 26—may be most readily accounted for on the ground that S. Luke purposely omitted it as containing matter which seemed to him less interesting than other information which he possessed. Both S. Matthew and S. Luke had a considerable amount of material before them. They were limited as to the size of their work by custom and convenience. It should be the length of the ordinary papyrus roll.[1] Therefore in dealing with S. Mark they shortened considerably the narratives they derived from him. In addition, S. Luke omitted

[1] An extremely interesting discussion of the space occupied on a papyrus roll by the various New Testament books will be found in Sir Frederic Kenyon's *Textual Criticism of the New Testament*, pp. 33 ff. [ed. 2].

those sections which seemed to duplicate the preceding chapters. It would be beside our purpose to go further in this direction; it is sufficient to recognize that the Gospel of S. Mark, as we have it, but without the twelve concluding verses and with perhaps a slightly different text, lay before the writers of the First and Third Gospels, and was one of their principal sources of information.[1]

The problem of the second source is not so simple. There is no doubt that the First and Third Gospels have much in common which is not derived from S. Mark's Gospel. It is remarkable, however, that while S. Mark's Gospel is taken as a framework for both S. Matthew and S. Luke, and the matter in it is reproduced very largely in its original order, the remainder of the common matter appears in these two Gospels in different orders, and often even with a different context. It may further be noted that the great mass of it consists not of incidents, but of discourses, and it is now generally believed that this second source was a collection of speeches, and that the narratives were probably only introduced as having formed the occasion of striking sayings of our Lord. Many attempts have been made

---

[1] On the Synoptic problem, see Hawkins, *Horae Synopticae;* Stanton, *The Gospels as Historical Documents;* Sanday and others, *Oxford Studies in the Synoptic Problem.*

to reconstruct this source, but wiser caution is now beginning to be exercised. It is recognized that, supposing we did not possess S. Mark's Gospel, it would be quite impossible to reconstruct it with any amount of accuracy from the other two. It is obvious, therefore, that the problem of reconstructing the second source which we do not possess is one to which only a tentative answer can be given. All that we can say with any definiteness is that it probably contained all the matter common to the two Gospels which is not found in S. Mark. It is on these lines that it has been reconstructed by Professor Harnack. Anything beyond this becomes most precarious.[1]

This it is important to recognize, for it makes it impossible for us to say what the source did not contain. For example, there is a considerable portion of S. Matthew's Gospel not found in S. Luke, which bears a very close resemblance to portions of the "common matter." We may believe that a considerable part of this came from the same source; but to make use of this as if it did would be unjustifiable. It would be equally unjustifiable to argue as if it did not occur in this source. To take an instance. It is well known that S. Matthew makes long additions to the eschatological discourse which is derived from S. Mark, and that

[1] See Harnack, *Sprüche und Reden Jesu.*

most of these additions do not occur in S. Luke. Some few do, many do not. We must not, however, assume that they did not come from the common source. It is clear that S. Matthew was interested in such eschatological matter, while to S. Luke, as a Gentile, it was less attractive. S. Matthew, therefore, would be likely to insert it, S. Luke would not. On the other hand, S. Matthew may have derived it from some other source. We must, in fact, recognize the limits of our knowledge. We must be content with the progress, and it is real progress that has been made. It is probable that S. Mark's Gospel was used by the authors of the other two, and that they also used the common source which we call " Q." The latter we may reasonably conclude contained a collection of our Lord's discourses and certain other matter. It probably did not contain any narrative of the Passion. Beyond that we have no knowledge of its contents.

Besides these two sources there can be no doubt from the statement made by S. Luke in his preface that there were other documents lying before him. Both he and S. Matthew have material derived from sources other than those we have referred to. We have not any direct evidence of the character of these sources, and any conclusions we may arrive at concerning them is only conjectural. To conclude then this part of our investigation, we shall have four documents to consider : two primary ; two, to a certain extent, secondary, being constructed out of the other two.

1. The Gospel of S. Mark.
2. The source we call " Q."
3. The Gospel of S. Matthew.
4. The Gospel of S. Luke.

III

Our next step is to ask what is the date of these writings. A convenient starting-point is the Gospel of S. Luke; here again critical investigation has made definite progress. It is now recognized very widely, even by writers who cannot in any way be called conservative, that the Third Gospel and the Acts of the Apostles were both compiled by the same author, that that author was the companion of S. Paul, and that he was present at the close of his missionary journeys, and was an eye-witness of what he records on these occasions. As Dr Moffatt puts it :

" This conclusion [that the we-sections represent the writer's own notes or memoranda] has now been put practically beyond doubt by the exhaustive researches of Hawkins and Harnack, which support the hypothesis that the diarist

was the author of the Third Gospel and the
Acts, and that the ἡμεῖς passages are either *bona
fide* extracts from his journal or *bona fide*
reminiscences." [1]

In fact, it is now established on grounds that are
as sound as anything historical can be, that it
was a companion of S. Paul, and therefore S.
Luke, who wrote the Third Gospel and the
Acts of the Apostles. This gives us a firm
starting-point. It is, of course, compatible with
any date for these documents between the
year 62 and the end of the first century; at the
same time it makes the latter date very improbable. Until recently it was customary to
consider that S. Luke's Gospel was written
shortly after the year 70. It was thought that
in certain passages the language had been

[1] Moffatt, *Introduction*, p. 295. It is important to emphasize the fact that the investigations which make this conclusion certain, are primarily those of Hawkins, on which
Harnack's work is based. It is one of the humorous
characteristics of some of those who claim to be our guides
in criticism, that they only recognize the value of English
work when it is adopted by Germany. They have no
standard of value of their own. As a matter of fact, the
attitude towards the dates of the New Testament books
which is gradually being reached by many German scholars
has been consistently and intelligently held by English
scholarship. It is Germany that is adopting our conclusions.
But our modern augurs will continue no doubt to demand
an allegiance to the latest German theory without a smile on
their face.

modified owing to the fall of Jerusalem. There have, however, always been a considerable number of writers who have felt that the natural date of the Acts of the Apostles was some time during the life of S. Paul. It is pointed out that on any other hypothesis the ending is very difficult to explain. It is really remarkable that S. Luke could leave S. Paul living in his own hired house in Rome, and say nothing about what happened after that date; in particular, that if, as is universally believed, S. Paul suffered martyrdom, that event should have been left unrecorded. This argument has been pressed by Professor Harnack with his accustomed vigour; he shews, and I think correctly, that there is not a word in the Acts of the Apostles that implies a later date, and that the arguments for placing S. Luke's Gospel after the fall of Jerusalem are in themselves of a most precarious character. He maintains that S. Luke wrote his Gospel and the Acts in the life-time of S. Paul, and that that is the reason why the Acts ends so abruptly. The only hypothesis which would carry weight against this is the suggestion of Sir William Ramsay that S. Luke intended to write another work. At the same time I must express my own opinion that I am not altogether convinced by Professor Harnack's argument. The reasons for placing the Gospel, and therefore the Acts later than

the year 70, seem to me stronger than he
suggests, and in particular the sense of perspective shewn by S. Luke's narrative in the Acts
of the Apostles suggests a later date.[1]

Within certain limits we can fix the date of
S. Matthew's Gospel. It is quoted early in the
second century, and on that ground alone it
would not be possible to place it later than the
year 100. If we turn to the subject-matter, its
character suggests that it comes from a time
very close to the events that lead up to the
great overthrow of the year 70. It was probably
written between the year 60 and 70 : in any case
not much later than the latter year.

The fact that we can fix within certain limits
the date of the Gospels of S. Matthew and S.
Luke suggests a date for that of S. Mark. It
must clearly have been earlier than either of
the others. It was written before the fall of
Jerusalem, probably some little time before, and
we have a good and early tradition that it was
written by S. Mark and reproduces the teaching
of S. Peter. In one form this tradition seems
to suggest that it was written while S. Peter
was still living. A second form places it after

---

[1] Harnack, *Lucas der Artz*. The position which Professor
Harnack now adopts was defended with great ability some
years ago by the Rev. R. B. Rackham in his edition of the
Acts of the Apostles (Methuen & Co.)—the best modern
edition of that work.

the deaths of S. Peter and S. Paul. The whole subject has been discussed at considerable length by Professor Harnack, who is compelled by his theory concerning S. Luke's Gospel to assign to it a date about the year 60. At any rate we may content ourselves with accepting as sufficiently accurate for our present purpose a date earlier than the year 70.

There has been much speculation as to the date and character of the source called "Q." It could hardly have been written much later than the year 60, and the tendency of critics is to put it considerably earlier. Sir William Ramsay indeed thinks that it was written during the lifetime of our Lord, but his view has not obtained general acceptance. His argument is that a document which contains no reference to the Passion must have been written before the Passion. But the object of the work was to collect discourses of our Lord, and we have to recognize that we must not expect a writer to include what was not part of his plan. The literary character of the contents cannot be used as an argument in any direction; nor can it be argued as some have done that the absence of the Passion narrative and of narrative generally means that the Early Church thought little of the death of Christ, or that they took no interest in the record of our Lord's life. They undoubtedly already possessed some

book which contained such information. Some
one, recognizing that, filled up a need by
providing a record of our Lord's discourses.

There has been much discussion as to the
relation of this document to what are called
the "Logia" of S. Matthew. An early writer,
Papias, tells us that S. Matthew wrote the
"Logia" of the Lord in the Aramaic tongue,
and that each one interpreted them as he was
able. There has been considerable dispute as
to the meaning of the word "Logia." Some
have translated it "Discourses," some have
thought that it meant a complete gospel. The
word really means "Oracles" and was regularly
used for Old Testament scriptures. It might,
therefore, be employed equally correctly for a
gospel or for a collection of discourses. Probably the general trend of criticism is in the
direction of a belief that the common source of
the Gospels of S. Matthew and S. Luke was the
"Logia" of S. Matthew, but that there were
two different but similar translations. Such an
hypothesis will explain both the resemblance
and the difference between them. It is better,
however, to avoid the use of question-begging
names, and therefore we shall adhere to the
somewhat barbarous appellation of " Q " for this
second source.[1]

We have, therefore, four documents to use

[1] " Q " stands for the German word *Quelle*, a source.

in our investigations. Two we may consider primary, two derived. We have a collection of the discourses of our Lord written very early, translated probably from the Aramaic, and perhaps originally written by S. Matthew. We have a Gospel written by S. Mark before the year 70, containing teaching derived more or less directly from S. Peter. We have two Gospels, one written by a companion of S. Paul, the other by an unknown author who probably resided in Palestine. Neither of these Gospels can be much later than the year 70. Both these writers make use of other sources besides those we have mentioned, and we have no ground for thinking that these other sources were either later or less valuable than those of which we have greater knowledge.

The question may be asked, and reasonably asked: How far can we consider that we possess these Gospels in at all their original form? It may be pointed out that they were written more than one thousand eight hundred years ago, that we can have little opportunity of testing and controlling the text during the earlier period of their transmission, and we know that there was some tendency to interpolate documents. What reason have we for trusting the text before us. The answer must lie in the knowledge that we possess of the history of the New Testament text, and the

very varied character of the documents by
which it has come down to us. We have far
more evidence for the text of the Gospels as it
has been restored by careful textual criticism,
than for any other ancient work. We have
many early manuscripts. We possess a number
of ancient versions or translations, two of which,
at least, were made in the second century, and
have thus transmitted the text from that period
by independent channels and we have quotations made in patristic authorities from the
second century onwards. We can trace the
history of the text back to the second century;
we know that as early as that there were at
least two types of text in existence, and we
know the limits of time within which they
appeared. There are many thousands of variations recorded, and it is very probable that
most of them go back to a period before the
year 200. When we know so much about the
text and its variations in the second century,
we may reasonably conclude that it is unlikely
that many variations exist of which no trace
has been left in our textual authorities. Now
although there are some passages of importance
which are affected by the various readings,
although there are perhaps places where the
existence of a considerable number of variations
may be best explained by what Westcott and
Hort call "primitive Error," yet the limits

within which the variations occur shew that
there has been no fundamental change in the
general character of the text. About some
details there may be uncertainty, but about the
general character of our Lord's discourses or
the narrative of His life, there is on textual
grounds no doubt at all.

We have sketched above the main results
of investigations as to the date and composition
of the first three Gospels. We have shewn that
they were written at the beginning of the
second Christian generation, that they were
based, as S. Luke tells us, on information
derived from the original preachers of the
Gospel who had been eye-witnesses of the
events they recorded. There can be no doubt
on critical grounds that we possess the narratives
of the life and teaching of our Lord substantially as they were told to the first Christian
generation.

This conclusion is supported by the character
of their contents. There is an eloquent passage
in Dr Sanday's *Bampton Lectures* in which
he describes the great change made by the
destruction of Jerusalem. The whole life of
Palestine as it had existed before that date
was then swept away. It is that life which
the Gospels—not only the Synoptic Gospels,
but also that of S. John—reflect. So far as
our knowledge goes they present us with an

accurate picture of Jewish life and thought at the
time when our Lord was upon earth, and by no
power of historical imagination could it have been
derived except from those who had lived that life.[1]

Here is further strong testimony to that
effect. It comes from Dr Abrahams, University Reader in Talmudic and Rabbinic Literature at Cambridge :

"One of the most remarkable facts about the
writings of recent Jewish critics of the New
Testament has been that they have tended on
the whole to confirm the Gospel picture of
external Jewish life, and where there is discrep-
ancy these critics tend to prove that the blame
lies not with the New Testament originals but
with their interpreters. Dr Güdemann, Dr
Büchler, Dr Schechter, Dr Chwolsohn, Dr Mar-
morstein have all shewn that the Talmud
makes credible details which many Christian
expositors have been rather inclined to dispute.
Most remarkable of all has been the cumulative
strength of the arguments adduced by Jewish
writers favourable to the authenticity of the
discourses in the Fourth Gospel, especially in
relation to the circumstances under which they
are reported to have been spoken."[2]

But we have not only the evidence of environment, we have also the evidence of style and
thought. There is in the Synoptic Gospels,

[1] Sanday, *Bampton Lectures,* p. 283 ff.
[2] *Cambridge Biblical Essays,* p. 181.

and to a certain extent also in S. John, a
definite form of religious teaching and phraseology which is peculiar to them. The earliest
epistles of S. Paul date from a period not
much after the year 50, but they contain only
reminiscences of this phraseology. Take as an
instance the term "Son of Man." It occurs
constantly in the Gospels, it never occurs in
the epistles, only once in the Acts, twice
in the Apocalypse. Take the expression
"Kingdom of Heaven." We have echoes of
its use in the epistles, but the whole of the
Gospel teaching hangs on this phrase. A
regular word used in the Gospels is "disciples."
It is found frequently in certain parts of the
Acts; it disappears entirely from the rest of
the New Testament. Many similar instances
might be added, and the full force of the
argument might be seen by comparing one of
our Gospels with one of the earliest apocryphal
gospels, that called the "Gospel of Peter." It
is based upon our Gospels and borrows a good
deal from them, but it represents the thought
and language of a later date.

We may pause here one moment to remind
ourselves of the remarkable point which we have
reached. During the last eighty years the
whole of the early Christian history has been
in the melting pot. Every traditional view has
been combated. The composition of all the

Gospels has been placed in the second century.
Their contents have been described as wholly
mythical. In the above paragraphs we have
sketched briefly the conclusions which have now
been reached on this subject, conclusions with
which the larger number of writers would
probably agree, conclusions arrived at as the
result of critical investigation. The result so
far as regards these books has been to place
traditional opinion on a sounder basis. On one
point, indeed, the traditional view is not accepted.
Few would now consider the First Gospel to
have been written by S. Matthew. That name
probably attached to it because it contained the
Logia written by that Apostle in its most
complete form. But the authorship of the
Second Gospel by S. Mark, of the Third by
S. Luke, the early date of all three and their
general historical character are not only recognized increasingly, but defended on critical
grounds.

IV

On the other hand, the position of the
Fourth Gospel is at the present moment one of
great uncertainty. Whatever may be a writer's
opinion, he would have no justification for
considering that his conclusions were agreed on.
There has been much conjecture. Many un-

substantial hypotheses have been built up. But there has not been sufficient scientific work, similar to that bestowed on the Synoptic Gospels, devoted to that of S. John.

Certain points, however, must be emphasized. Those who are acquainted with the history of criticism of this Gospel, will remember how fifty years ago it was customary to believe that it dated from a period late in the second century. Since that time there has been going on that study of the patristic authorities of the second century to which we have referred. The methods of that examination have been scientific, and on one point at any rate, some certainty has been arrived at. It is now admitted on all sides that the Gospel must have been in existence at the beginning of that century. Dr Moffatt, for example, tells us that "the carefully marked sequences" of the Fourth Gospel "were familiar and popular in Asia Minor in the opening of the second century."[1] It is admitted now by the majority of critics that it was known to all the prominent writers of the second century from Ignatius onwards.[2]

There is a tendency further to recognize more definitely the historical value of the work. For instance, Dr Edwin Abbott now says:

"I find that the Fourth Gospel in spite

[1] Moffatt, *Introduction*, p. 226.   [2] *Ibid.*, p. 557.

of its poetic nature, is closer to history than I
had supposed. The study of it, and especially
of those passages where it intervenes to explain
expressions in Mark altered or omitted by
Luke, appears to me to throw new light on
the words, acts, and purpose of Christ, and to
give increased weight to His claims on our
faith and worship."[1]

It is acknowledged also that the fact that
so much of the scene of our Lord's history
is laid in Jerusalem may be correct. As Dr
Moffatt says :

"There is good evidence to shew that Jesus
had a ministry in Judea, during which He visited
Jerusalem, prior to His final visit, and that the
narrative of the Fourth Gospel on this point
goes back to a nucleus of primitive tradition
from which they have been worked up."[2]

The evidence also accumulates that the writer
must have had first-hand acquaintance with the
topography of Palestine before the year 70, and
that the fundamental basis of thought is Jewish
and not Hellenic. We have already quoted
Dr Abrahams to this effect, and his statements
are corroborated by Dr Oesterley and Mr Box
in their recent work on Judea in the time of
our Lord. If all these statements are true, it
is hardly possible that the Gospel is really what

[1] Abbott, *The Fourfold Gospel* (*Diatessarica,* x. 1), p. viii.
[2] Moffatt, *Introduction,* p. 541.

it is asserted by some to be—an imaginative reconstruction of the Gospel history.

On the other hand, many critics are determined, if possible, to disprove the Johannine authorship. It is well known that there is a remarkable consensus of evidence coming from writers who lived in the second century, to the effect that John, son of Zebedee, the beloved disciple, survived all his contemporaries and lived to an old age at Ephesus. This statement is associated with the tradition that he there wrote the Gospel that bears his name. This tradition is early, and comes from many different writers. But an old theory that this John was not the Apostle, but a certain John the presbyter, has been revived in recent years, and some support has been found for it in a doubtful quotation from Papias preserved in two writers of the fifth and ninth centuries. The question will require much fuller investigation than it has yet received. It need only be said now that the evidence on which this new theory is supported would be treated with contempt if it were brought forward in support of a traditional opinion.

It is recognized more clearly than formerly was the case that the theological teaching of the book has undergone some translation into the thoughts and ideas of a later period, and that the comments of the Evangelist are mixed up with sayings of our Lord. Personally, however, I am of opinion that a careful examination of the whole question will ultimately prove that the information contained in the Gospel was derived from an eye-witness, and that that witness was undoubtedly " the disciple who testified these things." We do not, however, know enough to say whether he was directly the author or only the source from which the author derived his information.   This disciple was, I believe, John the son of Zebedee, and the main outline of our Lord's teaching represented in this Gospel is derived directly from the teaching of our Lord.

In the present state of critical opinion, it would not be legitimate to rely on this or in fact on any theory about S. John's Gospel as in any way proved. It is necessary so far as possible that the testimony we make use of should be of a character the value of which is generally recognized ; and the evidence of S. John's Gospel must therefore occupy a subordinate place in our enquiry.

The final group of documents that we must refer to are the epistles of S. Paul, and here again we are on firm ground. It is a commonplace in investigations such as that on which we are engaged to emphasize the universal acceptance of the four principal epistles.   They were accepted, it is always emphasized, even by Baur, and no serious writer has since doubted their genuineness and authenticity. Moreover, the tendency of criticism has been to increase the number of accepted epistles. For the purpose of this enquiry, however, the four principal epistles about which there is no reasonable doubt are alone of importance.

Our enquiry then will be mainly based on an examination of the three Synoptic Gospels, the Acts of the Apostles, and the four principal epistles of S. Paul.

LECTURE V

THE EVIDENCE FOR MIRACLES

The Evidence of "Q." The Character and Evidence of S. Mark. S. Matthew and S. Luke. S. John. The Epistles of S. Paul. The Acts of the Apostles. Summary.

In our last lecture we discussed the result of literary criticism on the history and authority of the Gospels. To-day, I propose to examine directly the evidence for miracles; and, as our task is a long one, I will begin at once without further preface.

I

First let us examine the evidence of "Q." We shall take for that purpose the reconstruction of it by Professor Harnack. Not that we consider that this has any particular claims to represent the original document more than others, but because it is safe. It confines itself entirely to matter common to the two Gospels. All that it contains we may be fairly certain

came from the common source; but we have no
grounds for saying that it contains the whole of
that source: most probably it does not.[1]   "Q,"
so far as we can judge, was a collection of discourses. It might, therefore, very well contain
little or no evidence on the subject of miracles,
and it is remarkable, considering its character,
how much it does contain, and how important
that information is.

At the threshold of our Lord's ministry
comes the story of the Temptation.[2]   We are
not concerned to defend its historical character
as a narrative of fact to be interpreted literally.
In all probability the story is a purely symbolical
representation of the temptations to which our
Lord was exposed.[3]   It is the theological
significance that is for us so important. It
implies a consciousness on the part of Jesus of
supernatural powers, and the temptation to
which He is exposed is that of using them in a
way inconsistent with the whole character and
purpose of His mission. He might have used
His powers for gratifying the wants of Himself
and others; He might have used them for a
thaumaturgic display. He might appear (as
tradition said He would) suddenly in the Temple

[1] Harnack, *Sprüche und Reden Jesu.*

[2] Harnack, *op. cit.*, p. 89, § 2.   S. Matt. iv. 1-11; S. Luke
iv. 1-13.

[3] See Origen, *De Principiis*, IV. i. 16 (iii. 1, ed. Koetschau).

floating down from one of the lofty pinnacles, and thus giving a clear sign of supernatural origin. He might, above all things, have been (as every Jew would expect) a conquering Messiah to build up that great kingdom with Jerusalem as its centre, which should embrace the whole of the earth and substitute the rule of the Chosen People for that of the hated foreigner. There was no one from whom the story could have come but our Lord Himself; no one who would have had the spiritual experience; no one who would have had the psychological insight to realize in what form the temptation would come to Him. The story must have come from Himself, and it shews us that Jesus was conscious that He possessed supernatural powers, that His temptation was to use them in a way that people expected—'to give a sign,' 'to be King,' to shrink from subordinating in all cases the power He possessed to the higher and more spiritual end of His work. This narrative will be to most of us strong evidence that Jesus was conscious of the possession of powers that we call supernatural.

We come next to the story of the healing of the Centurion's servant.[1] This is one of the few narratives which appear to have belonged to

[1] Harnack, op. cit., § 13, p. 91.   S. Matt. viii. 5-10; S. Luke vii. 1-10.

this source, and it is reasonable to believe that it was inserted on account of the remarkable saying of our Lord to which it gives rise. It was, however, selected by S. Matthew as an instance of a miracle, and substituted for one recorded by S. Mark, which he omitted. The importance of the story lies not merely in the actual miracle, but in the evidence that it gives of the widespread belief in our Lord's miraculous power. Unless that belief had prevailed the incident could not have occurred. It shews that Jesus was believed to be able to heal the sick, that this belief had spread so widely as to be accepted by a Roman centurion—a foreigner —and that this centurion's faith is so strong that he believes that our Lord can heal at a distance. His authority in the spiritual world was that of a Commander of an army—He had but to speak the word. Even if the miracle had been invented, incidents and sayings such as these have an originality quite unlike the ordinary results of thaumaturgic mythology. What had Jesus done to impress the people in this way ? Of course, it is true that attempts have been made to explain away the story ; but take the narrative as we have it, excepting the miracle. Its authenticity would not be doubted. The only reason for disbelieving it is that people disbelieve miracles. That is, it is good evidence for a miracle.

The next episode that concerns us is the
Baptist's message from prison and our Lord's
answer.[1] John in prison has heard of the works
of Jesus. He wonders whether one whom he
has greeted as the Messiah is really what he
had believed Him to be. Has He really shewn
signs of who He was? So he sends to ask,
"Art thou He that cometh, or are we to look
for another?" Our Lord's answer is twofold.
He appeals to the miracles He has accomplished,
to the works of mercy He has done, to the
Gospel He has preached, and He does so in an
answer reminiscent of a Messianic passage of
the Old Testament—"The blind receive their
sight, the lame walk, the lepers are cleansed,
the deaf hear, the dead are raised up, and the
poor have good tidings preached to them."
Here we have our Lord definitely appealing,
as was natural when dealing with John the
Baptist, to the miracles He had accomplished.
The only method of evading the evidence is
to explain the whole episode figuratively; but
that is difficult, for the story clearly refers to
the works and not to the preaching of our
Lord, and the original passage in Isaiah has
been so altered as definitely to refer to the
miraculous. We can if we will disbelieve this
evidence, because it is evidence in favour of

[1] Harnack, *op. cit.*, § 14, p. 91. S. Matt. xi. 2-11; S.
Luke vii. 18-28.

miracles. If we make up our minds to do so we can disbelieve anything. But it is hardly possible to conceive stronger evidence that our Lord claimed to work miracles, and that in relation to those who followed Him He was prepared to base His claims on them. It has further been remarked that all the miracles referred to are good works, and that there is no reference to miracles of a type that the Pharisees might call "a sign," a mere thaumaturgic display, and that, as always in our Lord's ministry, works of mercy are definitely coupled with His spiritual work.

The next episode is one of similar character and import. Again our Lord Himself refers to His miracles: "Woe unto thee, Chorazin! Woe unto thee, Bethsaida; for if the mighty works had been done in Tyre and Sidon which were done in you they would have repented long ago in sackcloth and ashes." Here again our Lord is represented as referring to miracles that He has wrought, and as condemning those who have disbelieved them. It is clear that He meant 'miracles,' or He would not have had sufficient ground for condemning the cities; it is clear, so far as evidence can prove it, that He believed He had worked miracles in those cities.[1]

[1] Harnack, *op. cit.*, § 23, p. 94. S. Matt. xi. 21-23; S. Luke x. 13-15.

The final incident we must refer to is the story of our Lord healing a man possessed of the demon of deafness, and a discourse on demoniacal possession that follows.[1] The story is, as always in this source, only introduced as being the occasion for a discourse—a discourse which is found in a somewhat different form in S. Mark as well as in "Q." We cannot of course say how much of the discourse as it exists in S. Mark was also in "Q;" we must be content with the evidence that in that source were passages which represent our Lord as recognized by His adversaries as well as by His followers as having remarkable powers of "casting out devils," and also recognize the claim which He based upon them of triumphing over the kingdom of evil. The suffering of human beings from what was at that time considered to be demoniacal possession was looked upon as a visible sign of the power and rule of the Evil one, and there was no part of His activity which seemed a more definite sign of the reality of our Lord's spiritual mission than His power of healing those who were possessed with devils. He claims to cast out devils "in the Spirit of God," and looks upon what He has done as a sure sign that the Kingdom of God has come.

[1] Harnack, *op. cit.*, § 29, p. 95.   S. Matt. xii. 22, etc.; S. Luke xi. 14, etc.

Our examination of this source has been more minute and detailed than we shall generally find necessary, for it has been claimed that "Q" gave no evidence for miracles. According to the usual hypothesis "Q" was mainly a collection of discourses. It contained little narrative. In these circumstances it might have been quite natural that there should be no reference to miracles in it at all. As a matter of fact we find that of the few narratives which were introduced as providing circumstances which led to striking sayings of our Lord the greater number are in some way or other miraculous in character. Further than that the discourses themselves shew that our Lord was believed, and believed widely, to work miracles, that He himself claimed to do so, that to a certain extent He rested His claim to be the Messiah on them, and spoke of them as a sign of the coming of the Kingdom. Of course there is nothing to prevent us from saying if we wish that our Lord was mistaken, that the people were deceived, that He was an impostor, or that the documents are untrustworthy. But we shall only do so because we do not intend to believe the evidence recorded. There is no ground at all for doubting them. The document is admitted to be good, to have contained a true record of His teaching. It is by some thought to be the earliest record of

our Lord's words; it contains many of His
most characteristic and original sayings. The
miracles are in most cases not directly related
but referred to as recognized facts. They
are inextricably bound up with the spiritual
character of our Lord's mission.   It is difficult
in fact to find any evidence stronger or more
remarkable than this source gives.

II

We come next to S. Mark's Gospel. It
is undoubtedly for us the most important source,
and we must seek to obtain any information
we can as to its origin or authority.

We learn from the preface to S. Luke that
there were many narratives embodying the
Christian tradition of the life of our Lord as
it had been delivered by eye-witnesses, and it
is quite clear from the use that they make of
it, that both S. Matthew and S. Luke considered
S. Mark to be the most valuable of all these
documents.   This may be looked on as some
corroboration of the statement made by Papias,
which in its origin cannot be much later than
the beginning of the second century:

" Mark, who was Peter's interpreter, wrote down
accurately, though not in order, all that he
recollected that Christ had said or done.   For

he was not a hearer of the Lord, nor a follower
of His : he followed Peter, as I have said, at a
later date, and Peter adapted his instruction
to practical needs without any attempt to give
the Lord's words systematically. So that Mark
was not wrong in writing down some things in
this way from memory, for his one concern
was neither to omit nor to falsify anything he
had heard."[1]

From the preface to S. Luke's Gospel we
also learn that it was customary for Christians
to be instructed in the life and teaching of
our Lord, and this statement is corroborated
in two passages from the Acts which describe
the scope of this teaching. In the speech of
S. Peter at the election of S. Matthias the
qualifications of Apostleship are described as
follows :—

"Of the men therefore which have companied
with us all the time that the Lord Jesus went
in and out among us, *beginning from the baptism
of John, unto the day that he was received up
from us,* of these must one become witness with
us of his Resurrection."[2]

Witness primarily to the Resurrection, more
generally to the life and teaching of Jesus
was a definite function of Apostles. So when
S. Peter is addressing Cornelius and his house-

[1] Moffatt, *Introduction,* p. 186 ; Eus. *H.E.* III. xxxix. 15.
[2] Acts i. 21, 22.

hold, he is represented as referring to the life and message of Christ as something that his audience is acquainted with.

"The word which he sent unto the children of Israel, preaching good tidings of peace by Jesus Christ (he is Lord of all), that saying ye yourselves know, which was published throughout all Judea, *beginning from Galilee after the baptism which John preached*: even Jesus of Nazareth, how that God anointed him with the Holy Ghost and with power: who went about doing good, and healing all that were oppressed of the devil; for God was with him. *And we are witnesses of all things which he did both in the country of the Jews and in Jerusalem.*"[1]

These passages seem to be sufficient to prove that regular instruction in the life of our Lord was part of the preparation for baptism, and that there was a recognized narrative based upon the witness of the Apostles. No doubt each Apostle would tell his story in his own way; but it would be the leading Apostles who had been in close intercourse with our Lord whose narratives would be the most attractive, and gradually an accepted tradition would grow up. The story would be told in a particular way which would be remembered. Events would be dwelt upon if they contained moral or

[1] Acts x. 36-38.

doctrinal teaching. The tradition that S. Mark's Gospel is based upon this narrative as told by S. Peter, and that S. Mark has given us this common Christian tradition in a literary form is quite in accordance with probability. There is no reason to think that he may not have obtained information from other sources as well. In fact, there is some evidence that he did. It is sufficient for us to know with reasonable certainty that we have a good example of the life of Christ as it was told by the first generation of Christians.

One further question naturally arises. How far during these thirty years had the narratives been written, or had they been only transmitted by memory? Both methods were available. Society in Palestine in the time of our Lord was literary; there was considerable diffusion of education and a considerable amount of popular literature. Not only were the Scriptures read in every village, but the Apocryphal literature clearly represents a popular literature, and it had considerable influence. Christian communities, we know, quite early communicated with one another by letters, and it is probable that they would also have preserved their memorials in writing, whether the speeches of our Lord or, as in the Acts, the early speeches of S. Peter. But there was also a teaching tradition. Memories were trained. The responses of the

N

rabbis were learnt by heart and repeated. It
was customary for a pupil to commit to memory
and to teach what he had learned from his
master. Both methods of preservation therefore
existed, and both were probably used ; we have
no evidence to enable us to be more exact in
our conclusions. The most reasonable suggestion is that the Gospel traditions had been
transmitted during those thirty years, partly
by tradition, partly in writing, and that a
recognized form had been attained from which
in important particulars it would not be customary
to deviate.

S. Mark's Gospel tells us little of its own
composition. If we had only S. Matthew or
S. Luke's Gospel it would clearly be impossible
for us to reconstruct S. Mark, and that should
make us recognize the limits of our power of
literary analysis. The various attempts that
have been made to distinguish different sources
have been, so far, quite unsuccessful ; nor does
it seem likely that objective data will be found
sufficient to enable us to do so. Two points,
however, demand some discussion. The first
is the existence of what are called 'doublets.'
The really important question is whether the
stories of the feeding of the five thousand and
the four thousand are different accounts of the
same event. It certainly is not improbable
that they are so, and in that case the reference

to these events by our Lord would again
represent conflation. Certainly the narrative
of the four thousand has much the appearance
of being a shorter account of the same event as
that of the five thousand. Now if this be true,
S. Mark had probably more than one source
written or oral. We cannot get further than
that, for no possibility of separating them has
yet been discovered.

A second point to notice is the statement
of Papias that Mark wrote 'not in order.'
It is generally agreed that this does not mean
'not in chronological order,' but 'without careful arrangement,' and it may be suggested that
this exactly corresponds with the character of
the narrative as we possess it. It reads like
a volume of reminiscences. There is no particular attempt to write in chronological order.
The Gospel reads as if it were composed just
in the way that reminiscences arrange themselves; the stories come from one who had
been connected with Jesus during His lifetime,
and so the events are mainly narrated in the
order in which they occurred, or were remembered. The events of certain days and
times were more vivid than others. Occasionally
notes of time are given which do not seem
to have any relation to the general arrangement.
But the chronological order is not entirely
adhered to. Events or discourses are grouped

also according to their subject, or from some subtle association which we do not know. I venture to think that it is in some such way as this that signs of arrangement or disarrangement can be explained.

A few more remarks may be added as to the general character of the narrative. While the writer clearly intended to write the life of one whom he looked on as Son of God, he never makes any attempt to prove a thesis or make out a case. He believes it is unnecessary for him to prove. Hence, while the other Gospels shew clearly a purpose and point of view in their writer, S. Mark is simply a chronicler. He gives a narrative which reflected things as they seemed to have happened. He makes no attempt at toning down or heightening effect. He is vivid, picturesque in his language ; the descriptions read as if they came from one who had seen the event; persons are referred to as if their thoughts and feelings had been known. The narrative, in fact, must have come from one who describes what he sees before his eyes. The picture of the events in which he had taken part was still vivid.

We now come directly to the question of the evidence for miracles in this Gospel. And first let us look at it generally. We are intended to get the impression that our Lord's ministry in Galilee was miraculous in the most complete sense. The few stories told us are only to be taken as instances selected possibly for their striking character. What is described in detail in one or two cases we are to gather happened constantly. " At even when the sun did set they brought unto him all that were sick, and them that were possessed with devils, and he healed many that were sick with divers diseases." [1] " He went into their synagogues throughout all Galilee preaching and casting out devils." [2] He enters a boat because the crowds throng Him, "for he had healed many : insomuch that as many as had plagues pressed upon him that they might touch him." [3]   When He arrives at the land of Gennesareth " straightway the people knew him, and ran round about that whole region, and began to carry about on their beds those that were sick where they heard he was. And wheresoever he entered, into villages, or into cities, or into the country, they laid the sick in the market-places, and besought him that they might touch if it were but the border of his garment ; and as many as touched him were made whole." [4]

It is this miraculous power that draws attention to Him.   " What is this ? a new teaching ? with authority he commandeth even the unclean spirits and they obey him." [5]   People

---

[1] S. Mark i. 32, 34.   [2] S. Mark i. 39.   [3] S. Mark iii. 10.

[4] S. Mark vi. 53-56.   [5] S. Mark i. 27.

came to Him from all parts hearing what great
things He did. While it attracts some, it has
not always that effect. "Whence hath this
man these things? and what is the wisdom
that is given unto this man? And what mean
such mighty works wrought by his hands? Is
not this the carpenter, the son of Mary? . . .
and they were offended in him."[1]   Some
of His friends said that He was beside himself.[2]
The people of Gerasa besought Him to depart
from their borders.[3]   The scribes that came
down from Jerusalem said, "He hath Beelzebub,
and by the prince of the devils casteth he out
devils."[4]   Herod when he heard of the marvels
said, "John the Baptist is risen"; so Jesus
retires into solitude.[5]

Now we have to notice throughout that
particular stress is laid on the miraculous. His
teaching indeed attracted also, and that too
might also have the contrary effect; but it was
the miracles that most conspicuously attracted
and repelled. Their reality was never in question; people had no doubt that they happened,
no doubt that they implied supernatural power,
but the problem was: Did they come from
heaven or from hell? Those who were opposed
to the teaching argued the latter.

But Jesus Himself also appealed to the

[1] S. Mark vi. 2, 3.   [2] S. Mark iii. 21.   [3] S. Mark v. 17.
[4] S. Mark iii. 22.   [5] S. Mark vi. 14.

testimony of the miracles. Take the story of
the paralytic man. Jesus is represented as
impressed by the faith of those who were so
determined to bring the man near to Him.
But He does not immediately heal him. His
first promise to him is, "Thy sins are forgiven." It is natural that such a remark
should call forth questions. Jesus perceives
the drift of their thoughts, and immediately
goes straight to the point: "Why reason ye
these things in your hearts. Whether is easier,
to say to the sick of the palsy, thy sins are
forgiven; or to say, Arise and take up thy bed
and walk? But that ye may know that the
Son of Man hath power on earth to forgive sins
(He saith to the sick of the palsy) Arise, take
up thy bed and go unto thy house." [1]

Now the whole narrative as we have it is
well worth pondering over. As it is told us, it
is entirely inconsistent with any other theory
than that our Lord claimed divine powers, and
justified that claim by an appeal to something
which His hearers must have looked on as
miraculous. He acts with dignity and certainty.
There is no misgiving or hesitation. It is
not a question of undisciplined utterances, or
vague and uncertain powers. It is a confident
claim to spiritual authority exhibited both in
the moral region of forgiveness and the material

[1] S. Mark ii. 1-12.

region of cure. And if we study other
narratives we find just the same confidence.
Jesus is always represented as clear, definite, and
decisive in all His actions.

If this story is not true it must have been
definitely written to express an idea; we are
clearly not in the region of unconscious myth.
The story is given us to shew that Jesus claimed
to do what God alone could do, and that He
justified His claim. Apart from difficulties that
might be raised on *a priori* grounds because of
these claims as to miracles, the narrative bears
all the mark of 'vraisemblance.' It is narrated
with such vividness that we can see the events
happening; it has detail which is most unlikely
to have been invented; it is strong, clear,
and simple. It is as difficult to believe that
the story was definitely invented as that it
grew up unconsciously; and it is difficult if we
accept it, to be satisfied with any compromise.
Jesus claimed to be divine and to work miracles,
and people believed that He did work them.

We cannot go through all the miracles
recorded in detail; we can only sum up the
general points of evidence. The great majority
of the stories will be found to bear just the same
character as the one we have described. They
are vivid and picturesque in detail; they are
performed with a quiet calm and dignity, and
almost invariably are associated with the

spiritual side of our Lord's mission. They have been divided into 'miracles of healing' and 'wonders.' Twelve of the former are recorded, and they give the impression of having been selected or remembered as typical. Three of them are described as "possession by unclean spirits," four as defects of sight, hearing, or speech, two paralysis, one fever, one leprosy, one issue of blood. It is now generally admitted by most writers that the evidence for these events is good, but it has been urged that they must be explained as the result of natural processes. Mr Thompson, for example, writes: "The evidence for works of healing is good evidence, but is not evidence for miracles."[1] We shall deal more fully in a later lecture with the explanations offered; at present we will simply point to the narrative of the paralytic as shewing that our Lord Himself, at any rate, believed that the works He did were signs of His divine authority.

The other miracles are classed as "wonders." They are the calming of the wind and sea, the bringing to life of the daughter of Jairus, the feeding of the five thousand (and the four thousand), the walking on the lake, and the making of the fig-tree wither. Now with regard to these, so far as regards the evidence that we have considered at present, they are on exactly

[1] J. M. Thompson, *Miracles in the New Testament*, p. 41.

the same level as the other stories. They are narrated in the same vivid and simple way; they are accepted and looked on as miracles. The difference between them and miracles of healing is not one of evidence, but lies in the character of the event. If the one is believed, and not the other, it is on *a priori* grounds. And this is particularly true of the narrative of feeding the multitude. If, as is widely believed, the two stories are doublets, that throws the evidence back to a very early period in the development of Gospel narrative. We have two accounts, clearly independent, differing from one another as independent accounts will in detail, but both bearing witness to the important fact. There is no more sign in one than in the other of a mythical origin.

A marked characteristic of the miracles is the insistence laid on faith. "Jesus seeing their faith," in the story of the paralytic. "Why are ye fearful? Have ye not yet faith?" He says to the disciples in the storm. "Daughter, thy faith hath made thee whole." "All things are possible to him that believeth." "Have faith in God. Verily I say unto you, Whosoever shall say unto this mountain, Be thou taken up and cast into the sea; and shall not doubt in his heart, but shall believe that what he saith cometh to pass; he shall have it."

And as faith seems to be the condition of

miracles being wrought, so absence of faith
prevents them. When Jesus came to His own
country the people did not believe on Him;
they considered His works to be impostures
or the result of demoniacal agency; they are
offended at Him. Jesus says that a prophet is
only without honour in his own house. "And
he could there do no mighty work, save that
he laid his hands upon a few sick folk and
healed them. And he marvelled because of
their unbelief." This passage is remarkable.
With a boldness which is characteristic of a
Gospel which has the appearance of representing
things just as they happened, we are told of a
case where Jesus could not work miracles, and
this frankness emphasizes to us the truthful
character of the whole narrative. Had the
author of the Gospel been trying to make out
a case, had he been doing anything else but
representing things as they were remembered,
he would certainly have omitted this. Here
and elsewhere he is speaking the truth. It
certainly seems somewhat arbitrary on the part
of Schmiedel to be prepared to accept this statement, and to argue from it that our Lord
never performed miracles. To most people this
narrative of failure will make them give greater
credence to other statements. Similar in
character is the story of the failure of the
disciples: "And I spake to thy disciples that

they should cast it out ; and they were not able.
And he answereth them and saith, 'O faithless
generation, how long shall I be with you ; how
long shall I bear with you.'"

Similar in character seems the command so
often given to those who were healed not to
reveal the fact.   The leper is told to say nothing
to any man but to go shew himself to the
priest.   When Jairus' daughter is raised, He
charges them that "no man should know this.'
When the devils recognize Him, He charges
them that they should not make Him known.
Although He works miracles, although He
appeals to them at times for evidence of His
spiritual power, He always avoids on all
occasions any appearance of thaumaturgic or
magical display.   His miracles are part of
His spiritual work : they are part of His
teaching as works of mercy, as giving spiritual
help in accordance with the character of His
mission.   He feeds the multitude, when they
need it, because He has compassion on them.
He will never work a sign—that is something
so public, so clear and decisive that no one
can doubt that He is the Messiah.   "And
the Pharisees came forth, and began to question
with him, seeking of him a sign from heaven,
tempting him.   And he sighed deeply in his
spirit, and saith, Why doth this generation
seek a sign ?   Verily I say unto you, There

shall be no sign given unto this generation." [1]
This is not a fragment of true history embedded
in a legendary narrative, as we have been told,
but an indication of the limits within which
our Lord restrained the powers that He
possessed. It harmonizes entirely with the
story of the Temptation. The self-restraint and
reticence of Jesus in relation to His miracles is
not the least important of the characteristics
which distinguish the Gospel narratives from
all the many legendary accounts of miraculous
display.

To sum up. In S. Mark's Gospel we have
an early source for our Lord's life which has
the appearance of being a simple, vivid, and
truthful picture, as it was narrated by one who
had been present at the events. It represents
Him as being divine, as the Son of God, as
claiming to have more than human power. It
represents Him as working miracles. The
people believe that He does so. Friends and
enemies alike do so. He claims to do so, or
rather appeals to His miracles as part of the
corroboration of His mission. The narratives
are of various kinds; they are told in a natural
manner — they are closely interwoven with
the whole fabric of the Gospel. We cannot
separate the miracles from the non-miraculous.
No one would hesitate to believe the stories

[1] S. Mark viii. 11, 12.

except for their remarkable character. As they depend upon human witness, no doubt there may be mistakes here as elsewhere, but the evidence is good.

III

We may, I think, couple together the two Gospels of S. Matthew [1] and S. Luke, since from our point of view they have much in common. They are both literary productions, the works of writers who had definite purposes and arranged their material in accordance with those purposes. While in S. Mark or " Q " we are dealing with chroniclers or recorders, in these two Gospels we are dealing with historians or theologians.

S. Luke tells us that he had various sources before him, and that he had constructed his narrative with a view as far as possible to accuracy. S. Matthew equally clearly had various sources. But while both had a purpose before them, it was not the same. S. Luke is primarily a historian, S. Matthew is rather a theologian.

We can study S. Luke's characteristics best in connexion with the work in which he

[1] It is unnecessary to say that the First Gospel is for convenience called S. Matthew's, without implying any theory of authorship (see above, p. 176).

has wider scope. In the Acts of the Apostles
he has clearly conceived the development of the
Church. He marks out the stages of its progress.
He exhibits to us the characteristics of various
types of teaching. He shews an accurate
acquaintance with local government and other
similar matters. So also in the Gospel he brings
his narrative into contact with secular history
wherever possible, perhaps not altogether accurately. In particular he has collected information about the Herods. As regards, however,
any development of our Lord's ministry, he does
not add to, but rather confuses, what we may
learn from S. Mark. He preserves, indeed, the
chronological order of that Gospel better than
does S. Matthew, who is indifferent to chronology
and influenced by other motives; but, except
as regards the difference of place, he does not
seem to see any development in the character of
the ministry. This is a significant fact. S. Luke
had undoubtedly attempted to get the best
information both from writings and from eye-
witnesses; he had visited Jerusalem, he had
talked with those who had seen the Lord, he
was clearly an acute and intelligent man. He
had grasped the idea of historical development;
but neither in what is called the development of
the Messianic consciousness, nor in the growth
of opposition, nor in stages of progress, had any
idea of development impressed itself upon the

narrators.   They may have only gradually learnt
to know their Master, but they looked back on
the life as throughout that of the Messiah, the
Son of God, always in opposition to a section
of the people.   The signs of development we
find in S. Mark are photographed unconsciously.
We seem to see certain stages in progress, and
are probably right in doing so, because the narrative simply represents things as they happened.
But this was hardly obvious to the disciples
themselves, and the additions and re-arrange-
ments of S. Luke and S. Matthew obscure rather
than emphasize what appears in S. Mark.   The
marked characteristics, then, of the Acts do
not appear in the Gospel, but S. Luke had
clearly purposed to write a history as a scientific
Greek historian would.

S. Matthew was rather a theologian.   He
was primarily interested in the words rather than
the work of our Lord, and he is particularly
anxious to shew that our Lord fulfilled Old
Testament prophecy.   He therefore from time
to time stops in his narrative to shew how
different prophecies had been fulfilled.   He
groups together discourses, and to a certain
extent events, in accordance with the subject-
matter.   A conspicuous instance is the Sermon
on the Mount; here we have concentrated a
large amount of material which in the Third
Gospel is scattered through the ministry and is

connected with different circumstances. S. Matthew cares about the teaching, S. Luke about the historical situation in which the words were spoken. Moreover, a desire to place at the beginning of the Gospel a general survey of our Lord's teaching leads to a departure from the recorded chronological order. The whole process is, in fact, exactly similar to what might be followed by a modern historian who opened an account of the ministry with a sketch of the main features of the Gospel, and would be considered to increase rather than diminish his merits by doing so. Other instances are the charge to the Apostles, the Parables of the Kingdom, the denunciation of the Pharisees, and the eschatological discourses.

Such are the main characteristics of these two writers, and the questions we have to ask are how they used their sources, and whether in addition to the information to be obtained from those sources which we have examined, they give additional and valuable evidence about miracles.

The first question is an important one. We know now that both used S. Mark. Did they use it in a way that leads us to trust them? The question becomes of greater importance as it has been made the ground of accusation against them. It has been stated that, " In Matthew and Luke—Gospels based upon Mark

o

—most of these stories reappeared, but in a more miraculous guise. On examination we find that the editors of both these Gospels were in the habit of heightening the miraculous element in the old tradition, and of omitting or mollifying features that clashed with it. This at once weakened their evidence, and suggested that a similar process had been at work in the case of Mark. In the new miracles that they added, Matthew and Luke went even further in the same direction."[1] It is this statement that we have to examine.

Let us first see how S. Matthew uses S. Mark. In the first place he uses it very completely. There are, in fact, only about seven paragraphs of importance that he omits, but of these four deal with miraculous evidence. This does not look *prima facie* like an excessive desire to accumulate stories of the miraculous. But apparently to omit a miracle is as bad as to insert it. Mr Thompson, for example, writes :

" S. Matthew felt himself justified, without any fresh evidence, but simply from a particular standpoint of devotional and theological development, to omit some incidents from the account of our Lord's life which seemed to be unedifying. He thus encouraged the tendency to set up ideas as to what Jesus ought to have done,

[1] Thompson, *op. cit.*, p. 209.

instead of the plain tradition as to what He did or was."[1]

There seems to us really no justification for this statement. We have no evidence that S. Matthew thought the stories unedifying; what seems to be the case is that he collected together a certain number of instances of miracles as illustrations of what our Lord did. The majority of these he takes from S. Mark, but he substitutes in one or two cases stories from other sources which he preferred, the chief being the story of the centurion's servant, which we have already considered. The others he omits as not necessary. There was, when S. Matthew wrote, ample evidence of the miracles, and he did not think it necessary to take up space by inserting every story that came to him. But critics are hard to please. If the author of the Gospel inserts a miraculous incident it shews a tendency to exaggerate; if he omits one it shews a tendency to set up ideas as to what Jesus ought to have done. But at any rate, so far, we have not found any great desire to exaggerate miracles.

How does he treat the narratives of S. Mark that he gives us? Let us ask first, What do we expect him to do? Do we expect him to take a pair of scissors and cut out a story, or do we

[1] Thompson, *op. cit.*, p. 64.

expect him to tell it in his own words? The
latter is what any modern historian would do,
and it is what S. Matthew does. He tells the
story to a large extent in his own words, and
therefore he changes the style. A second
point is that he abbreviates. This we must
emphasize, for it gives the most natural explanation of the greater number of changes which
are made. S. Matthew was limited in the
size of the Gospel that it was convenient
he should write. He had a large amount
of material before him; he was far more
interested in the discourses than in the miracles;
he therefore considerably shortens the miracles.
And this becomes clear by comparison of the
two narratives. The majority of those in
S. Mark have a vivid picturesqueness of detail
which may imply an eye-witness, and certainly
implies a gift of story-telling. S. Matthew
omits all these vivid details which give life, and
contents himself with the salient facts. His
procedure is clearly that of a second-hand
narrator. Perhaps he occasionally corrects what
seem to him errors, sometimes he adds explanations or details; in some cases he may have
had another account, although that is not often
the case; generally he simply shortens. Take
the story of the healing of the leper. In
S. Matthew it is told in 63 words, in S. Mark
in 97. In the healing of the paralytic there are

in S. Matthew 97 words, in S. Mark 196; in the story of the Gadarene swine in S. Matthew, 136 words, in S. Mark 285. This difference in length holds good generally of the narratives; on the other hand, the discourses are, where-ever possible, lengthened, and information accumulated.

This being S. Matthew's usual procedure, it naturally leads to omission of personal detail, and makes us hesitate to ascribe a 'tendency' to him. It is widely stated, for example, that he omits what is discreditable to the disciples. Now it is quite true that some things that he omits might be considered so, but whatever force there may be in this is taken away if, as we find, he inserts other statements which might be con-sidered discreditable, or if he fails in other cases to omit. For example, in the description of the walking on the sea he does omit the comment : " For they understood not concerning the loaves, for their heart was hardened," but he does so to make room for the story of S. Peter's attempt, and that contains a much more severe rebuke : "O thou of little faith, wherefore didst thou doubt ? " [1]

The story of S. Peter's confession is, from this point of view, of great interest. S. Matthew clearly has a second source, and he amplifies the narrative considerably ; and it is true that

[1] S. Matt. xiv. 22-33.

from this source he adds the famous words,
"Blessed art thou Simon Bar-jona" and all
that follows.   But had he had any purpose such
as to spare the disciples, he would surely have
omitted the very stern rebuke that follows ;
instead of that he amplifies it.   "But he turned
and said unto Peter, Get thee behind me
Satan : for thou art a stumbling-block unto me :
for thou mindest not the things of God, but
the things of men." [1]   The stern words "thou
art a stumbling-block" are added by S. Matthew,
and the historian who records this saying cannot
have had any great desire to omit what was
discreditable to the Twelve.   It is true that on
one occasion he omits the words : "they disputed with one another who was the greatest,"
but not long afterwards he does not hesitate
to say that "they were moved with indignation." [2]   In fact, so ineffective and half-hearted
would have been the way in which S. Matthew
carries out this supposed tendency, that we
cannot really believe that it exists.

Again it is asserted that out of motives of
reverence words are omitted that ascribed to
our Lord human emotions ; and, in particular,
questions which might seem to imply ignorance.   The instances again are not very conclusive, and if we study what is not omitted
we shall hardly feel inclined to lay stress on

[1] S. Matt. xvi. 23.   [2] S. Matt. xx. 24.

the motives. It is true, for example, that in one
place the words "he marvelled at their unbelief"
are omitted, but elsewhere in S. Matthew we
read, "when Jesus knew it he marvelled." [1]
It is true that in one account the words
"How many loaves have ye" are omitted, but
in the other account the words are retained. [2]
It is true the words "looking upon him he
loved him" are omitted, but several times we
are told that "Jesus was moved with compassion." [3]   He may omit the words, "he
sighed deeply in spirit," but he does not scruple
to say, "he began to be sorrowful and sore
troubled." [4]   In fact, we doubt whether anyone
reading the two Gospels with care would notice
any difference between the two conceptions of
Jesus' human nature.   And similarly with
regard to miracles it is true that S. Mark says,
"they brought unto him all that were sick
and them that were possessed with devils. . . .
And he healed *many* that were sick with divers
diseases, and cast out *many* devils"; while in
S. Matthew we read, "they brought unto him
many possessed with devils; and he cast out the
spirits with a word, and healed *all* that were
sick." [5]   But I do not believe the alteration
to be an exaggeration, conscious or unconscious;

---

[1] S. Matt. viii. 10.   [2] S. Matt. xv. 34.
[3] S. Matt. ix. 36.   [4] S. Matt. xxvi. 37.
[5] S. Mark i. 32-34; S. Matt. viii. 16.

it simply comes from running together two sentences. If there were a tendency to exaggerate miracles there would be other instances; but the tendency is to shorten, not exaggerate such passages.

The real fact is, I believe, that the whole of this criticism is based on an erroneous conception of the primitive Church. There is an assumption that in order to make Christ such as they desire, the Evangelists found it necessary to alter the actual portrait of Him that they possessed; that there was the consciousness of difficulty, and the uncertainty of belief which characterizes modern critics. Neither S. Mark nor S. Matthew had any such difficulties. They both believed that Jesus was the Son of God, and wrote their Gospels on that assumption; they both believed that He worked miracles and found them recorded in various sources before them. They had no need either to heighten the effect or to exclude anything. It is the absence of exaggeration concerning miracles throughout which is most striking, and there seems to us no evidence for the following statement of Mr Thompson:

" It is doubtful whether any of the evidence is quite free from a tendency to exaggerate the miraculous element. This tendency was natural but disastrous; in place of the rich reality of the facts it sets up a one-sided theory. In the name of reverence it disparages the soul of reverence, which is truth."[1]

As a matter of fact the result of our comparison of S. Matthew and S. Mark shews us that S. Matthew omits four stories containing miracles, and in almost every case where he records them he shortens his narrative considerably, so as to obtain more space for discourses which seem to him of so much importance. As a result of this procedure many vivid touches are lost. His other source contains evidence as to miracles which he uses without laying any particular stress on them. It is on the teaching that he always lays stress, and he uses the miracles as a portion of the facts which shewed him that Jesus was the Messiah; but he neither exaggerates nor lays undue stress on them.[2]

We may deal with S. Luke more briefly. His method of treating S. Mark's Gospel is to leave out a large section, and he has less need therefore to shorten the several narratives. He omits seven miracles recorded by S. Mark. In dealing with the individual stories he aims chiefly at reconstructing the circumstances in which they occurred. He is more concerned with the historical situation than is S. Matthew, and

[1] Thompson, *op. cit.*, p. 71.
[2] On the relation of S. Matthew and S. Luke to S. Mark, I may refer to a paper by Dr H. J. White, which will shortly be published.

where possible he reconstructs it from the narrative. This can be seen, for example, in the story of the paralytic.

S. Luke had probably three main sources. In addition to S. Mark's Gospel and to "Q," there was also probably a special source of great interest and value for reconstructing our picture of Jesus. For instance, Professor Bacon writes of it as follows:

"But how little should we have from Mark alone to explain the popular support which gave to the movement of Jesus its Messianist character, and afterwards recruited to the standard of the crucified Nazarene a great following from the 'people of the land,' were it not for the Special Source of Luke, with its constant depiction of Jesus as the champion of the 'little ones,' the unrecognized 'sons' or 'daughters of Abraham,' the spiritually disinherited masses, publicans, women, Samaritans, outcasts from the synagogue, scattered sheep, lost ones!" . . . "We need even more the Special Source of Luke, with its humanitarian view of Jesus: His championship of the cause of the lost sheep, the house of Israel, His yearning 'to seek and to save that which was lost.'" [1]

Now as regards the miracles, this source exactly resembles the others which we possess; generally it describes our Lord's ministry as

[1] Bacon, *Beginnings of Gospel Story*, p. xxxvii.

miraculous. Amongst those who followed our Lord were " certain women which had been healed of evil spirits and infirmities, Mary that was called Magdalene, from whom seven devils had gone out."[1] When the Seventy are sent forth the injunction is : " And into whatsoever city ye enter, and they receive you, eat such things as are set before you : and heal the sick that are therein, and say unto them, The Kingdom of God is come nigh unto you."[2] And we have on their return a special warning against pride in miraculous power : " Howbeit in this rejoice not, that the spirits are subject unto you ; but rejoice that your names are written in heaven."[3] We have also the special message of our Lord to Herod : " Go and say to that fox, Behold I cast out devils and per- form cures to-day and to-morrow, and the third day I am perfected."[4] We have also seven narratives of a miraculous or quasi-miraculous character. Six correspond in character to those contained in S. Mark and in " Q," and the signi- ficance is this, that here we have the support of an independent report of tradition about our Lord's life, and it contains just the same type of evidence as do the other sources.

As a result of examining S. Matthew's and S. Luke's Gospels, we arrive at the conclusion

[1] S. Luke viii. 2. [2] S. Luke x. 8, 9.
[3] S. Luke x. 20. [4] S. Luke xiii. 32.

that when they are using a source which we possess, so that we can follow their methods, they act as honest historians, impressing, of course, as all historians do, their own characteristics upon the material they employ; that they do not alter the conception of our Lord's personality or exaggerate the miraculous; and that S. Matthew, in particular, shews comparatively little interest in that side of our Lord's activity. They both had other sources of information. From these they derived a certain number of narratives similar in character to those obtained from the known sources, and all these narratives alike represented naturally and simply our Lord's ministry as miraculous in character. We can find no evidence of a non-miraculous nucleus from which the miraculous element has grown, nor can we find in any New Testament historian, whose writings we possess, any attempt to exaggerate or invent miracles.

IV

For those who believe that S. John's Gospel was written by the Apostle of that name, the son of Zebedee, and is intended to be an historical work, and that the Apostle was an honest man, there can hardly. I think, be any problem concerning miracles, so far as evidence goes. The Gospel explicitly tells us that Jesus claimed to be the Son of God, and that the works that He did bear witness to Him. Only seven miracles, or, including the miraculous draught in the last chapter, eight, are recorded ; but they are selected with care, are told with great picturesqueness of detail, and are inter-woven with our Lord's most spiritual teaching.

It will hardly, I think, be worth while to discuss further the critical question of the authorship or the historical character of the Gospel ; we must recognize that a great diversity of theories exists, that negative critics feel great uncertainty, that there are some who believe that the Gospel is in no way an historical work, but is to be looked upon as symbolical from beginning to end, and that it is spiritual teaching alone that we are intended to gain from it. It will, I think, be more helpful to our purpose if I confine myself to examining two of the miracles recorded : one, the feeding of the five thousand—an account of which is contained in the other Gospels, and which there-fore was clearly not an invention of the author ; the other, the raising of Lazarus, to which there is no parallel.

The author of the Fourth Gospel seems to have selected the feeding of the five thousand for narration both as a remarkable sign and

because it was the basis of the discussion on the
bread of life. The story is told in a vivid and
picturesque manner. We cannot lay very much
stress upon that, but it certainly seems more
natural that when the names of the Apostles are
indicated it should imply actual reminiscences
rather than symbolism. What we cannot help
feeling about so much of this symbolical interpretation of S. John's Gospel is how great a
misfortune it is that the writer took so little
trouble to give any indication of what he meant,
and that it has remained undiscovered all these
years.[1] The interesting feature in S. John's
account is that he clearly makes this miracle
a great crisis in our Lord's history. If things
happened as they are described to have done
this is the one occasion when anything like a
sign which might be looked upon as Messianic
was worked. It had a natural and remarkable
effect. It made the people determined to
accept Him. " When therefore the people saw
the sign that he did, they said this is of a truth
that prophet that cometh into the world," and
as an inevitable result of this they are desirous
of making Him king. Jesus sees what is likely
to happen, and avoids it. He withdraws Himself and sends His disciples away, as Dr

[1] *Cf.* Tertullian, *Adv. Marcion,* i. 20. O Christe, patient-
issime domine, qui tot annis interversionem praedicationis
tui sustinuisti, donec scilicet tibi Marcion subveniret.

Latham suggests, lest they should be contaminated by this worldly movement. Equally naturally many of those who had followed Him were so disappointed with His refusal to take the position that was demanded of Him, and with His use of a somewhat unintelligible spiritual teaching instead of having courage enough to take upon Himself His kingdom, that they went back and walked no more with Him; this again naturally gives occasion to the test of faith implied in the confession of S. Peter.

Now all this is very natural; it suggests that S. John had a considerable interest in history, and a far clearer conception of events than S. Mark. Moreover, it may be quite reasonably held that there is a reference to this misconception in the rebuke which S. Mark tells us was administered to the disciples because they could not understand the meaning of the loaves. They, like the Jews, were inclined to see only the marvellous event: they interpreted it in accordance with the current Jewish expectation of the Messianic kingdom. Many affirm that the hope of Israel is that "Messias shall come and raise the dead, and that they shall be gathered together in the garden of Eden, and shall eat and drink and satiate themselves all the days of the world." Do not these considerations suggest that possibly in S. John we may have an account with far greater insight than that given us by the other Gospels.[1]

And now let us turn to the story of Lazarus. It is needless to say that it has been exposed to much criticism, and we are hardly prepared,

---

[1] *Cf.* with this Abbott, *The Fourfold Gospel,* p. 47 (*Diatessarica,* x. i.). "Now this misunderstanding, according to John, did actually possess the great mass of the Jews who partook of the mystery of the Feeding of the Five Thousand. They entirely missed its meaning. John alone describes the failure that followed, and the attempt to make Christ a king, and His consequent withdrawal from the multitude. We shall have to consider whether John is not right, and all the Synoptists wrong—Mark being the only one of them who retains a vestige of the truth. If we decide in favour of John, we shall have to go further and reject the Marcan and Synoptic view—or at all events the view that would be naturally attributed to the Synoptists, if John had not written—that Jesus never spoke of the mystical Bread of the brethren till the night on which He was delivered up.

"Not, indeed, that we must consequently accept, as coming from the lips of the historical Jesus, every word of that long discourse about the mystical Bread which John puts into His mouth as being uttered in the synagogue at Capernaum, almost immediately after the Sign of the Five Thousand. But, though we reject the words, we shall be prepared to accept the thought. Piecing together Marcan scraps of tradition with the aid of what we call John's Targumistic exposition of it, we shall (I believe) arrive at the conclusion that a Eucharistic doctrine expressed in a Eucharistic practice was inculcated by Jesus at an early period, and only repeated with special emphasis — not introduced as quite a novel thing—on the night of the Last Supper."

nor do I think that my readers would be
prepared, to wade through all the suppositions
and possibilities which are suggested to explain
it. I will content myself with considering
what is, I believe, the strongest argument, as
it is put forward by Professor Burkitt. How
did it come to pass that the Synoptists left
out this—the most conspicuous of all miracles?
Can we find room for it in the other narratives?
So Mr Burkitt writes:

"But where are we to put the scene into the
historical framework preserved by S. Mark?
Can any answer be given, except 'there is no
room'? If the events occurred as told in the
Fourth Gospel, if they were as public as the
Fourth Evangelist insists, so fraught with influence upon the action both of friends and foes, they
could not have been unknown to a well-informed
personage like 'Mark,' nor could he have had
any reason for suppressing a narrative at once
so public and so edifying. It is true that
'Mark' does not record the Lord's Prayer or
many of the most noteworthy sayings of Jesus,
but these were not public events like the
Raising of Lazarus. Is it possible that anyone
who reads the continuous and detailed story of
Mark from the Transfiguration to the Entry
into Jerusalem can interpolate into it the tale of
Lazarus and the notable sensation which we
are assured that it produced? Must not the
answer be, that Mark is silent about the raising
of Lazarus because he did not know of it? And

if he did not know of it, can we believe that, as a matter of fact, it ever occurred? For all its dramatic setting it is, I am persuaded, impossible to regard the story of the raising of Lazarus as a narrative of historical events." [1]

Now let us turn to the Synoptic Gospels. They tell us that Jesus came to Jerusalem, and they represent Him as welcomed by great crowds of people and led in in a triumphal entry; they tell us on the other hand how the leaders of the Jews made up their minds to seize Him. How was it that all this happened so? They do not tell us that he had ever been at Jerusalem, but we find a long triumphal procession from Jericho to the city. There were men waiting by the roadside to see Him; there were preparations made for His coming, the ass and the colt were ready; He was known and looked for. Now these events as described in the Synoptic Gospels hardly seem possible if their story is complete; but if Jesus had already visited Jerusalem, if He was known there, above all, if the story of the raising of Lazarus be true, we have a natural sequence of events.

And does not this harmonize with what we have already learnt about S. John? If our arguments with regard to the feeding of the multitude are right, we find that S. John had a

---

[1] Burkitt, *The Gospel History and its Transmission*, p. 222.

far more correct conception of the course of
events than the writers of the other Gospels. He
has remembered and described things as they
happened. The ordinary Synoptic narrative does
not trouble itself about crises; it contains a
number of stories as they were told as part of
their teaching by the Apostles.   Its object is
evangelistic. A philosophical or historical conception did not trouble the Apostles when they were
preaching the Gospel. But behind the Fourth
Gospel there is a better tradition and a deeper
interest.   If that is true in one case, then may it
not be true in others ?   The raising of Lazarus
is represented as leading up to the Crucifixion.
Does it not fit into a natural sequence of events ?
We study the account in S. John, and we see
how the opposition to our Lord grows. Jesus
has been teaching in Judaea; He has aroused
great opposition there ;   He is well known.
The story of Lazarus increases this opposition :

"Many, therefore, of the Jews, which came
to Mary and beheld that which he did,
believed on him.   But some of them went
away to the Pharisees, and told them the things
which Jesus had done.   The chief priests
therefore, and the Pharisees gathered a council,
and, said What do we ? For this man doeth many
signs.   If we let him thus alone, all men will
believe on him : and the Romans will come
and take away both our place and our

nation. . . . So from that day forth they took counsel that they might put him to death."[1]

Then comes the triumphal entry, and again we get the progress of events recorded : "The Pharisees therefore said among themselves, Behold how ye prevail nothing : lo, the world is gone out after him."[2] Clearly here S. John's Gospel seems to supply a hiatus in the narrative of the Synoptists.

And the silence of the other Gospels is not so significant as has been represented. All of the accounts of the life of Jesus are fragmentary. Only a selection of the miracles which Jesus was reported to have worked are recorded. A considerable amount of evidence shews us there must have been a Jerusalem Ministry as well as a Galilean Ministry. The Synoptic Gospels are concerned only with the Galilean Ministry, and therefore this narrative would naturally not occur in them. Nor, if the other miracles of raising the dead — Jairus' daughter, and the widow's son at Nain—were recognized as true, would this appear so much more remarkable. In relation to Jerusalem the raising of Lazarus was of supreme importance ; not necessarily so to the Galilean disciples. The disciples, curiously enough, are hardly referred to in S. John vii. and viii.,

[1] S. John xi. 45-53.   [2] S. John xii. 19.

not at all in chapter x. In chapter vii.
His brethren are represented as suggesting
to our Lord that He should go up and shew
Himself to—we may presume—His Jerusalem
disciples. It is probable that many of the
Galilean disciples, and among them perhaps S.
Peter, were not with Jesus on this visit to
Jerusalem. A miracle described by S. John
is told in such a way as to make it appear far
more important than equally wonderful events
quoted in the other Gospels. We have, then,
a Johannine, not a Petrine, tradition. That
does not imply that the Marcan narrative is
false; it may be inadequate. It was certainly
incomplete, and it did not realize the full
sequence of events, or the most important
causes of the final catastrophe.

I have said that the criticism of the Fourth
Gospel is in a transition state. I do not,
therefore, wish to put forward any opinion too
dogmatically; but I would venture to suggest
that it is a little difficult to believe that these
stories were narrated by the author of the
Gospel not as historical facts, but as allegories;
that he had no good means of information and did
not desire them. It is true that he emphasizes
the spiritual teaching of our Lord, and the
spiritual significance of the miracles, as do the
other evangelists; but he believes that he is
relating what is historical. And if the sugges-

tion made above be correct, there will be
considerable grounds for thinking that his
historical information may be better than that
of the other Gospels.[1]

V

We have now examined the evidence of the
Gospels, but that does not exhaust the New
Testament. We have also the evidence of S.
Paul, and of the Acts of the Apostles. That of
S. Paul, at any rate, appears to be first hand.
There is no doubt as to the genuineness of
the writings. They are not anonymous or
pseudonymous. They bear on every page marks
of the character of the writer. They are the

---

[1] In the above remarks I have been considerably indebted
to Mr Brooke's essay in the *Cambridge Biblical Essays*, p. 329,
and to Dr Abbott's remarks in the work quoted above. At the
same time it is interesting to me to find that I used the
same arguments some thirty years ago in lectures that I
gave at Oxford. See Abbott, pp. 155-163.

It may be noted that a tradition in the Babylonian
Gemara runs as follows: "Tradition reports that Jesus was
crucified (hanged) on the evening of the Passover, an
officer having during the preceding forty days publicly
proclaimed that this man who, by His imposture, had seduced
the people ought to be stoned, and that anyone who could
say aught in His defence was to come forward and speak ;
but no one doing so, He was hanged on the evening of the
Sabbath."

evidence of a man who, by what he accomplished, shewed that he had the character and power which demand that we should receive what he says with respect. His witness seems to prove that he considered miracles a regular and recognized phenomenon of the Christian life, that he claimed himself to work miracles, and looked upon them as part of the signs of an apostle.

The first passage to be considered is one in the Second Epistle to the Corinthians. " For in nothing am I behind the very chiefest apostles, though I be nothing. Truly the signs of an apostle were wrought amongst you in all patience, by signs, and wonders, and mighty deeds." [1] You will notice in the first place that here we are introduced to the regular phraseology of the New Testament. The combination, " signs and wonders," is that habitually used to describe what we speak of conventionally as miracles. There can be no doubt at all that S. Paul means to refer to miracles, and that this regular phraseology of the New Testament means what were looked upon by the writer as marvellous occurrences.

The second passage, very similar in character but varied in phraseology, occurs in the Epistle to the Romans : " For I will not dare to speak of any things save those which Christ wrought

[1] 2 Cor. xii. 11, 12.

through me, for the obedience of the Gentiles, by word and deed, in the power of signs and wonders, in the power of the Holy Ghost."[1] An attempt has been made to destroy the authority of this passage, by suggesting that there are some doubts as to the genuineness of the two last chapters of the Romans. This is not correct. There are some doubts, it is true, as to whether they formed part of the original edition of the Epistle to the Romans or were added at a later date, but there are none at all as to their being the work of S. Paul. The only difference in this passage from that we have already considered is that S. Paul definitely states that the miracles were worked by himself, and that he varies the expression slightly, saying that these marvellous events had been wrought in the power of signs and wonders, and he particularly ascribes them to the power of the Holy Ghost.

The third passage occurs in the Epistle to the Galatians. "He therefore that ministereth to you the Spirit, and worketh miracles among you, doeth he it by the works of the Law or by the hearing of faith?"[2] This passage is not quite so explicit as those we have considered, and it is to a certain extent ambiguous. It may be interpreted in a more objective sense to mean working miracles among you, or it may mean

[1] Rom. xv. 18, 19.   [2] Gal. iii. 5.

rather giving inward power. In the one case
it implies that God had given the Galatians the
gift of the Spirit, and that the reality of the
gift had been shewn by miracles worked among
them. In the other case it means that the
reality of the gift had been shewn by their
consciousness of more than ordinary powers
that had been given them. The regular use of
the word implies in any case that that which
was given them was looked upon as miraculous.

It may be convenient in this connexion to
refer to one more passage. The writer of the
Epistle to the Hebrews—a Christian of the
second generation—tells us how the Gospel had
been received from those who first heard it:
"God also bearing witness with them, both by
signs and wonders, and by manifold powers, and
by the Holy Ghost according to his own will."[1]
Here we have a second witness confirming the
claim made on his own behalf by S. Paul.

The remaining group of passages which we
are to consider occur in S. Paul's discussion
on spiritual gifts in the First Epistle to the
Corinthians. Gifts which are there described as
given by the one Spirit, are the word of wisdom,
the word of knowledge, faith, gifts of healing,
workings of powers, prophecy, discernment of
spirits, and the interpretation of tongues;[2] and,
again, God is said to have set in the Church

[1] Heb. ii. 4.   [2] 1 Cor. xii. 8-10.

apostles, prophets, teachers, powers, gifts of
healing, helps, governments, and kinds of
tongues.[1] You will notice that in these
passages the same word—" powers "—is used that
we have come across elsewhere, that it is used
regularly throughout the New Testament to
imply miraculous working, and that these
powers appear to be distinguished from gifts
of healing.

Now if we put all these passages together, it
becomes evident that S. Paul was quite clear
that through him or his agency, direct or indirect, what both he and those to whom he was
writing regarded as miracles were worked, and
were the signs of his apostleship. He looks upon
powers and healings as signs of the work of the
Spirit in the Church. So confident is he of the
reality of what he refers to that he speaks of it
as something which will be recognized by others
as a proof and sign of his apostolic mission.
The force and power thus exhibited had been
part of the motive which had induced his
hearers to accept the message which he brought
them.

It is unnecessary to say that various attempts
have been made to disparage this testimony.
For example, the author of *Supernatural
Religion* has devoted a lengthy chapter to
examining it. It will be apparent at first

[1] 1 Cor. xii. 28.

sight that his argument, like many other arguments in the same work, loses very much effectiveness by its excessive vehemence. He is always trying to prove too much in order to make out his case. For instance, if we remember the regular usage of the New Testament, it becomes futile to try and prove that signs and wonders and powers do not mean miracles. It is curious how much there is in what are called critical writers which makes them ready to accept any argument, however indifferent, and be prepared to explain away any passage, however clear and definite. They are often quite as unintelligent as the least instructed champions of orthodoxy. A good deal of this work, in fact, need not be discussed, but one particular point must be touched upon, for it is not only this writer that makes use of it; it is becoming a commonplace of criticism.

It is claimed that the temperament of S. Paul was such that his evidence on points of this sort could be of no value. "The History of Christianity after the death of its Founder," says this writer, "would sink almost into commonplace if the grand figure of Paul were blotted from its pages. But it is no detraction to recognize that his nervous temperament renders him peculiarly susceptible of those religious impressions which result in conditions of ecstatic trance, to which, as we actually learn from himself, he was ex-

ceptionally subject. The effects of this temperament probably first made him a Christian ; and
to his enthusiastic imagination we owe most of
the supernatural dogmas of the religion which
he adopted and transformed." [1] You will notice
that the last statement is somewhat beside our
purpose.

This description of S. Paul demands some
consideration. It is pointed out that he describes
a vision, whether in the body or out of the body,
and that that was clearly an hallucination ; it was
equally an hallucination that he could work
miracles. Further, it is argued that S. Paul
believed in the genuineness of the supernatural
origin of the divine Charismata, and that he in
like manner believed in the reality of his visions
and revelations. " He has equal reason or want
of reason in both cases." [2] Now a moment's consideration will shew that the two events do not
stand at all on the same level. It is quite true
that S. Paul describes a vision that he had, and
it is possible that that vision may have been a
dream or hallucination, but the evidence in the
two cases is entirely different. In the one case
S. Paul has only described his own experience,
whether real or not. In the other he is appealing to events which were known and understood
by his readers. It is difficult to believe that

[1] *Supernatural Religion*, edition 1879, iii. 394.
[2] *Ibid.*, iii. 395.

S. Paul was such a deluded person that he could write to the Roman and Corinthian Christians and remind them of miracles which had taken place among them when, as a matter of fact, nothing of the sort had happened, and they would not in the least understand what he was referring to. Of course we do not know very exactly what his readers thought of the letters except this, that they considered them of such value that they preserved them, and that the Church almost immediately began to treat them as inspired. But supposing that S. Paul had been such a mistaken and deluded person as he is made out to be, it is difficult to believe that his influence would have been what it was, that he would have been able to accomplish what he did accomplish, and that the result of his life's work would have been as great as it was. Of one thing, I think, we may be quite clear: that both S. Paul and his readers believed firmly that these miracles had taken place, and looked upon them as a sign of the workings of the Divine Spirit.

There is a further point on which I should like to dwell. The author of *Supernatural Religion* denies S. Paul's evidence just because he appears to have been not quite normal. But surely the whole claim of those who believe in the divine character of the Christian revelation would be that S. Paul was not quite normal;

that he had received, in a way which he regarded as supernatural, the gift of the Spirit; that this gift had been so powerful as to enable him to be a great missionary of the new religion, and had enabled him to win souls to Christ where Christianity had never been preached before, in city after city. Our claim is that we are dealing with phenomena which were not normal; that S. Paul was in a real sense inspired with the gift of God's Spirit; that it transformed his personality, and worked in him and through him; and that it was this that enabled him to do what he did.

Looking at his testimony, in fact, from an objective point of view, we find that it is of value not only because it represents his sincere belief, but also because it was corroborated by the general conceptions of the apostolic age as to missionary activity. Looking at it from the subjective point of view, we see that S. Paul was clearly a man of abnormal temperament; that it was just because he was carried away by the Spirit that he was able to preach the Gospel as he did. The result of the evidence, in fact, is to make us feel that S. Paul, like the rest of the Church, believed in the reality of the miracles that he claimed to work; that these were in their eyes part of the supernatural sign of his teaching, and they were ascribed to the power which came from the gifts of the Spirit.

With the narrative of S. Paul we must compare that of the Acts of the Apostles. It was written by a companion of the Apostle; quite possibly it was written at Rome during his imprisonment, and it was the work of a man of culture and understanding and historical sense. Here is a writer who possesses a supreme historical faculty. He was a philosopher, an acute observer, a clear-headed Greek physician, who became a Christian and accompanied S. Paul in many of his voyages; he shared his perils and dangers with him; even in the Apostle's last imprisonment he remained faithful. He depicts from the inside the history of what he realizes to be an extraordinary movement; he believes that the whole history is the result of the supernatural work of the Holy Spirit, and that the miracles which he knows to have happened are a normal expression of the indwelling energies of that Spirit. Is not this belief of his a strong evidence that he was right? Here we have given the testimony of an eye-witness, a participator in the scenes he describes, bearing witness to the truth of what he tells us. Of course we may say he was mistaken, but there must be some limit to such incredulity. It is difficult to see the reason for not accepting his testimony. Some attempt has been made to suggest that in the latter part of the narrative there are fewer miracles than in the earlier. It

is a little difficult to harmonize this language
with the accusation made against the author of
inventing a parallelism between the story of S.
Peter and S. Paul. His evidence consists first
of all of a general statement with regard to
miracles on the lines of such statements in the
Gospels, and then of some twelve accounts of
different miraculous events, as to which it may
be noted that one half occur in the earlier part
of the book, and the other half in the latter.
These are partly miracles of healing, partly
what S. Paul would have called "powers." And
a review of this evidence shews us that the
conception of apostolic history which we find
in the Acts corresponds exactly to that which
we obtain from a study of S. Paul's epistles.
From them we learn that S. Paul himself
claimed to work miracles, and looked upon them
as a sign of his apostleship; that he believed
that his life was under the special guidance
of God; that he was directed by warnings and
by visions. The supernatural environment in
which he seemed to live is clearly depicted for
us in the story of his companion given in the
Acts, and by both alike it is referred to the
real gift of God's Spirit.

VI

We have now finished our survey of the New Testament, and our study of it will suggest the following conclusions :—

1. All evidence, without exception, tells us that our Lord's life and activity were characterized by events such as are described as miraculous. We have various gospels, themselves probably the work of writers of the first and second generations of Christians. These have been, in the process of criticism, analyzed, and we are taken back to certain sources, which in their turn seem to represent a selection from narratives about our Lord which were current in the Christian Church during the first generation. So far as we know, all these, without exception, bear witness to the miraculous character of our Lord's work. It is probable that these writings contain the testimony of our Lord Himself, while tradition traces two main sources to S. Peter and S. Matthew.

2. When analyzed this evidence is complex in character. We have, first of all, general statements of the miracles wrought by our Lord. These alone might not be of great value. We have then a number of actual miracles recorded ; so far as we can see, these are in no case more than a selection from those which

Q

had been described. Each source we have in a fragmentary form. From each source we get new evidence, and the aim of the writers seems in all cases to have been not comprehensiveness, but the selection of typical and striking incidents.

3. But further than this the narrative is built up on, and implies, miraculous powers. The Apostles themselves looked upon the miracles as part of the basis of their faith. It was by miracles, we are told, that the crowd was attracted, while it was from disappointment at the absence of anything sufficiently striking that many left our Lord. There is teaching recorded which would be meaningless unless our Lord had power to work miracles. Moreover, He Himself, in all our documents, claims to have such power.

4. Attempts have been made from time to time to get back to a non-miraculous Christianity —to a nucleus which would represent the pure teaching of Jesus before it had been contaminated with supernaturalism. None of these efforts has had the slightest success. Objective critical grounds for rejecting the miracles have never been found. When the criticism comes to be examined, it is found to assume the impossibility of miracles as one of its axioms. It can hardly be said that the reason is adequate, if we first reject the testimony of a work because

it is miraculous, and are assured that miracles do not happen ; and then say we cannot believe in the miracles because our documents are untrustworthy and the evidence is insufficient.

5. We find abundant and first-hand evidence that the same miraculous power existed in the Church in the apostolic age. S. Paul himself claims to have worked miracles, and this power is definitely and consistently represented as derived from a gift of God's Spirit.

LECTURE VI

THE RESURRECTION

Character of the Evidence. Testimony of S. Paul. The
Empty Tomb. The Appearances. The Moral Evidence.
Explanations. Theory of Harnack. Fraud or Deception.

I PROPOSE in the present lecture to discuss the
evidence for the Resurrection of our Lord. It
is, of course, the most conspicuous and striking
of the miracles of the New Testament; it is
also that for which there is the strongest
evidence. It is bound up with the whole conception of Christianity as it is commonly understood, and it is consequently exposed to the
most searching attacks of criticism.

There are two primary points which I would
ask you to notice. The first is that, whatever
may have been the grounds for it, the belief in
the Resurrection was universal in the Early
Church. It was clearly looked upon as the
fundamental fact on which the Christian message
is based, and as the ground of Christian hope.
Our Lord is represented as foretelling His

Resurrection, and all four Gospels contain narratives about it, but it occupies even a higher place in the other writings of the Apostolic Church. The author of the Acts of the Apostles considered that the main function of an apostle was to be a witness of the Resurrection. When Matthias was appointed S. Peter says: "Wherefore of these men which have companied with us all the time that the Lord Jesus went in and out among us, beginning from the baptism of John, unto that same day that he was taken up from us, must one be ordained to be a witness with us of his resurrection." Through all the early speeches in the Acts S. Peter is represented as proving the Messiahship of Jesus by the fact of the Resurrection. "This Jesus did God raise up, whereof we all are witnesses." Equally clear is the character of S. Paul's teaching: "but God raised him from the dead: and he was seen for many days of them that came up with him from Galilee to Jerusalem, who are now his witnesses unto the people."

Similar evidence is given by S. Paul's epistles. S. Paul himself bases his claim to the title of apostle on the fact that he was a witness of the Resurrection. "Am I not an Apostle?" he says; "have I not seen the Lord?" In two or three minutes we shall analyze the evidence that he has collected as to the fact. At present I ask you to notice that he looks upon the preaching of the Resurrection as one of those fundamental beliefs that he shared with all other Christian preachers. "Whether then it be I or they, so we preach and so ye believed." All depends upon the belief in the Resurrection. "If Christ hath not been raised then is our preaching vain, your faith also is vain. Yea and we are found false witnesses of God; because we witnessed of God that he raised up Christ: whom he raised not up, if so be that the dead are not raised. For if the dead are not raised, neither hath Christ been raised; and if Christ hath not been raised your faith is vain." So far as our evidence goes the belief in the Resurrection of Jesus Christ was an essential part of the preaching of Christianity, one of those doctrines about which there was no question or difference of opinion in the Church as a whole.

Then, secondly, I would ask you to notice the character of the evidence on which it was believed. It was based on two facts: on the one hand, the fact of the empty tomb, on the other the appearance of the Risen Lord. It was that combination that gave particular cogency to the argument. Supposing, for example, that the curious reconstruction of the history which we owe to Professor Kirsopp Lake was true, that the two beliefs were independent in their origin, that the earliest appearances were in Galilee to the Apostles who had fled thither without any knowledge of what the women had discovered, that it was only later when they returned to Jerusalem that the women gave the account of their discovery, it would make the coincidence even more remarkable. I have referred in a previous lecture to criticisms which have attempted to estimate mathematically the evidence against a miracle. What are the mathematical chances against a coincidence that the women should think the tomb empty, when it was not empty, and the disciples should think they had seen the risen Lord when they had not seen Him, and that these two blunders combined should produce the Christian Church.

I

We now come to the evidence, and we will begin with that of S. Paul. The First Epistle to the Corinthians is one of the earliest books of the New Testament. It is not an anonymous work, nor one that comes to us without credentials. Its authenticity cannot be seriously disputed. We know what type of man S. Paul was; we know that, while he was a man of intense religious zeal and earnestness, he was also a

man of intellectual power. He was not likely
to believe without adequate grounds, and his
belief was so strong that it had compelled
him to change completely his creed and life.
To turn Saul the persecutor into Paul the
Apostle demanded very genuine and real
evidence. The basis of his belief was twofold :
his own experience, and the information that he
had received from the Early Church. He
himself had seen the risen Lord in a vision on
the way to Damascus ; that vision had been so
strong and clear that it had transformed his
whole life. But although he was thus convinced,
he was not satisfied without collecting evidence
from other sources, and he narrates various
appearances of which he gives us an account.
Here is his evidence :

"Now I make known unto you, brethren,
the gospel which I preached unto you, which
also ye received, wherein also ye stand, by which
also ye are saved, if ye hold that word, in which
I preached unto you, unless ye have believed in
vain. For I delivered unto you first of all that
which I also received, that Christ died for our
sins ac ording to the Scriptures ; and that he
was buried ; and that he rose again the third
day according to the Scriptures ; and that he
was seen of Cephas, then of the Twelve ; there-
after, he was seen of about five hundred brethren
at once, of whom the greater part remain until
now, but some have fallen asleep ; then he

was seen of James, then of all the apostles ; last of all he was seen of me also as of one born out of due time. For I am the least of the apostles that am not meet to be called an apostle because I persecuted the church of God. But by the grace of God I am what I am : and his grace which was bestowed upon me was not found vain : but I laboured more abundantly than they all : yet not I but the grace of God that was with me. Whether then it be I or they, so we preach, and so ye believed." [1]

Now with regard to this evidence there are certain points which I would wish to emphasize. We may, I think, in the first place be quite confident that S. Paul knew of the empty tomb. For some time it was the custom to maintain that he did not. Now it seems to be more generally accepted that he did. It is true that he does not specially and definitely mention it, but when he says that the Lord rose " on the third day " he implies the belief, for the only reason that the Church had for dating the Resurrection was the fact that on the third day the tomb was found empty. Various other explanations have been suggested, but they are not of a character to win acceptance. It has been suggested that as S. Paul says our Lord rose again on the third day, according to the

[1] 1 Cor. xv. 1-11.

Scriptures, it means that this belief was a deduction from the Old Testament and not based on fact; but apart from the fact that the reference to the Scriptures qualifies the whole sentence, no text could be cited which could have caused this belief to grow up. S. Paul speaks of the Death, the Burial, the Resurrection of our Lord as according to the Scriptures: in no case does he mean that the evidence for them was the Old Testament prophecy. He means that these facts were the fulfilment of prophecy. Still less convincing are the attempts made to base the belief on folklore, or on a calculation of the time which was supposed to elapse before the body would become corrupt. There is not the slightest trace of evidence for any such theory, nor of the influence of such methods of thought; and they are obviously only suggestions made to explain away the historical account. We may take it, therefore, that S. Paul implies by his reference to the Resurrection on the third day that he knew the story of the empty tomb.

This story is also implied in S. Paul's theory of the Resurrection. He believed that Jesus had risen, the first-fruits from the dead, and his conception was that at the Resurrection our natural bodies would be transformed into spiritual bodies. "We shall not all sleep, but we shall all be changed." The day will come—S. Paul believed very soon—when our Lord would come down from heaven; the dead in Christ would rise from their tombs, but with their bodies changed and glorified; all those who were alive on earth would be caught up in the sky and experience the same transformation. The particular point of importance for us is that as he believed that the dead would be raised with their bodies transformed, so he believed that our Lord had risen, and that His body had become a spiritual body. He had no conception, nor was it in the least in accordance with his manner of thought, that the body should remain in the grave, and the soul or spirit should survive apart from it like a disembodied ghost.

The second point of importance to notice is the stress that S. Paul lays on the fact that our Lord had appeared to five hundred brethren at once, of whom the greater part remain unto this present, but some are fallen asleep. Here he is clearly emphasizing the fact that he is appealing to the evidence of living persons. There were eye-witnesses to be seen if anyone would like to consult them. There is a second reason why emphasis must be laid on the appearance to five hundred brethren. It has been maintained that these appearances were subjective, of the nature of psychological hallucinations. S. Paul, it is said, included the appearance to himself with the others. Now clearly that appearance might be some sort of subjective hallucination: a person so constituted as S. Paul, with a highly strung nervous temperament, subject to visions, might have imagined the experience which he recounts. But any sort of explanation of such a character is excluded in relation to an appearance, whether to twelve or to five hundred people at once. There must have been some objective cause for a crowd of people having the same impression at the same time. To conclude, S. Paul shared with the Early Church the belief that the tomb had been found empty, and that the risen Christ had appeared on various occasions to His disciples. He had undoubtedly received information from eye-witnesses. He believed that the appearances were real, that Christ appeared in such a way that He might be recognized. His body was spiritualized and transformed, but it bore all the marks and characteristics of His human body. It was not merely a vision.

II

We now turn to the evidence of the Gospels. There is one point of considerable importance about this. It may be accepted as certain that S. Mark as we possess it is mutilated. According to the oldest manuscripts it ended with the

eighth verse, and the last twelve verses were an
appendix containing a summary of the evidence
of the Resurrection written at a later date and
inserted to take the place of something which
was obviously missing.   Moreover, it appears as
if the copy which S. Luke had before him, and
perhaps even that of S. Matthew were both
imperfect.   The result of this is that while the
accounts in the first three Gospels of the burial
and of the finding of the empty tomb were
based on a known source, there is no known
original source for the Resurrection appearances
mentioned in the four Gospels.

The evidence of the Gospels divides itself
under two headings—the empty tomb, and the
Resurrection appearances.   It is around the
empty tomb that controversy has circled during
recent years, and that we must consider first.

Our conclusion as to the whole question of the
credibility of the Resurrection narratives, as of
other narratives in the Gospel, depends upon
the extent to which minor discrepancies may
be held to vitiate a narrative.   It is obvious as
we read them that there are differences between
the narratives.   It is probable also that some
imaginative and legendary details have crept in,
and as is often the case in history, especially
when we are dealing with narratives of an
extraordinary character—such as stir up people's
minds—it is a little difficult to reconstruct

the exact course of events. But on no ordinary
canon of criticism should we be justified in
rejecting evidence on the grounds of variation in
detail, if the fundamental facts are such as all the
writers agree upon.

Now all the Gospels give a definite and clear
account of the finding of the tomb empty. The
narratives in the three Synoptic Gospels are
primarily based on that of S. Mark; but as each
adds details which clearly they would not have
been likely to invent, they must have known the
story also in other forms, whether written or
oral. The account in S. John is more independent, and places the weight of the evidence on
S. Peter and another disciple (as generally
believed, S. John himself), and the narrative, like
the narrative of the Fourth Gospel generally,
has a simplicity and minuteness which must
imply very great imaginative art if it is not
based on historical reminiscences.

S. Matthew also gives the story of the
sealing of the tomb and the setting of a
watch. Now that incident appears to be one
of those later additions to the narrative contained in S. Matthew's Gospel which must be
looked upon as less certain, and having, perhaps,
grown up in the Jewish controversy. But the
important fact for us is the indirect evidence
that it gives that the story of the empty tomb
was early and widely circulated; for such an

explanation would never have developed unless
the rumour had also been widely circulated that
the disciples had come by night and taken away
the body of Jesus. But such a rumour would
never have grown up unless Christians had
asserted their belief in the empty tomb, nor if
the tomb had not been empty would it have
been necessary to invent such an explanation.
If it had been possible to point to an unopened
tomb, no such story would have arisen. It must
be recognized as a fact that there was an empty
tomb known, or there would have been no reason
to invent other stories to account for the disappearance of the body.

Further evidence for the belief of the Church
may be found in the speech put into the mouth
of S. Peter in the Acts, in a narrative which
was almost certainly based upon an early
document. Our Lord's body had not been
allowed to see corruption. It has already been
pointed out that S. Paul implies this belief ; and
its universal existence in the Early Church may be
learnt not only from the traditional formula, " He
rose again on the third day," but also from the
fact that from a very early period the Christian
Church celebrated the Lord's Resurrection on
the first day of the week. When S. Paul wrote
to the Corinthians, the first day of the week
was the day of importance to the Church. It
was on the first day of the week that the Church

was gathered together at Troas to break bread, and very soon "the Lord's Day" took the place of the Sabbath. Now, some event of great importance must have been necessary to lead the Church to substitute another day for the Sabbath, and the cause that all our evidence suggests is that on the first day of the week the tomb was found empty, and that therefore that was the day on which our Lord was believed to have risen from the dead.

It is now widely recognized how strong this evidence is, and the tendency is not to deny the fact, but to explain it away, and various explanations are suggested. Professor Lake thinks that the women made a mistake, they went to the wrong tomb: someone or other, who must have known what they were about, told them that our Lord was not there but in some other tomb. They did not take the trouble to make any further investigation, but jumped to the conclusion that the Lord was risen, and were so frightened that they immediately went away. Later they imagined the rest of the message. I cannot help thinking that this will be looked upon as a most extraordinary suggestion. Mr Streeter, in *Foundations*, writes as follows:—

" The discovery of the empty tomb, assuming the story to rest on adequate historical evidence, which personally I believe to be the case, is often supposed to determine the decision in favour of the traditional theory. This, however, is not really so, for with a little ingenuity it is not difficult to imagine more than one set of circumstances which might account on purely natural grounds for the tomb being found empty. Various suggestions have been put forward, as, for instance, that the Romans, fearing a possible disturbance, took advantage of the Sabbath quiet to remove the body out of the reach of the disciples. Of course neither this nor any other one definite suggestion has any claim to be regarded as *in itself* particularly probable, but where a natural explanation of an event is at all possible, there must be very special reasons for falling back upon an explanation of a supernatural character.[1]

I cannot help thinking again that these statements are of a most remarkable character. It is admitted that the evidence is good ; it is admitted that there is no evidence for any explanation that is offered, but it is suggested that as the fact is one of an extraordinary character, we must assume that there must be some explanation which is possible. Now this statement is at any rate sufficient to convince us that we are not dealing with an event for which there is no good historical evidence. The only ground for contesting it is that it is difficult to believe. But if we accept Mr Streeter's

---

[1] *Foundations,* p. 134.

position, and remember what he believes about our Lord, he surely lands us in an argument of a very extraordinary kind. He is quite prepared to believe in the Resurrection as a spiritual fact; he is prepared to believe that it was made known in some way or other to the disciples; he is prepared to accept generally the belief that our Lord Jesus Christ was the Son of God, and the truth of the Christian religion as built up on these facts. But he believes at the same time that something which was either a fraud or a blunder or a misconception was the cause of the belief of the disciples, to whom we owe all the evidence on which our religion is based. I venture to think that such a belief is quite impossible. The real difficulty which underlies the position of Mr Streeter and various other writers may be shewn from the following quotation given by Mr Lake from an unpublished work of Dr Rashdall. We have no right to talk of "suspension of natural law."

"The disappearance or absolute annihilation, the reanimation, or the sudden transformation into something not quite material and yet not quite spiritual, of a really dead body, would involve the violation of the best ascertained laws of physics, chemistry, and physiology. Were the testimony fifty times stronger than it is, any hypothesis would be more possible than that.   But in the present state of our knowledge of the kind of causality which is discovered in the relation between mind and mind, or between mind and body, there is nothing to be said against the possibility of an appearance of Christ to His disciples, which was a real, though supernormal, psychological event, but which involved nothing which can properly be spoken of as a suspension of natural law."[1]

We have already dealt at sufficient length with the whole of this conception of natural law, but we must point out what inconsistency Dr Rashdall is involved in.   If any naturalistic theory of the universe which would make a miracle impossible were true, it would be just as difficult for a "supernormal psychological" experience to take place as any of the other events which he considers so difficult.   Either the world is subject to the sway of fixed and rigid laws, in which case no miracle is possible, or it is possible for God to reveal Himself to mankind, to become incarnate in the world, and to shew by visible signs that He is risen from the dead.   We have evidence, and strong evidence, for certain events.   If that evidence is true, then we have sufficient

[1] *The Historical Evidence for the Resurrection of Jesus Christ*, by Kirsopp Lake, M.A. (Oxon), Professor of New Testament Exegesis and Early Christian Literature in the University of Leiden, p. 269.

grounds for believing in the truth of the Christian religion and all that it involves. But Dr Rashdall would have us reject all the evidence that is before us because of *a priori* theories, and then suggests that we can believe the religion on grounds which he has invented himself, and for which there is no authority at all. We cannot play fast and loose with our evidence in this way.

I would therefore venture to suggest to you as a result of this discussion, that that event which formed some of the strongest evidence on which the disciples were ultimately convinced that the Lord had risen—the discovery of the empty tomb—was a real event for which we have good historical evidence, and that the reasons for not believing in it are not the failure of the evidence, but the difficulty created by *a priori* conceptions.

III

The second point which we have to consider with regard to the Gospel narratives is the account of the Resurrection appearances. Now here the historical difficulty is in one aspect much greater than regards the empty tomb. There is undoubtedly a difficulty in harmonizing the narratives, in particular the relation between

the appearances in Galilee and those at
Jerusalem. It is difficult to be quite clear as
to the movements of the disciples. It would
be impossible to go into this subject minutely,
nor is it, from our point of view, of much
importance; for it is admitted that undoubtedly
appearances—whatever may have been their
character—took place. Supposing that all the
accounts harmonized completely, we should at
once say that all came from the same source,
probably from one original document, and that
would carry little weight. The impression that
these stories of the appearances of our Lord
gives us is that they come from those who
had had experience of the events, that they
were afterwards written down, while later an
attempt was made to construct a connected
narrative. S. Paul gives a summary of the
more important appearance of which he had
information, but, it must be remarked, with no
determination of locality at all. What S. Mark
originally contained we do not know; the
present ending is a later summary based probably on S. Luke and S. John, or at any rate
agreeing with them. S. Matthew gives a
Galilean appearance. S. Luke in his capacity
as an historian has formed a clear idea of how
the Gospel arose in Jerusalem. He confines the
appearances entirely to that city, and he ignores
if he does not entirely neglect the possibility of

any having happened in Galilee. S. John in the Gospel gives us an exact account of appearances at Jerusalem, in the Appendix of events in Galilee, and his story reads like an independent and direct reminiscence. There were undoubtedly a large number of clear and definite stories narrated by those who had seen the risen Lord, and the Apostles believed that they had good evidence for the faith that they preached.

Now the corroborative line of argument which makes us believe that these stories represent a real experience is that something must have happened to explain and account for subsequent events. We know that the arrest and death of their Lord and Master had been almost too much for the faith of the disciples; they forsook Him and fled. They were overwhelmed with a sense of failure and defeat. Something happened which transformed their thoughts, which changed their lives, and turned them into enthusiastic preachers of a living Christ. What was the cause of this change? The reason which they give is one that appears sufficient and adequate. They had seen the risen Lord, they knew that He who was crucified lived. The Resurrection had power to change those timid Galilean peasants into fearless Evangelists. If you take away the Resurrection you cannot account for the preaching of the Gospel. If you leave the Resurrection, you have adequate and sufficient cause for what happened afterwards.

It is needless to remark that every attempt has been made to explain away the evidence. It would not be possible, and it would hardly be profitable, to go into all the criticism which has been applied to the Resurrection narratives. What I would draw your attention to is how mutually destructive of one another are the various theories put forth. There is one set of critics who are so impressed by the reality of the evidence for the empty tomb and the character of the stories of the risen Lord, that they suggest that He had not really died upon the Cross, that His disciples had recovered His body, and that He had revived and afterwards made appearances to His disciples in a dramatic and striking manner. It is really impossible in the face of the story of the Crucifixion, the Death, and the Burial of our Lord, to believe that this is true. It is still more impossible to believe it on moral grounds. But the chief value of drawing attention to these theories is that they serve to bring out how striking the evidence for the Resurrection really is. The existence of such an hypothesis shews that its authors do not feel that the ordinary explanation of subjective appearances in any form is sufficient to account for the facts. The story of the

discovery of the empty tomb is too strong,
the appearances are of such a character, the
evidence is so wide and varied, the circumstances
attending them are such, that no theory of subjective vision is sufficient. An hypothesis to be
accepted must be one that will give an adequate
explanation of the facts, and will account for
the origin of the different narratives. Neither
of the two lines of explanation is capable of
doing that.

Nor will any of those which would suggest
what we may call a modified supernaturalism.
There are some people who are willing to believe
in the supernatural if it is not too obviously
asserted. Such a position is that of Professor
Harnack as put forward in his lectures on
the Nature of Christianity. He would have
us distinguish the Easter *Faith* and the
Easter *Message*. We are to accept the faith
whatever difficulties we may have about the
message.

"The Easter *message* tells us of that wonderful event in Joseph of Arimathaea's garden,
which, however, no eye saw; it tells us of the
empty grave into which a few women and
disciples looked; of the appearance of the Lord
in a transfigured form—so glorified that His
own could not immediately recognize Him; it
soon begins to tell us too, of what the Risen One
said and did. The reports became more and
more complete, and more and more confident.

But the Easter *faith* is the conviction that the
crucified one gained a victory over death; that
God is just and powerful; that he who is the
firstborn among many brethren still lives. Paul
based his Easter faith upon the certainty that
' the second Adam' was from heaven, and upon
his experience, on the way to Damascus, of
God revealing His Son to him as still alive.
God, he said, revealed him 'in me'; but this
inner revelation was coupled with 'a vision'
overwhelming as vision never was afterwards." [1]
And then later, he goes on: "Either we must
decide to rest our belief on a foundation unstable
and always exposed to fresh doubts, or else we
must abandon this foundation altogether, and
with it the miraculous appeal to our senses.
But here, too, the images of the faith have their
roots in truth and reality. Whatever may have
happened at the grave and in the matter of the
appearances, one thing is certain: *This grave
was the birth of the indestructible belief that
death is vanquished, and that there is a life
eternal."* [2]

It is a little difficult to follow accurately
what Professor Harnack means, but apparently
he would have us accept the belief that Jesus
lives, and the hope of immortality based upon
that belief, but dispense with all the evidence
in favour of this belief in the Gospel. But on

[1] Harnack, *What is Christianity*, p. 161.
[2] *Op. cit.*, p. 162.

what evidence do we base our belief if we discard the evidence given ? No doubt the Apostles as ourselves had such spiritual experience as helped them to believe, and they found that their life in the faith corroborated that faith. But clearly and undoubtedly the Church believed that its Master had risen because they had seen Him, had spoken with Him, and even touched Him. The tomb was empty and He had come to them. I do not think that we have grounds for accepting the belief if we reject the evidence given, and the evidence has been rejected because the belief has been held to be impossible. S. Paul believed not only because of his own personal experience, but because he had behind him the belief of the Church. The belief of the Church existed and was known to him before his conversion. The conversion did not mean accepting an individual opinion, but joining a number of persons who had like faith with him, and then he found that they had good grounds for that faith. We cannot, of course, interpret the facts of Christianity in terms of spiritual experience unless we have real experience of our own. Neither the testimony of a book nor that of a society can make faith real unless there be a reality in ourselves ; but the religious experience necessary for that reality is conditioned by the experience of the Church and by the body of facts which are necessary to give the intellectual basis which makes it possible.

I have not thought it necessary to consider one line of argument. In the early days of attacks upon Christianity, when people's minds were more crude perhaps than they now are, it was suggested that the whole story arose from the deception of the disciples. There are few persons who would have the courage to hold, or at any rate to teach, such a theory nowadays, for we have learned that certain things are morally impossible. If we have any belief in divine providence, it would be quite impossible on any theory of the divine government of the world to believe that a religion which had had such a transcendent influence on the human race could be built up on direct and conscious fraud, nor would it be consistent with what we know of human nature. There are some things which are impossible.

We read how some power came which transformed those Galilean peasants into great preachers of the Gospel of Christ, which sent them out into the unknown world with this new message, which gave them courage to lay down their lives for what they believed to be the truth. To suggest that such a history should be built up on conscious fraud, that men's lives should be transformed by what they knew to be untrue is to make impossible demands on our

credulity. The reality of the preaching of
Christianity and the lives of its preachers is
sufficient evidence that they believed what they
taught, and the evidence that they give us is
sufficient to convince us that they had good
grounds for their belief.

THE RESURRECTION 265

sufficient to convince us that they had good
grounds for their belief.

LECTURE VII

THE VIRGIN BIRTH

Character of the Evidence. The Text of the Narratives.
Importance of the Gospel Testimony. The Argument
from Silence. The Church Tradition. Ignatius.
Aristides. Justin Martyr. The Ascension of Isaiah.
The Odes of Solomon. Jewish Calumnies. Explana-
tions. The Place of the Virgin Birth in Christian
Theology.

THE miracle of the Virgin Birth differs from
that of the Resurrection in two important points.
The testimony for it is not so good, and it never
had the same evidential value for Christianity.
All the Apostles were witnesses of the Resurrection; they had, as they believed, good grounds
for accepting what they taught. If the facts
as reported are true, they had good grounds.
The tomb was empty, they had seen the risen
Lord in His glorified body. He had spoken
with them in a manner that could leave no
doubt in their own minds as to His identity.
As regards the Virgin Birth there was not, and
there could not be, any such evidence. We

believe it not for the particular evidence in its favour, but because it comes to us as part of the Christian tradition, and harmonizes with that tradition.

Nor did the belief play any part in the preaching of Christianity. The Apostles could put forward the Resurrection as good ground for believing that Jesus was the Messiah. It was not the only reason for which men accepted its message, but it formed a part—and an important part—of the body of evidence which influenced people's minds. Few, or none, accepted Christianity because of the Virgin Birth. It was not part of the ordinary preaching ; but converts would learn of it during the period of instruction, and it was enshrined in the Creed into which they were baptized. It came to them with authority as part of the Church's teaching, but they did not believe because of it.

I am not sure that its value as a witness has not been greater as time has gone on, and that the beautiful figure of the Virgin Mother appealing to and arousing some of the highest human sentiments has not been one of the strongest influences in creating religious devotion and elevating the purity of human life.

I

The evidence for the Virgin Birth is primarily the witness of the two Gospels, S. Matthew and S. Luke, which give an account of the Nativity. We must, to begin with, refer to certain textual questions that have been raised concerning each narrative.

In the Sinaitic MS. of the Syriac Version— the discovery of which, some twenty years ago, attracted so much attention—the concluding verse of the genealogy in S. Matthew runs as follows :—" Joseph, to whom was betrothed Mary the Virgin, begat Jesus who is called the Christ." Now it has been argued that this variant, which harmonizes with some others known, probably implies an original which simply stated that Joseph begat Jesus, and that in any case the use of the word ' begat ' implies that the compiler of the genealogy did not accept the story of the Virgin Birth. On the first point it may be noted that while we cannot be quite certain as to the original form of the reading, there is not the slightest evidence of its ever having existed in any form which did not call Mary the Virgin ; while secondly no stress can be laid on the term ' begat,' for it is clearly used throughout the genealogy to imply legal relationship. The whole genealogy is official ;

many links are left out, and in all cases the
word is used without any reference to its
physical meaning. But there is a further reason
that suggests that the compiler of the genealogy
believed in the Virgin Birth. We will quote
Dr Moffatt's *Introduction*:

"A further apologetic motive is evident in
the introduction of the women's names,
especially of Rahab, Tamar, and Bathsheba.
They reflect the Jewish slanders which the
author desired to rebut, not only by stating
what he believed to be the truth about Mary,
but by arguing that, even on the Jewish level,
women of irregular life played an honoured role
in the history of the Davidic lineage. Mary's
character, he proceeds to argue, was not
irregular. How much less, therefore (the
inference is), are Jewish objections to her and
to Jesus justified!"[1]

The genealogy thus harmonizes with and is a
fitting introduction to the story in the first
chapter, and that story is of such a character
that the belief in the Virgin Birth cannot be
eliminated from it. "No hypothesis," says Dr
Moffatt, "of literary criticism or textual
emendation can disentangle the conception of a
virgin birth from a story which is wrought
together and woven on one loom."[2]

---

[1] Moffatt, *Introduction*, p. 251; see Allen, *Expository
Times*, xi. 135 f.; Zahn, *Einleitung*, 271-275, 290 (E. T., ii.
533-539, 563).   [2] *Ibid.*

If the suggestion that the reference to the women in the genealogy arose from the existence of Jewish calumnies be at all well founded, it will shew how early these calumnies came into existence, and by consequence that the story of the Virgin Birth is not, as has been asserted, a late introduction into Christian history.

A similar attempt has been made, in this case with even less external justification, to eliminate the Virgin Birth from the story in S. Luke. It is argued that verses 34 and 35 in the first chapter may be omitted, and that to do this will improve the story. The words are, "And Mary said unto the Angel, How shall this be, seeing I know not a man? And the Angel answered and said unto her, The Holy Ghost shall come upon thee, and the power of the Most High shall overshadow thee: wherefore also that which is to be born shall be called Holy, the Son of God." Now, it must be stated at once that there is no reason for omitting these words except alleged internal evidence. There is no external authority of any value for doing so. It is true that verse 34 is omitted in one Latin MS.; that seems to arise from a confusion of the text, and on no theory of textual criticism would it be legitimate to omit a verse on such authority. Not only is there no evidence for omitting verse 35, but it is one of the earliest supported verses in

S

the New Testament, being quoted by Justin Martyr. [1]

But a careful study of the context will shew that the verses cannot be omitted, and even if they were omitted the Virgin Birth is implied in the rest of the narrative. If Mary had not been known as the Virgin the word would not have been used, as it is twice in verse 27, "to a virgin betrothed to a man whose name was Joseph, of the house of David; and the virgin's name was Mary," nor would there be any point in verses 36 and 37, which imply that a miraculous event is happening in the case of Elizabeth as in the case of Mary: "And behold Elizabeth thy kinswoman, she also hath conceived a son in her old age: and this is the sixth month with her that was called barren. For with God no word shall be impossible." I think we may add also that Mary's words in verse 38 are exactly consistent with the announcement made to her: "And Mary said, Behold the handmaid of the Lord; be it unto me according to thy word." For the angelic message implied that she would have to endure suspicion and reproach from those who were ignorant.

If it had not been for the prejudice which is felt in many minds against the idea of the Virgin Birth, I am quite sure that no one would

[1] See page 283.

have attempted to eliminate the evidence from either Gospel on textual grounds ; and this investigation will furnish an instance of the manner in which critics feel themselves justified in playing with texts to prove their point. If in the case of orthodox doctrine such essays at textual criticism were made, they would be treated with contempt, and we have an equal right to be contemptuous. There are certain recognized rules of evidence, and within certain limits scientific principles of textual criticism have been established. It is not legitimate to depart from these principles even for the sake of disproving an article of the Christian creed.

I do not think that there is any real doubt that both the Gospels contained from the beginning the story of the Virgin Birth, and it is important to emphasize how early this evidence must be. In the first place the two narratives are clearly independent. It has been asserted that in some points they are inconsistent with one another. That inconsistency is only gained by reading into one or other narrative statements that are not made. For example, it is never asserted in S. Matthew that Bethlehem was the original home of Joseph and Mary, nor is it necessarily implied. For our purpose that does not matter, for the important point to us is that the belief in the Virgin Birth, which is contained in two quite independent documents,

must be older than either, and independent of
them both. Had the belief been of later
growth, it would have been developed in one
particular circle, and in one particular form.
As it is, clearly it is not dependent on either
of these sets of stories.

For that reason it is not necessary to discuss
the credibility generally either of S. Matthew
or S. Luke's account, for whether they are
true or not in some of their details, does
not affect the point. The belief in the Virgin
Birth is independent of the details of the two
stories. There has, of course, been a large
amount of discussion about the taxing of
Quirinius, and that is just one of those points
which exercise the ingenuity of the classical
scholar. But it does not touch the heart of
the question. It may be that S. Luke was
mistaken. In that case his method is clear.
He was anxious when he could to connect
his narrative with the course of general
history. He inserts names and details where
he could. If in some of his calculations
regarding the secular history he is mistaken,
this does not take away from the credibility
of his sources. Then he is also anxious to
account for the birth at Bethlehem. He knew
that Joseph and Mary had lived at Nazareth.
How did it happen that the birth took place
at Bethlehem? He suggests an explanation.

But it was an explanation of facts which he knew on other grounds. The birth at Bethlehem is known to us from an independent source—the Gospel of S. Matthew. S. Luke, then, did not invent the birth at Bethlehem as part of the story, but he received it as part of Christian tradition, and then tried to harmonize it with facts of secular history. These two facts, then—the Virgin Birth and the birth at Bethlehem—are part of Christian tradition independent of the particular form that the story assumes whether in S. Matthew or in S. Luke. There is no reason to doubt their truth, even if there may be difficulties about any special Nativity story.

To conclude—the two Gospels which alone contain any account of our Lord's birth witness to an early Christian tradition which stated that He was born of the Virgin Mary.

II

Great stress has been laid on the argument from silence. It has been pointed out that nothing is said on the subject in S. Paul's epistles, in the earliest Gospel, or even in S. John. It is argued, therefore, that the Virgin Birth is a late tradition that gradually grew up.

Now the argument from silence is always precarious. How little stress can be laid on it in this case a single instance will shew. There is no reference to the Virgin Birth in the Acts of the Apostles. This is really quite natural, because it was not part of the ordinary apostolic missionary preaching. It would not be likely that it should be. It did not give any proof to outsiders. It was something that the convert would learn later, and would then harmonize with his other beliefs ; but it was not part of the missionary preaching of the Apostles such as S. Luke gives in the Acts. There was therefore no need for it to be mentioned; but we know that S. Luke also wrote the Gospel, and he wrote it before the Acts. Therefore he clearly knew of the Virgin Birth as part of the Christian teaching. If we had not the Gospel but only the Acts, it would at once have been argued that the author of that book had no knowledge of the Virgin Birth. This is an instance which brings out how little stress can be laid on the argument from silence. The writers of the books of the New Testament composed their works to meet the needs of their own day, and did not write to assist people in the twentieth century in the particular controversy in which they might be engaged.

A slight consideration will shew that neither in S. Mark nor in S. John would an account of the birth of Jesus be natural. S. Mark's Gospel is based upon the preaching of the Apostles, the witness that they gave of the things that they had seen and known from the time of the baptism of John, and in all probability it was on the particular witness of S. Peter that it mainly rested. Now he could not be a witness as regards the birth, and therefore it would not be part of his normal teaching ; and it is significant that S. Luke himself recognized these limits when describing the election of Matthias and the qualifications of an Apostle. In the same way the Gospel of S. John claims to contain the special witness of "the beloved disciple." There again a story of the Nativity would be quite out of place, nor can either Gospel be quoted against the belief even if we cannot lay stress on the passages which have been adduced in its favour. Nor again would it, we believe, be legitimate to lay stress on the various reading of S. John i. 13, "who was born not of blood, nor of the will of the flesh, nor of the will of man, but of God," although it is accepted by many leading critics of the present day, and would undoubtedly be a more natural statement than the ordinary reading. It is difficult to understand what is meant by saying that ordinary human beings were born "not of blood, nor of the will of the flesh, nor of the will of man." We must

content ourselves with asserting that there is
nothing in either Gospel which could make
us doubt the story of the Virgin Birth, and
that it was not in accordance with the plan
of the writers that they should give any
account of the Nativity. All the books of the
New Testament are very short, and it is obvious
that the writers in producing them must in
each case have confined themselves to the
particular purpose they had in view.

Similarly it is never safe to argue from the
silence of S. Paul. His letters were in all
cases occasional documents. They assume the
ordinary Christian preaching and the ordinary
knowledge of the Gospel history. They were not
written to provide future ages with a complete
idea of what Christianity was, and in a sense it
must be considered accidental that any particular
point of early Christianity is found in them.
Supposing that 1 Corinthians had not survived,
it would have been the customary thing to argue
that S. Paul knew nothing at all about the Lord's
Supper. S. Paul's Christological doctrine was
of such a character that it would be natural for
him to believe that our Lord was born in a
remarkable manner. Stress is by some laid on
the words "born of a woman, born under the
law," but the phrase 'woman-born' is so pro-
verbial that it would hardly be legitimate to
base anything on this expression. It is more

important to emphasize the general statement of S. Paul that the Second Man was from heaven, and his conception of our Lord as free from any taint of Adam's sin such as might be engendered by ordinary human birth. We may not have sufficient evidence to assert that S. Paul must have known the story and must have accepted it, although the fact of his relation to S. Luke would make it extremely probable. We can argue quite definitely that he had such a conception of the person of Christ, of His heavenly origin, of His freedom from sin, as might seem to justify the belief in His supernatural birth.

III

The belief in the Virgin Birth is one of those historical facts in relation to which tradition corroborates and strengthens the testimony of the New Testament. It appeared in the earliest form of the Roman creed, which is placed by Kattenbusch as early as the year 100 and cannot be much later, the words being, "He was born of the Holy Ghost from the Virgin Mary." This corresponds with the fact that we find it part of the regular Church tradition from the beginning of the second century. So Ignatius, writing to the Ephesians:

"For our God, Jesus the Christ, was conceived in the womb by Mary according to a dispensation, of the seed of David but also of the Holy Ghost; and He was born and was baptized that by His passion He might cleanse water. And hidden from the prince of this world were the virginity of Mary and her childbearing and likewise also the death of the Lord —three mysteries to be cried aloud—which were wrought in the silence of God."[1]

And again in his letter to the Smyrnaeans:

"Fully persuaded as touching our Lord that He is truly of the race of David according to the flesh, but Son of God by the Divine will and power, truly born of a virgin and baptized by John that all righteousness might be fulfilled by Him."[2]

One of the earliest Christian Apologists was Aristides, the discovery of whose work about twenty years ago created so much interest. He says:

"The Christians, then, reckon the beginning of their religion from Jesus Christ, who is named the Son of God Most High; and it is said that God came down from heaven, and from a Hebrew virgin took and clad Himself with flesh, and in a daughter of man there dwelt the Son of God."[3]

---

[1] Ign. *ad Eph.* 18, 19.   [2] Ign. *ad Smyr.* 1.

[3] Aristides, Syriac Version, chapter ii.   In the Greek (chapter xv. ed. Robinson) the text is as follows: "Καὶ ἐκ παρθένου ἁγίας γεννηθείς, ἀσπόρως τε καὶ ἀφθόρως, σάρκα ἀνέλαβε, καὶ ἀνεφάνη ἀνθρώποις, ὅπως ἐκ τῆς πολυθέου πλάνης αὐτοὺς ἀνακαλέσηται."

The third testimony may be selected from the writings of Justin Martyr, in particular because of the testimony it gives to the verses of S. Luke referred to above.

" The words, then, ' Behold a virgin shall conceive' signify that the Virgin should conceive without intercourse; for, if she had had intercourse with any one whatsoever, she would have been no longer a virgin. But the Power of God coming upon the Virgin overshadowed her, and caused her, being a virgin, to conceive. And the Angel of God, who was sent to the virgin herself at that time, brought her good tidings saying, ' Behold thou shalt conceive in thy womb of the Holy Ghost, and shalt bring forth a Son, and He shall be called the Son of the Most High, and thou shalt call His name Jesus, for He shall deliver His people from their sins,' as they who have related all the things about our Saviour Jesus Christ taught." [1]

It is unnecessary to continue our quotations later. These are sufficient to shew that this was a regular part of the normal Christian teaching as far back as we have evidence to go upon. There are, however, two writings of a more Apocryphal character which are worth referring to.

Among the many curious Apocryphal writings preserved, one is the Ascension of Isaiah. It is a composite work. The following passage seems

[1] Justin Martyr, *Apol.* i. 33.

to have been proved to belong certainly to the original Greek form of the work, and probably also to its archetype. I do not, however, feel certain as to the statement of Dr Charles that it must have been known to Ignatius. The following is the quotation:—

"After this I saw, and the angel who spoke with me, who conducted me, said unto me: 'Understand, Isaiah son of Amos; for this purpose have I been sent from God.' And I indeed saw a woman of the family of David the prophet, named Mary, a virgin, and she was espoused to a man named Joseph, a carpenter, and he also was of the seed and family of the righteous David of Bethlehem Judah. And he came into his lot. And when she was espoused, she was found with child, and Joseph the carpenter was desirous to put her away. But the angel of the Spirit appeared in this world, and after that Joseph did not put her away, but kept Mary and did not reveal the matter to any one. And he did not approach Mary, but kept her as a holy virgin, though with child. And he did not live with her for two months. And after two months of days while Joseph was in his house and Mary his wife, but both alone, it came to pass that when they were alone Mary straightway looked with her eyes and saw a small babe, and she was astonied. And after she had been astonied, her womb was found as formerly before she had conceived. And when her husband Joseph said unto her: 'What astonied thee?'

his eyes were opened and he saw the infant,
and praised God, because into his portion God
had come.   And a voice came to them: 'Tell
this vision to no one.'   And the story regarding
the infant was noised abroad in Bethlehem.
Some said: 'The Virgin Mary hath borne a
child, before she was married two months.'   And
many said: 'She has not borne a child, nor
has a midwife gone up to her, nor have we
heard the cries of pains.'   And they were all
blinded respecting Him, and they all knew
regarding Him, though they knew not whence
He was.   And they took Him, and went to
Nazareth in Galilee."[1]

Very similar testimony is that given in
the newly discovered *Odes of Solomon*.   It is
particularly remarkable that this passage should
occur in one of the odes for which we have
not only the testimony of the newly discovered
Syriac Version, but also that of Lactantius,
who not only quotes it, but gives its number
in the collection.   The following is the passage :—

"The Spirit opened the womb of the
Virgin, and she received conception and brought
forth ; and the Virgin became a Mother with
many mercies ; and she travailed and brought
forth a Son, without incurring pain ; and because
she was not sufficiently prepared, and she had
not sought a midwife (for He brought her to

---

[1] *The Ascension of Isaiah*, ed. Charles, xi. 1-15 ; see
Introduction, pp. xxii., xxiv.

bear), she brought forth, as if she were a man,
of her own will; and she brought Him
forth openly, and acquired Him with great
dignity, and loved Him in His swaddling clothes,
and guarded Him kindly, and shewed Him in
majesty." [1]

Dr Rendel Harris is of opinion that the
Odes of Solomon should be placed in the First
century, but when he comes to this passage
he feels inclined to date it later. It is impossible,
he says, that the doctrine of the miraculous
birth should be so highly developed in the
first century, and he suggests, therefore, that
it would be necessary to depress the date of
this ode to the second century. There is, of
course, underlying this, the assumption that the
belief in the Virgin Birth was a later addition
to Christianity, since it would have been quite
impossible for such a legendary amplification
to be introduced earlier. Personally I am
not of opinion that the Odes of Solomon
should be put so early as Dr Rendel
Harris would place them. I believe that they
date from early in the second century, and
that they represent just the same fantastic
development of Christianity of which we find
some trace in Ignatius, and which grew later
into the Apocryphal Gospels. But the important
point for our purpose is to note that if in quite

[1] *The Odes of Solomon,* ed. by Rendel Harris, xix. 6-10.

early documents like the Ascension of Isaiah and the Odes of Solomon we find these developments, it is an additional testimony that the belief dates from the early days of Christianity, and was not, as has been suggested, a later addition.

Still more important for our purpose are the Jewish calumnies which were noticed by Celsus in his argument against Christianity, and are referred to by Origen in his work against that philosopher. The following are the passages:—

"After these things he introduces a Jew disputing with Jesus Himself and refuting Him, as he thinks, on many points; first of all, as having invented the birth from a virgin. He reproaches Him as having been born in a Jewish village, of a woman in the country who was poor and worked with her hands. He says she had been turned out of his house by her husband, a carpenter by trade, having been convicted of adultery. Then he says that she, having been thus cast out by her husband, and wandering about in disgrace, brought forth Jesus in secret: and that He, having hired Himself out into Egypt owing to His poverty, and there having learned certain magic rites on which the Egyptians prided themselves, returned to His own country highly elated with this, and by means of them proclaimed Himself God."[1]

---

[1] Origen, *Contra Celsum*, I. xxviii.

Again, later, he returns to the same subject :

" But let us return again to the place where
the Jew is introduced, where it is recorded that
the Mother of Jesus was thrust out by a carpenter
who was betrothed to her, as having been convicted of adultery and bearing a son to a
certain soldier named Panthera, and let us see
whether those who have blindly invented these
stories of the adultery of the Virgin and of
Panthera, and of the carpenter who thrust her out,
did not invent all these things to overthrow the
miraculous conception by the Holy Ghost; for
they could have falsified the history in some
other way owing to its marvellous character,
and not have unconsciously joined in establish-
ing that Jesus was not born of an ordinary
marriage.   It was naturally to be expected that
those who could not believe in the marvellous
birth of Jesus would invent some false story ; but
they did not do it in a plausible manner, for
by preserving the tradition that the Virgin did
not conceive from Joseph, they made clear the
falsity of their position to those accustomed to
criticism." [1]

There can, I think, be no doubt that Origen
is right and that this story which Celsus reports
as a Jewish calumny was invented because of
the belief in the Virgin Birth in order to throw
contempt and discredit on the story.   The name
of the soldier ' Panthera ' was clearly a corruption
of Parthenos (virgin).   How early this calumny

[1] *Op. cit.*, I. 32.

arose we cannot tell; certainly it was not late in arising, and it implies, of course, that the Christian story of the Virgin Birth was earlier. It is interesting to notice that here, as in the case of the Resurrection, the false reports spread by the Jews have strengthened the evidence for the Christian tradition.[1]

There are only two instances so far as I am aware of any disbelief among Christians of the Virgin Birth. It was accepted not only by the orthodox but by the great body of heretics as well. There were, however, certain Ebionites or Jewish Christians who denied it. There were some Jewish Christians who accepted the belief that Jesus was God; others, on the other hand, allowed that He was the Messiah, but said that he was only a man born of Joseph and Mary. These latter seem to have been a small and unimportant body of people, and represented the extreme wing of Jewish Christianity. There is, however, no evidence at all for the belief that they represented, as has been asserted, a more primitive Christianity. They represented rather the opinion of certain Jews who tried to compromise between Judaism and Christianity, but wished to preserve all their Jewish habits and their Jewish prejudices. Cerinthus also is stated

[1] It is I think quite possible that this tradition arose from the knowledge that our Lord was not the son of Joseph. See *Church Quarterly Review*, October 1914.

T

to have held that the man Jesus was the son of
Joseph and Mary. That was because he believed
that it was only at the baptism that the Christ
descended upon Him.

To sum up this part of our investigation.
There can be no doubt that the Virgin Birth
was part of the orthodox tradition of the
Christian Church throughout the second century,
and that it was looked upon as part of the
Christian creed. It was accepted not only by
the orthodox, but by the great body of heretics.
Already legendary details similar to those which
we find in the late Apocryphal Gospels are
beginning to grow up round it, while the attacks
upon it made by the Jews, and the calumnies
that they circulated, combine to strengthen our
belief in its early date and its original character
as part of the primitive Christian tradition.

IV

Various theories have been put forward to
account for the belief in the Virgin Birth. It
has been suggested that it arose from a desire
to find a fulfilment for the well-known passage
in Isaiah, and attention has been drawn to the
stress laid by S. Matthew on the fulfilment of
prophecy. It is, of course, quite true that the
author of the First Gospel is most anxious to

impress on us the fact that Jesus as the Messiah of the Jews fulfilled the Old Testament; but there is sufficient evidence to shew in almost every case that it was not the prophecy that suggested the narratives, but the narratives came first and were found to be the fulfilment of the prophecy selected.

If we study the Gospel as a whole, we shall see that S. Matthew, in those parts of the narrative which he derived from S. Mark, in various cases appends passages from the prophets to incidents which he thinks were the fulfil-ment of them. And if we examine the passages quoted in the first two chapters, it will make it very difficult to believe that the story was invented to fulfil the prophecy. It was, for example, quite natural and in accordance with the then prevailing views about the use of Scripture for anyone who knew of the flight into Egypt to quote the well-known passage from Hosea, "Out of Egypt have I called my Son," as a prophecy fulfilled; but it would have been hardly natural for him to invent the narrative in order to find a fulfilment of that prophecy, for the original passage does not refer to the personal Messiah but to Israel: "When Israel was a child, then I loved him and called my son out of Egypt." A student of the Old Testament who knew of the massacre of the Innocents might naturally find an analogy in the

well-known text in Jeremiah about Rachel
weeping for her children. But it is not a passage
which *prima facie* has any Messianic bearing, and
it would not have been natural to invent the
narrative in order to find a fulfilment to that
prophecy. And so again if the story of the
Magi had arisen to fulfil the Isaianic prophecy,
they would have been made kings, as in fact later
Christian tradition made them, and not Magi.

We have further to remember that in the
passage from Isaiah, which is quoted in relation
to the Virgin Birth, the word used in the
original does not mean a virgin, but a young
woman of marriageable age ; that there was
no expectation so far as we can judge of a
Virgin Birth ; and that it was, so far as we can
judge, inconsistent with ordinary Jewish expectations and prejudices. Naturally, if the story
of the Virgin Birth were known, a passage
which might be so quoted would be selected as
representing an analogy from the Old Testament. The Christian controversialist who
searched the Old Testament for proofs and
prophecies, seeking to find them according to
Jewish methods of exegesis, would bring
forward passages which were not completely
relevant, or would impose on them a more or
less unnatural interpretation ; but such passages,
which are so obviously misquoted and had not
originally a Messianic reference, would not be

likely to create such a story when that fulfilment was not expected.

Another source for the growth of this story has been sought in the analogy of Greek mythology. Now it was quite natural that this analogy should come to be pressed later, and we see references to it in Justin Martyr, where he points out the difference between the two conceptions; but to find traces of any Hellenic influence in S. Matthew or in the early chapters of S. Luke is exceedingly difficult. The First Gospel bears all the traces of having been written under undoubtedly Jewish influences; the author of it seems to look only to the fulfilment of Jewish prophecy. The early chapters in idea and thought are essentially Jewish. The genealogy, the story of the Magi, the birth at Bethlehem, the lamentations of Rachel, shew no traces of Hellenic ideas. To find Hellenic influence in these entirely Hebraic surroundings would be most strange. It is true, of course, that S. Luke was probably a Greek, and his Gospel is more universalist in character than any of the others; but it is particularly remarkable that the early chapters shew throughout an Aramaic colouring. They are written throughout from a Jewish point of view; they are full of references to Jewish customs. Whether this came from tradition or from the use of an early Aramaic source we do

not know; what is clear is that there seems to
be no trace in the chapters as a whole of Greek
influence. Greek mythological influences and
conceptions were entirely different in character
from the ideas which are present in the Gospels,
and just those sections which give an account of
the Virgin Birth are the ones where there is the
least trace of any other than Jewish influence.

The attempt to find an analogy with the
Buddhist birth-stories, which are really late in
origin and have most probably grown up under
Christian influence, seems far-fetched; as also
does the industry with which stories of other
analogies are sought out. It is curious how
the very slightest and most obscure analogy
is raked up from any mythical source and
supposed to have influenced the narrative of
the Gospel. The analogy is generally so slight
that it rarely succeeds in convincing any but
those who have discovered it, and each new
investigator puts forward some new theory.
But a sort of vague idea is created that, where
there are so many suggested analogies, some
one or other must hold good. So we shall find
when we investigate the different explanations
of miracles or methods of explaining them away
which have been suggested, it is argued that
some one of the suggestions made must be true.
All this represents a very unconvincing type of
argument. It obtains any cogency that it has

because the assumption is made that the story in the Gospel is not historical, that, therefore, it must have grown up in some way, even if we do not know how. But is it not possible that the simplest and truest explanation is that the story is true ?

V

We stated at the beginning that the evidence for the Virgin Birth is not of the same character as that for the Resurrection, that it could not be so widely known, and that we accepted the belief as part of the Christian revelation as a whole. But if the evidence could not be so cogent as in some cases, so far as it goes it is good, and I would suggest that so far from our having any reason for discrediting it, the fact of the hold of the story on the Christian consciousness, and its connexion with Christian theology, are good reasons for accepting it.

I would suggest first of all that the extraordinary hold that the birth-stories of Jesus have had on the Christian mind is some evidence for them. Christianity was to be a religion for all peoples ; it is a religion, not a philosophy ; a religion capable of being embodied in simple stories which appeal to the human mind, to the simple and untaught as well as to the educated and thoughtful. It may be argued that the

stories have had their day. I think not. I
think that probably most of us will feel that
however lofty may be the theological and
philosophical conceptions which have been built
up round Christianity and appeal to our intellectual needs, it is still the simple Gospel
narratives which have the greatest hold upon
our heart. Our own religion is simple, and a
simple story means much more for us than an
elaborate dogmatic statement. A Christmas
hymn can stir us far more than many a Christmas
sermon. Of course it might be argued that we
are dealing with myths, true in idea but not in
history. I do not think it likely that such
prominent parts of the Gospel would be untrue,
nor do I see any particular grounds for thinking
that they are.

For they are not the sort of story which the
ordinary mythopoeic tendency would build up ;
what the natural human consciousness might
invent may be seen in the Apocryphal Gospels
and Acts, and there is no part of the story
where the contrast between the Gospels and
Apocryphal writings is more conspicuous than
in the stories of the Nativity. Even the two
specimens of incipient Apocryphal development
which have been referred to above will be
sufficient to mark the contrast, and anyone
who desires to see how great it is should study
the Protevangelium of James, or the summary

of all the Apocryphal stories given in the *Annals* of Baronius. If God teaches mankind through stories why should not the birth of Jesus and the incidents attending it have been such as to give these lessons. The Gospels are throughout on the plane of the simplest and purest human nature, and are not influenced by any ideas of academic propriety.

And as the stories appeal to the natural religious instincts of man, so it has always been felt that they harmonize with Christian theology. I am not prepared to say as some would say that the Incarnation could only have happened in the way that it has done. I do not personally care for those *a priori* methods of argument; but I think we may simply say that we feel the Virgin Birth does take its natural place in the scheme of Christian theology.

It emphasizes in the first place the way in which the Incarnation is a new departure in the history of mankind. We have shewn that such a conception is quite in harmony with the analogy of nature, that there have been periods when something new has come into the world. This is what we believe happened at the Incarnation, and it is not out of harmony with that thought that when human nature took a new step in development, as a sign of the new departure an event such as the birth of our Lord in a marvellous way should take place.

And then it has created the whole of the Christian ideal of motherhood. It is very remarkable that there has never been anything which we may call Manichean in the Christian aspect of the Virgin Birth. The emphasis has always been on the birth of our Lord and on the figure of the Virgin Mother, and what this belief has done for mankind has been to emphasize the fact that motherhood is the end and aim and ideal of Christian marriage. It is this conception which, working throughout Christian history, has built up the Christian ideal of marriage, nor, I believe, is there any thought or ideal more necessary than this at the present day.

And then, lastly, it harmonizes with the conception of the sinlessness of Jesus. What we learn about Him is that He took human nature to Himself, but human nature without any touch of sin; and Christian theology has felt that the fact that He was born not as we are, suits such a belief. It is not possible of course to say that He must have been born in that way, that He could not be sinless if He were not; but it is possible for us to feel that if He as God came in the world taking upon Him our human nature, but taking it upon Him not in its stained and corrupted form, His birth from the Virgin Mary is a fitting accompaniment of such theology.

To those who do not believe in the Incarnation, I am not now speaking. Before we ask them to accept the Virgin Birth they have much to learn about Christianity as a whole; but there are some who are prepared to accept the belief in the Incarnation but cannot believe in the Virgin Birth. I would suggest to them that they are really being led astray by their imagination. The Incarnation itself, the thought of God taking upon Him human nature, is a miracle so stupendous as almost to be impossible to realize. The additional fact that this event took place through the Virgin Birth makes little further demand upon our faith. From the naturalistic point of view it is really one of the least difficult of miracles; from the Christian point of view it is one of the most beautiful. It has been one of the greatest inspirations of Christian art, one of the purest influences on Christian life. The Church has, therefore, wisely retained it in her creed.

LECTURE VIII

EXPLANATIONS OF MIRACLES

Character of our Evidence. Possibility of Explanations.
Theory of Matthew Arnold. Problem of Possession.
Miracles of Healing. The Mythopoeic Faculty. Coincidence. Symbolical Interpretation. The Feeding of
the Five Thousand. Conclusion.

So far we have been examining the evidence
for the miraculous occurrences in the New
Testament, and the conclusion we have arrived
at is that the evidence is good. That is to say,
if the events recorded were not such as to cause
us difficulties in accepting them, we should
give them credence as we should other events
recorded in history. That does not mean that
every event must necessarily have happened
exactly as it is recorded. We know that there
are differences between the narratives in the case
of events which are not miraculous, and therefore
we cannot tell exactly how any event happened.
We do not claim any other authority for the
writers than that of being good historians, and
they would therefore be subject to the same

chance of error as other witnesses. They may have made mistakes in some cases, or there may have been some mistakes made by their authorities; but so far as we can judge they are good witnesses, and the evidence they give us is good evidence.

We have to come, then, to the statement made by Matthew Arnold that it really does not matter whether the evidence is good or not; we know how miracles came into existence. They are the natural product of the mythopoeic faculty of the human mind, and therefore we do not believe them. A moment's consideration will shew how very dangerous such a method of argument is. Supposing we were to apply it to history generally. We know how great the love of legend is; it is always creating picturesque events, and loves striking and interesting details. If for that reason we were, without any examination, to rule out from history everything which might be legendary, we should present a very jejune affair to our readers. There are some historians whose scepticism has been carried to a point almost as extreme as the above: they have eliminated a large amount of history. It is recognized now that such methods are not sound. We have no right to assume beforehand that events did not happen. We must examine the evidence carefully in all cases. And so with regard to miracles, we cannot assume that they are necessarily the result of the mythopoeic faculty, and can thus be explained away. We must examine the evidence to see whether it is adequate, and the explanations to see whether they are reasonable.

I

I propose first of all to examine one particular class of miracles, the problems in connexion with which demand our special attention— namely, the casting out of devils.

We may take it as generally admitted that the expression "possessed with devils" or "with a devil" was the ordinary term used to describe that class of disease which we now designate as 'nervous,' or more commonly group together under the heading 'insanity.' There was probably much at that date which intensified these evils. We must realize what would be the character of life in this country at the present day, if all those now confined in asylums were wandering at will over the country-side. Neglect, cruelty, contempt would all intensify the evil. The result must have been in many cases appalling. Whether or no there were special circumstances in that age, in the breaking up of the fabric of society and the failure of religious life, which increased the prevalence of insanity, is a further question. There are undoubtedly stages of civilization and conditions of society in which all mental evils seem to be intensified. At any rate it is quite clear that mental disease was in Palestine in the time of our Lord a terrible affliction.

Our Lord's attitude towards it was clear. In this as in all other matters affecting the scientific knowledge of the age, He adopted unreservedly current theories. However great a shock this may be to some, we must recognize that it is so. And if we are prepared to do this, it will become clear that there was no other attitude that would have been consistent with the character and purpose of our Lord's ministry. He came neither to teach a science nor a medical knowledge nor a biblical criticism which those whom He addressed would have been quite incapable of grasping. The psychological language which He used was that of His time. And have those who expect us to believe anything else ever asked themselves what He could have taught? Was it to be the psychology and medical knowledge of our own day? But do we really imagine that the last word has been said on any of these subjects, or that the theories of to-day will be the theories of to-morrow? Our knowledge and practice are most imperfect. We hardly know or can do more—in some cases we can do less, perhaps—than people did eighteen

hundred years ago. It is possible that we may
still find, we have perhaps begun already to find,
that for the cure of such cases a powerful
spiritual principle is the one thing needed. At
any rate of one thing we are certain. Our
knowledge at present is most imperfect, and
it is possible that supposing the purpose of the
Gospels had been to give a complete account
of demoniacal possession, it might be found to
be as inconsistent with the present stage of
medical knowledge as is their actual teaching.
Our attitude towards the personality of evil
in any form must be at present one of suspension
of judgement. The essential thing for us to
realize is that in this, as in other respects, the
message of our Lord was clearly and inevitably
given in the language, and according to the
ideas, of those to whom He preached.

May I be allowed in this connexion to refer
for one or two moments to the profoundly
interesting book on the teaching of Christ by
your own Bishop Moorhouse, in whose memory
the lectures I am now giving were founded.
He is one of those men of vigorous and able
mind who, although throughout his life engaged
in practical work, has done much to help us to
meet the many and difficult theological problems
which the new ideas of the generation to which
he belongs created for us. He points out
how largely indebted our Lord was "for the

forms in which He clothed His thought to the religious symbolism which was in use among His countrymen; and thus, at times, it becomes exceedingly difficult to determine how far He adopted contemporary modes of thought as His own, and how far He simply employed them as a vehicle of instruction, which would be intelligible to those who heard Him."[1] He suggests that the real explanation of Satanic influence is the theory put forward by Dr Martensen, Bishop of Seeland. "He believes that primarily the Satan of Scripture is a principle, and not a person, a spirit and a power which seeks to realize itself in persons."[2] The evil principle becomes incarnate in personalities human and superhuman, and this theory it is suggested "illuminates for us some of the obscurest sayings of our Divine Master."[3]

Now I am not prepared to say that I would accept this theory, but I think it is one we must ponder over. What I would put before you is that those possessed with devils were men subject to nervous diseases, some of which take now, as they did then, very strange forms; that the extent to which moral and spiritual causes have been at work is at present unknown; that

---

[1] *The Teaching of Christ, its Conditions, Secret, and Results*, by the Right Rev. J. Moorhouse, Bishop of Manchester [sometime Bishop of Melbourne], p. 114.

[2] *Op. cit.*, p. 128.   [3] *Op. cit.*, p. 129.

U

our Lord simply adopted the current theory in relation to them, and that this was in accordance with His normal methods; that no really satisfactory theory of these phenomena has yet been attained, and we must be prepared to widen our methods of investigation if we would learn what is the spiritual origin of spiritual disease.

It was the custom in our Lord's time to deal with these diseases by exorcism. Sometimes that was effective. It was here that His power appeared most striking. We are repeatedly told that He cast out unclean spirits. Many typical instances are given, and the power that He exercised was recognized as something different from anything that people had experienced. "What is this? A new teaching? With authority he commandeth the unclean spirits and they obey him." So great was His success that some believed or pretended to believe that He was leagued with Beelzebub, the prince of the devils. This accusation roused His indignation more than any other that was made. For the power by which He worked was, He said, the power of the Holy Ghost, "and whosoever shall blaspheme against the Holy Spirit hath never forgiveness but is guilty of eternal sin."

There is one more fact that we must notice, and that is the testimony which the devils are stated to have given concerning Jesus. "And he cried out, saying, What have we to do with thee, thou Jesus of Nazareth? Art thou come to destroy us? I know thee who thou art, the Holy One of God." "And he suffered not the devils to speak, because they knew him." And again, "And the unclean spirits, whensoever they beheld him, fell down before him, and cried, saying, Thou art the Son of God. And he charged them much that they should not make him known." And again, "What have I to do with thee, Jesus, thou Son of the Most High God?" It is difficult to believe that we are not reading an account of things just as they happened. But I prefer leaving these facts without further explanation. At the same time we must realize that it is part of what we have to include in any satisfactory theory that we may formulate.

Now it is generally admitted that these things happened, and that our Lord did heal those who were possessed with devils; but it is said that no miracle really took place, and we are told that it was only an instance of 'natural' law. We have already recognized that this phrase does not help us: it only means 'in accordance with experience.' Here were certain persons afflicted with diseases which were in various forms mental. We know that in certain cases such diseases could be cured by the influ-

ence of other minds on them. Both the disease
and its cure were mental, not material. In
certain cases to a slight degree one mind has the
power of influencing another—the process is
entirely spiritual. If therefore we find that there
is a great development of this power in any
particular circumstances, surely this is a sign to
us of a real gift of spiritual power to humanity.
That was the impression it created, and the
explanation Jesus gives. Whatever analogy
there may be to phenomena we are acquainted
with, the power exhibited was quite abnormal,
and it is only by having a very narrow conception of what is miraculous that we can refuse
to call it a miracle.

Before concluding this subject I may just refer
for one minute to the attacks which Professor
Huxley has made on these stories of the healing
of the possessed, and in particular that of the
Gadarene swine. Now with regard to that
particular instance on which he lays such stress,
I will frankly confess that I do not feel
altogether able to satisfy myself about it.
There are particular difficulties in the story
which I cannot explain, and I am glad to take
this opportunity of suggesting that we should
recognize that there will always be some things
we cannot understand, but that that is no reason
why we should allow particular difficulties to
overthrow a belief which has been built on a

broad and substantial basis ; nor should we be
anxious to accept inadequate explanations, but
rather we should learn to exercise in certain
things suspension of judgement. As regards the
accusations, as a whole, that Huxley brings
against the narrative of the Gospel, I would
say, that I cannot personally conceive our Lord
approaching these phenomena from any point
of view but that of His own times ; that nervous
diseases could only be dealt with through the
mind of the sufferer ; that our Lord probably
in no other direction did more to heal misery
than in this ; and that the spiritual power of the
Christian Church, which has undoubtedly enabled
it to cast out devils, has been one of the most
powerful vehicles for suppressing mental suffering. It gradually overpowers the spiritual evils
of the world and makes us feel how much
mental suffering is owing to the failure of
spiritual life. There are many cases where
medical skill can do little for the minds of
those afflicted, and I am sure that wise, spiritual
power wisely exercised does much more in the
world than anything else to save lives from
being wrecked.

II

I would next deal with miracles of
healing. In relation to these it is said that

the evidence for the works of healing is not
good evidence for miracles, the reason alleged
being that these so-called miracles represent
faith-healing, and that faith-healing is natural
law, and not miraculous. Now these statements
will, I think, make us reflect. For a long time
it was the endeavour of rationalistic critics to
shew that the evidence for these works of
healing was not good. The Gospel of S. Mark
was placed late, largely because it contains so
many miraculous cures. Renan, for example,
tells us quite simply that these things could
not be true because they were miracles.
Now quite suddenly the whole of the criticism
changes ; we are told that the evidence which
has been so long condemned is good, but it is
not evidence for the miracles. Does not this at
once suggest to us how worthless is much of
this criticism which claims to be historical ? It
was not really historical ; it simply attempts to
justify a position which is assumed on *a priori*
grounds. A further observation presents itself
to us. The evidence offered for other miracles is
exactly the same as that for miracles of healing.
We have been told that the former is not good,
and that the latter is good. When we come to ask
the reason, it is not because of any defect in the
evidence in the former case, but simply because
there are difficulties in believing the events recorded. It is not evidence but speculation.

Now we come to this question of faith-healing. It may be allowed that there are some phenomena which may be so described. There can be no doubt that in certain cases people who were ill, or fancied they were ill, have been cured by a visit to Lourdes. There are cases where the mental attitude of the patient has had a considerable influence on their cure. There is, then, a certain analogy between the miracles of healing recorded of our Lord and certain events which have happened within recent experience. Therefore, it is argued, these miracles are more credible; because they are more credible, therefore, the evidence is satisfactory; but since they are credible, they are not miracles. It will be noticed how, underlying all these discussions, is the assumption consciously or unconsciously made that a miracle cannot happen. Practically, the evidence is believed if the miraculous character of the event can be explained away.

We may admit to a certain extent the existence of the phenomena called faith-healing, but what are their characteristics? So far as we are acquainted with them, what they imply is the influence of the spiritual nature of man on the material. If we accept the materialistic explanation of the human mind, and believe that the whole of our mental equipment is merely a function of the brain, then we may

be right in explaining these phenomena as con-
forming to what is called natural law. But of
course if that assumption is true, there is no
place either for miracles or for religion in any
form. But if, as a vast number of persons
believe, and on good grounds, the spiritual
nature of man, his will, his mind—whatever we
may call it—is something which is not material
in its origin, but is representative in man of
that spiritual principle which is the ultimate
cause of material things, then the attempt to
bring all these phenomena within the sphere
of natural law (in the ordinary sense in which
the word is used), is entirely unjustified. They
represent in fact the influence of mind or spirit
on matter. Those who are so wedded to the
word 'law' may talk if they like of 'spiritual
law,' but that is not really a phrase with much
meaning. What really happens is that the
spiritual nature of man influences the material
nature somewhat abnormally. The influence
of the spirit on matter is of course something
which is continuously taking place. Whenever the mind acts through the medium of the
brain and the body, it is spirit working upon
matter. Whenever this spiritual power working
in us on the body leads to some variation in
physical phenomena, it is the influence of spirit
upon matter. Whenever the mind is so strongly
excited that it is able to help the body to throw

off disease, whether functional or otherwise,
again it is the influence of spirit upon matter.

Now what is clear, and the evidence and
instances given shew it, is that this power is
heightened and intensified by religion and
spiritual influence. That is what is meant by
faith-healing. The faith may be more or less
imperfect, but it intensifies the spiritual power
of every individual. It enables men to overcome the restraints and restrictions of their
material environment, and it increases their power
in a way which is sometimes normal, sometimes
abnormal. Now all this exists, we are told, at
the present day ; if it does so it is in a weak,
tentative, and uncertain manner. Religious
faith is slight, and exercises little power, and
there is also a certain amount of imposture
connected with this. But these instances
represent in a feeble manner what Jesus did.
Again and again He appeals to the power of
faith in His disciples. The power to do works
of healing or to cast out devils depended upon
their faith. So far the analogy is exact, but
the difference is also profound. If we are to
believe in any way at all the stories which are
told about Jesus, what exists at the present
time in a weak, feeble, and tentative fashion
existed in Him as strong, authoritative power.
He is confident of what He can do, and He
acts with authority.

If this be the case surely we have here real
evidence of the existence of a strong spiritual
force in the world abnormal in its character.
We are told that this is not miraculous. That
depends entirely upon what definition we have
given of miracles. What we do say is that it
is something which in its manifestations, judged
from the point of view of ordinary experience,
is abnormal. It represents a power analogous
perhaps to events which have happened at other
times, but exhibited in a manner of which we
have no record in the other cases. It harmonizes
with all else that we are told about our Lord.
We are told that there was authority in His
preaching and teaching; that we can see for
ourselves from what we read of Him. We are
told that He Himself based this authority upon
the fact that He was the Son of Man; we
are told that He claimed that these miracles
were an additional sign of the reality of His
divine mission. Surely all these corroborate
one another. They represent a consistent whole,
and it is only a purely pedantic and academic
use of terms which would deny that events like
these are miraculous, or that they have an
evidential value in relation to the mission, the
work, and the nature of Jesus Christ.

I would suggest then that the confession
that is now made that the evidence for these
miracles is good, is good and decisive evidence

of the reality of the miraculous. We are not at liberty on any scientific grounds to assume that this or that particular miracle could not have happened. We do not know on any grounds of experience what spiritual power can or cannot accomplish in the world ; and if this spiritual power represented the presence among mankind of Him who was the author of all spiritual life, then any attitude of incredulity on general grounds is illogical and unscientific. It may be quite right to admit that in this or that point a mistake may have arisen, but we are not justified in saying this could or could not have happened.

III

The second explanation which is given miracles is something as follows. In all times of religious excitement or religious movements miracles have been said to occur. There is plenty of evidence of their alleged occurrence in history. There is nothing really to distinguish miracles of the Gospel from any other miracles, and, therefore, as we are not prepared to accept the ordinary ecclesiastical miracles of history, we should not accept the Gospel miracles. Now if the theory which we have developed above be at all true, there is no reason why within certain limits we should not be prepared to accept what are called ecclesiastical miracles. That is to say, we are quite prepared to believe that in times of religious movements when man's spiritual nature is strengthened, the influence of their spiritual nature on their material environment will be intensified. Some ecclesiastical miracles may have happened; but we venture to say that in no way is the analogy either as regards evidence or character between the two classes of miracles really sound.

To survey the whole field would be impossible, but by good fortune our attention has been drawn in particular to the miracles recorded of S. Thomas of Canterbury, and we have been told that as regards both character and evidence they present a striking analogy to the Gospel narrative. It is, we think, hardly possible to maintain this statement after a careful study of the question. In the first place no miracles were recorded of Thomas Becket at all during his lifetime. In the earlier lives we are particularly told that there were none, and it is only in quite late documents that any reference occurs. The life of S. Thomas was that of a zealous, religious man defending the ecclesiastical position in the country with earnestness and zeal; no doubt making mistakes, no doubt with his faults. Then his career ended in a manner which increased his influence by his martyrdom. He became, in consequence, the champion of the ecclesiastical cause, and all the religious fervour of the later Middle Ages, in the peculiar manner in which it was wont to express itself, centred throughout Western Europe in his name. It was to him, or through him, that prayers were offered in times of danger, stress, or emergency. It was to his shrine that people came to seek his aid in curing disease. The cathedral at Canterbury was, we are told, at times of pilgrimage filled with those who came from all parts of England and Western Europe. There is still a road across the Downs known as 'the Pilgrims' Way.' Some of those who filled the cathedral at times of pilgrimage were cured. Books were written containing accounts of the cures: some of them edifying, some of them not so. We have, in fact, exactly the same phenomena as occur at Lourdes. Unless our idea of the universe is so materialistic that we do not believe in answer to prayer, we can still believe that many of the events thus recorded are true. We have seen that the influence of religious fervour may, and does, cure disease of various types. The whole phenomenon is in fact just what we have described above. But in dignity, in edification, and in power, the narratives are completely different from those of the Gospel. They do not represent a real analogy, and their

value is of exactly the same character as other
records of answer to prayer and of faith-healing.

IV

The third way of explaining away miracles
is that of coincidence. This is particularly
applied to the healing of the centurion's servant
as recorded in S. Matthew and S. Luke. The
circumstances, it will be remembered, are very
striking, and the incident is recorded because
it represents an instance of faith in one who was
not an Israelite. It was introduced into the
collection of discourses called 'Q' as an
introduction to a very remarkable saying of
our Lord. So widespread was the belief in
His power that a Roman soldier came to Him
to ask Him to heal his servant. He does not
even think it necessary for Jesus to come to him,
because he believes that His spiritual power is
as great in its sphere as that of the Roman
centurion, who can issue his orders to his
subordinates and knows that they will be
obeyed. Jesus comments on the greatness of
the faith shewn. He emphasizes the fact that
it is not by a Jew but by a Gentile, and
promises that what is asked shall be done.
When the centurion reaches home he finds
his servant restored to life.

Two explanations are offered of this event. One is that the record of the success of the miracle which is contained in somewhat different language in S. Matthew and S. Luke is not historical, and that no miracle ever happened. We venture to think that it is hardly credible that this story should have been remembered and recorded if it was one from which no successful result issued. It is making demands which are somewhat excessive on our credulity to ask us to believe in so much simpleness on the part of those who followed and narrated the acts of our Lord.

The other explanation is that here we have a coincidence, and stories are given to support this of what are called coincidences which have happened in life at other times. These other coincidences represent in one form or another the power of prayer; and are we as religious people willing to admit that prayer has no power in the world? If there be any reality in the spiritual order of the universe, prayer must have power. Of course it is quite possible that on any one occasion a coincidence might occur, but the chances against it are enormous, and chances against coincidences of this sort happening often in the life of our Lord or existing to such an extent as to create the belief in His miraculous powers, become incredible. It really makes a greater strain on our belief to ascribe

miracles to pure coincidences than to believe
that our Lord could exercise spiritual power in
the world.

V

The fourth explanation which is offered is
that miracles are symbolical. A very good
instance of this is the story of the walking on
the sea. This is described as follows :—

"However this may be, it seems likely that
S. Peter's confident undertaking to walk on the
sea, the failure of his faith, his rescue by Jesus,
and his return to establish the belief of his
brethren that Jesus is 'of a truth the Son of
God,' are a symbolical representation of S.
Peter's readiness to go with Jesus 'both to
prison and to death,' of his subsequent denial,
of his restoration and commission by the risen
Christ, and of the confirmation of the Early
Church in the faith of the Resurrection. If
such be the symbolism of the story, we shall
attach less importance to it in its present form,
as evidence for a fact of history." [1]

This same principle we find applied to other
miracles, and in particular in S. John's Gospel.
The turning of the water into wine at the
marriage feast in Cana of Galilee, the five
porches at Bethesda, the five husbands of the

[1] *Miracles in the New Testament*, by the Rev. J. M.
Thompson, p. 74.

woman of Samaria, are all given a spiritual
interpretation. It has always been remarked
that one of the characteristics of the miracles
of our Lord is that they were not only means
of doing good in His lifetime, but often formed
the basis of some of His most spiritual discourses.
That has generally been accepted as corroborative evidence of the reality of the miracles.
Jesus was not a mere magician or thauma-
turgist; He did not merely try to influence
people by the wonders He was able to accomplish. With perhaps one or two apparent
exceptions His miracles were always adapted to
the spiritual character of His mission. He had
come to seek and to save the lost, to shew the
love of God to man. He drew His spiritual
teaching from His miracles as from other
incidents in His daily life. Now we are asked
to reverse the process. The miracles are really
parables, whether parables of Jesus or parables
of the Early Church. They were not intended
to be looked upon as actual events. It was not
the spiritual teaching which was to be derived
from the miracle, but the miracle was created
by the teaching.

If we wish to find out whether any such
method of explanation is the true one, our aim
should always be to ascertain how far the
principle is capable of application. It will
generally be found that such an explanation

x

when adopted will explain in a way which is not
unnatural one or more miracles, but so soon as
we attempt to carry it out completely at all
it becomes frigid and unreal. No doubt the
story of S. Peter's walking on the water is
entirely in accordance with his character. With
his usual impulsiveness he rushes to his Master
at once, then the sea overwhelms him and it is
only through Jesus that he is saved. But surely
the fact that the story harmonizes with a person's
character does not prove that it was invented.
In this case the story is natural; but when we
get elaborate symbolical meanings attached to
such stories as the healing of the sick man at
Bethesda—to take an instance—we see how
unreal and frigid the general method is. It is
possible, of course, that the desire to be edifying
may have helped occasionally to mould the
story. We do not expect infallibility in any
record which comes to us through human hands ;
but once apply the principle of symbolical interpretation at all fully, and its unreality becomes
apparent. In particular it will not help us to
explain the general evidence for the miraculous character of our Lord's life. It was
because people believed that our Lord worked
miracles that they came to Him, and they
recorded miracles of Him because they believed
that He worked them. The general belief in
His miraculous character could not have been

created by symbolism, although symbolism
might make use of the belief. The idea of
symbolism would only extend to later possible
developments, and even then it generally appears
very far-fetched.

VI

There is one miracle to which we must
refer more particularly, namely, the miraculous
feeding in the wilderness. That is, of course,
one of the most difficult of the miracles in the
New Testament. At the same time it is also
one of the best supported. If, as is possible,
the feeding of the four thousand and the feeding
of the five thousand are doublets, being independent records of the same event, it is
obvious that the story must go back to the
very beginnings of the formation of the Gospel
narrative, and the record in S. John, with
the additional details that he gives makes the
event more probable. Now as to the explanations of it. They have been collected for us
by Schweitzer in his work on the *Quest of the
Historical Jesus*, and Mr Thompson gives us
a convenient summary of them :

" To the school of Bahrdt and Venturini it
is a trick carried out by a secret society. Paulus
explains it as the sharing of supplies among a

crowd of people, encouraged by Jesus' example.
Hase suggests that there is nothing more unnatural in the sudden increase of bread, than in
the gradual growth of corn from seed-time to
harvest.   Strauss believes that the story is a
myth, based on Old Testament parallels (the
manna in the desert, or the miracle of Elisha).
A disciple of Venturini suggests that rich friends
sent an unexpected supply of food into the
desert." [1]

How extraordinarily unreal and incredible
are explanations such as these, inconsistent with
one another, and all alike repugnant to common-
sense! Nor do we think that later suggestions are more credible.   Let us hear what
Mr Thompson says :

" What really happened was that Jesus, in
a parable analogous to that of the Sower,
compared His teaching to food—not to ordinary
food, but to miraculous food, which satisfies all
who receive it, and increases, instead of diminish-
ing, as it is more widely distributed (this explains
the twelve basketfuls left over, which otherwise
add a quite unnecessary miracle).   The change
of such a parable into a real event is not difficult
to understand." [2]

Then he goes on to suggest that the most
valuable clue to the meaning of the narrative
is supplied by the Eucharist :

[1] Thompson, *Miracles in the New Testament*, p. 45.
  Ov. cit., p. 46.

" Suppose an original incident, the exact nature of which we cannot now determine, but which must have been remarkable enough to impress itself upon the memory of the Apostles, to be compared with the stories of the Old Testament prophets (1 Kings xvii. 8-16 ; 2 Kings iv. 42-44) ; and to be regarded at a comparatively early date as a miracle. This incident may have been transformed, by the pious imagination of a later generation, into the original institution of the Agapê and Eucharist. Then the account of it would be assimilated to the actual experience of Christian worship." And he concludes, " It is difficult to see why, unless there was some such eccles- iastical motive for its preservation, the story of this miracle should have appeared six times in the Gospels, and always with such an amount of detail. The fact that it is so often described is not a sign that the Evangelists were par- ticularly sure that it happened, but rather that it was particularly appropriate to the needs of those for whom they wrote." [1]

It is really very difficult to believe that things should have happened in this way. As a matter of fact so far as historical evidence goes, the spiritual explanation comes second, and the miracle first. The miracle was widely known. The spiritual explanation comes only in S. John's Gospel, and the discourse in which it is contained is generally said by critics

[1] Thompson, *op. cit.*, p. 47.

to be unhistorical.   Now we are asked to believe
that there was unknown spiritual teaching
which was somehow or other transformed into
a miracle, and that then later new spiritual
teaching was derived from it.   But would
such spiritual teaching, or such a possible
institution of the Eucharist, of which we have
not the slightest evidence, have had the effect
upon the development of our Lord's career
which this event appears to have had ?   It was
clearly an epoch in its development, and that
because of the expectations which its miraculous
character created.   What we feel throughout
is that again and again a strain is put upon our
powers of belief by the attempt to explain away
a straightforward and natural story.

We have reviewed in this chapter the various
explanations which have been put forward for
these miracles of our Lord.   The ultimate
question is whether the explanations or the
miracles are the more probable under the conditions under which these events occurred.   We
have to remember that we are dealing with the
beginnings of a religion which has had a most
profound influence on the world.   We have to
remember the belief which the Church has
always held as to the Person of our Lord.   If
this belief be true, the difficulty of believing
in the miracles will for many persons at any
rate cease, the difficulty in believing in these

explanations will always be equally great; they will only gain an appearance of probability if we have already made up our minds that the miracles cannot have happened. It is argued that the miracles are not true, therefore it is necessary to find some origin for these stories, and the result is the following curious position :—

"It would be a mistake," says Mr Thompson, "to rely entirely upon any one method of interpretation where the subject-matter is so obscure. The tendency to transform natural events into supernatural, the love of assimilation, the ease with which an editor can give a new turn to a passage, and the influence of present interests upon the representation of the past— all these have played their part in the formation of the miracle stories as they now stand. If there is the greater difficulty in choosing the best method of interpretation, there is the greater confidence that by one or other it will be possible to arrive at an approximate reconstruction of the original non-miraculous facts."[1]

No passage can illustrate better than this the assumption underlying these explanations. It is assumed that the miracles are untrue, and therefore it is necessary to discover a theory which will explain how the stories grew up. It is only under such conditions that these

[1] Thompson, *op. cit.*, p. 51.

explanations are likely to appear credible.　They are not the reasons which have led to the miracles being disbelieved ; they are arguments which are discovered to support a belief which is already assumed.

LECTURE IX

THE NATURE OF MIRACLES

Summary of Preceding Lectures. Definition of Miracles.
What are They? Other Classes of Miracles. Miracles
of the Old Testament. Miracles of Church History.
Modern Miracles. The Evidential Value of Miracles.
At the Beginning of Christianity. Value of Miracles
at the Present Day.

WE have covered in the preceding lectures a
considerable amount of ground, and discussed
the question before us from various points of
view. It remains in our concluding lecture to
attempt to bring together the different threads,
and arrive at some conclusion as to the meaning
and purpose of miracles.

I

In our first lecture we suggested five main
lines on which miracles had been criticized.
First of all miracles are impossible because they
are violations of the law of nature. We dis-

cussed this question from the point of view of modern science, and shewed that 'laws of nature' could mean nothing more than the sum of our experience. Therefore to say that miracles were contrary to the laws of nature only meant that they were contrary to experience; but this they must be or they would not be miracles. Nor because anything is contrary to experience is it therefore impossible, because every new discovery means something which is contrary to experience. The uniformity of nature means only that like causes produce like effects. If therefore any new cause of whatever nature intervenes, a new effect will be produced. Nor is there any reason for eliminating freedom from nature; what indeed may be the origin or cause of phenomena we do not know, but there is no evidence to prove that the progress of the world has been the inevitable result of the forces existing from the beginning. New and incalculable forces and new phenomena have appeared as the world has developed.

The whole idea of inevitableness in the laws of nature has arisen from confusing the discoveries of science with philosophical systems which were supposed to be developed from it. All such reconstructions of nature are only attempts, generally quite inadequate, to explain the world from a particular point of view. The minds of men have been filled with mathematical and mechanical ideas. They have constructed a world on that basis, and have imagined that it is the real world. So it has been with the conception of God. They have constructed a mathematical and mechanical God, and then said that miracles were not consistent with His nature. But if we look upon God as Wisdom, if we realize that what we call the order of nature is merely the expression of His will, then there is nothing inconsistent in the idea of miracles with Him as we know Him. They would represent, if you like to put it so, the law of the divine wisdom.

Is it then improbable that there should be miracles ? We can attempt to answer this question from two points of view. We can ask, Does the course of this world suggest that at any period new and strange events should happen ? We ventured to suggest that it does ; that as a matter of fact there have been completely new departures in the history of the world. There was such a new departure when life appeared, there was such an one when the human being—a man with the power of thought —first came into existence. So it was not unreasonable to think that there should be a new and higher departure at a certain stage in the history of the human race accompanied by events which might seem marvellous. If, on the other hand, we look at it from the point of view which our conception of God would suggest, it was congruous that He, inasmuch as He loved mankind, should in His own time reveal Himself to man, and should give adequate signs of such a revelation. Moreover miracles would in relation to mankind be a natural means of accrediting a revelation. There is no reason, then, to think on *a priori* grounds that miracles could not take place. The real question was whether they had. We must examine the evidence without prejudice.

We then turned to the evidence for Christian miracles and found that it was good evidence, that criticism had failed to account on a naturalistic basis for the rise of Christianity, that the Gospels were early documents capable of giving good evidence, and that there was no sign of a primitive non-miraculous Christianity. Miracles harmonize with the spiritual message of Jesus. They were acts of mercy, they always conveyed a spiritual message. There was great self-restraint exhibited throughout our Lord's career, and the narratives harmonize with the conception of His person suggested by the story of the Temptation. So far as we could judge, these miracles, and particularly that of the Resurrection, had had a direct influence on the founding of the Church of the Apostles. Historically we found that a large part of the criticism of miracles had arisen because, on other grounds than historical evidence, people ceased to believe them. Although we had no reason for believing in the infallibility of the Gospels, they gave good evidence for the life of our Lord, and for miracles as part of His life. It might be, however, possible that in particular cases mistakes had arisen in relation to this or that miracle, as in regard to other historical facts.

We then finally discussed the question whether we could explain the way in which New Testament miracles had arisen. To say that because some miracles were false therefore all must be false, or because evidence in some cases was bad therefore all must be bad, was, we held, an unsound method of argument. We must ask whether, as a matter of fact, we can explain the miracles. With regard to the explanations offered, we noticed that that of faith-healing practically admits the miracle, and therefore the value of evidence for miracles; that in other cases the explanations were as improbable as the miracles, while the co-operation of so many different explanations seem exceedingly improbable. We may conclude in this connexion with a passage from Mr Knox in that work of his called *Some Loose Stones*, which hardly seems to be an over-statement.

" Orthodox theology explains all the miracles

recorded of our Saviour under one single hypothesis, He was omnipotent God. But the enemy of miracle is forced to give a variety of different explanations ; that the healing of the sick was faith-healing, the stilling of the storm coincidence, the feeding of the five thousand a misrepresented Sacrament, the withering of the fig tree a misrepresented parable, the raising of Lazarus a case of premature burial, and so on. Certainly it does seem odd that all these non-miraculous events should have combined to create a presumption of the miraculous." [1]

I think that a study of all these varied methods of eliminating the miraculous will convince us that they have been adopted to support a belief already formed against the miraculous. Men do not reject the stories because of the explanations, but they find out the explanations because they already disbelieve the stories. And in the ultimate analysis it is not reason which causes this disbelief but a limited imagination. Our minds are so clogged and warped by the overwhelming influence of ordinary experience that we cannot imagine or realize or believe what so completely transcends our experience. Once let a man's life be illuminated by the reality of faith which will lift him above the prejudice which sense creates, and he finds no difficulty in believing, for the

---

[1] *Some Loose Stones,* by Ronald Knox, p. 49.

belief is rational. But we allow our minds to
be so overpowered by the prejudice which
sensuous and material things create that we
cannot imagine anything happening contrary to
what we perceive, and therefore we do not
believe. But our disbelief is not rational. It is
the result of the tyranny of an imagination
limited by what our sense can teach it.

II

It will be remembered that at the beginning
of these lectures we decided to postpone the
question of definition until the end of our
enquiries. I do not know that I am yet
prepared to give a formal and precise definition
of what a miracle is, but I think that it may be
possible to go so far as to suggest a description
of what we mean by the miraculous on the
lines to which the preceding lectures have been
leading up. I would like to do it in the words
which I used some time ago when discussing
this subject at the Church Congress at Middles-
borough—"A miracle means really the supremacy
of the spiritual forces of the world to an extraordinarily marked degree over the mere material."

Now I would point out, to begin with, that
this definition seems to be in accordance with
the language of the New Testament. Through-

out, it is to the work of the Holy Spirit that
miracles are ascribed. According to S. Matthew
Mary was "found with child of the Holy
Ghost." According to the word of the angel
in S. Luke, "The Holy Ghost shall come upon
thee, and the power of the Most High shall
overshadow thee." Jesus will "baptize with
the Holy Ghost and with fire." He "was led
up of the Spirit into the wilderness." It is "by
the Spirit of God" that He "casts out devils,"
and to say that it is by Beelzebub is blasphemy
against the Spirit. It was through the Spirit
that our Lord was raised, and that same Spirit
will quicken our mortal bodies. Miracles are
worked in the power of the Spirit.

Now this truth will, I believe, best enable
us to understand what we mean by miracle,
and how God works miracles. Of course, it is
simple enough to say that miracles are worked
by God. God can do all things ; therefore, to
say that they are His work is sufficient. So
perhaps in a sense it is, but we must recognize
that God's revelation is intended to be rational
and will suggest to us an explanation of things
which is rational. Nor do hard and dogmatic
assertions of what God must do really tend to
win assent.

We believe that there is a spiritual nature
in man responsive to the divine Spirit, and the
spiritual nature can influence what we call our

material nature. It often does so; in our own experience we have probably known cases where its influence has been very great. It is not therefore unreasonable or irrational to believe that that spiritual nature can be so strengthened and inspired by God's Spirit as to make its powers more effective, and enable it still more to overcome weakness or cure the ills of our natural bodies. It is something that we believe as being in harmony with all that we know of spiritual life; only through God's Spirit working in and through Jesus Christ it is much intensified.

Nor is it out of harmony with all we know of the working of God in nature to believe that, as even Paulus thought, "Through holy inspiration Mary receives the hope and the power of conceiving her exalted Son, in whom the Spirit of the Messiah takes up its dwelling." Her nature was inspired and strengthened by God's Spirit, so that she could become the mother of Him who was the Son of God.

But as God is also the creator and sustainer of the universe, and as the Spirit of God works in the world, it is that Spirit which must represent the fundamental cause of all things. We know, in fact, nothing more of the material world than that it is the manner in which the universe is revealed to our senses. It is not therefore impossible or unreasonable that miracles should take place in nature, as well as in man. God's Spirit is working in nature. He who was incarnate as Jesus Christ was Himself the Word of God through whom all things were made. It was Tertullian, as we saw in our first lecture who first realized that it was not inconsistent with the nature of Jesus Christ that He as the Word of God should reveal Himself in and through His power over nature. We can, I think, then give a perfectly rational explanation of nature - miracles. A miracle is not inconsistent with the ordinary manifestations of phenomena, because it represents simply the ultimate nature of things asserting themselves.

I would here add one thing more. If I am asked whether this or that miracle is credible or not, the answer that I would give would be this: I do not see that we can set any limits to the power of God's Spirit; I cannot limit the power of God to suit the limitations of my own imagination. Only I would say to others that if this or that event seems to anyone incredible, there is no reason why a man should feel compelled to say or think that he believes it. This is surely one of those cases for the exercise of suspension of judgement. We have only to realize how limited our knowledge is, how very much our imagination is shackled by the particular experience to which we have been subject. If, then, to us the message of the Gospel and the revelation through Jesus Christ seems reasonable and true, I do not feel that we should trouble ourselves if some particular incident causes us difficulties. I have frankly confessed throughout, that while the evidence that we have for miracles as a whole is good, the character of the Gospel narrative is not such as to enable us to be certain that every event took place exactly as it is reported. There are discrepancies in some cases between the narratives, which make us feel that neither account can be absolutely accurate. What the limits of error may be, it may not be possible to judge, but no difficulty about any detail ought to prevent us from accepting the general teaching of the Gospel.

And then finally, it is, we believe, through the Holy Spirit that Jesus was raised from the dead in a spiritual body, and that we too, like Him, shall be raised. It is sown a natural body ; it is raised a spiritual body. With all that representation of ourselves in a concrete form by which we are known, through which our character is expressed, in relation to which all our human functions are developed, shall we be raised. Our Lord did not appear to His disciples as a disembodied spirit, but clothed with a spiritual body, and our resurrection must be not as a mere disembodied spirit, but

clothed with such a body as will express our
personality.[1]

III

I would venture to suggest that a conception
of miracles such as that given above may help
us in our attitude towards other miracles than
those of the New Testament.   And first, what
is our attitude towards Old Testament miracles ?
Here the fundamental point undoubtedly is that
the evidence for Old Testament miracles is not
good.   If we compare it for a moment with that
for the New Testament miracles, the difference

[1] In connexion with the above view of miracles, I may
perhaps refer to an article in the *Church Quarterly Review*,
vol. lxx. 1910, April, p. 117, by the Rev. Robert Vaughan,
a theologian whose work is less known than it should be.
He has thus summed up his views :

"Miracle is a revelation of the latent possibility of
things—of what they can become by divine activity within
them.   The whole of nature is by its creation so constituted
that it can, according to its very *nature*, become what it is
not in itself.   It has a capacity to receive what it does not
contain, and the isolated miracles, of Christ in particular, are
to reveal this capacity.   Such changes are not from the
thing as it is in itself—and therefore not properly products
of 'nature,' nor are they contradictions of the natural—for
things of nature are created with a fitness for such transformation and evolution ; but they are supra-natural by
virtue of a communication to their nature of a fresh activity
from their source."

in character is very great. The books of the Old
Testament, those for example which narrate the
miracles of Moses, were in their present form
probably produced nearly a thousand years after
the events they describe, and it is very doubtful
how far back the material out of which they
were put together reaches. The testimony for
the miracles of Elijah and Elisha is somewhat
better. The books in which they occur were
compiled within a few hundred years of the
events. They were undoubtedly put together
out of much older material, and these narratives
are written in the best style of Hebrew prose
and appear to be largely historical. But even
this testimony is very different from that for
the New Testament miracles. Broadly speaking, then, we can say that the evidence is not
good.

But having said that, there are other points
we must notice. The great body of Old Testament miracles, certainly those which would
claim to be accepted, centre round two epochs.
The one, the departure from Egypt and the
first religious creation of the nation ; the other,
the great religious revival connected with the
names of Elijah and Elisha. The events connected with the departure from Egypt are so
far back in history that it is very difficult for us
to know what really happened. But of this we
can be certain, that there was an original

creative period for the religion of the Jews, which first separated them from other nations, and set them on that strange line of development which had such a far-reaching effect on the future of mankind. Our difficulty in knowing what really happened is concerned as much with the non-miraculous as with the miraculous events ; but there is no reason for not believing that such an epoch in the history of what we believe to be true religion might involve the working of God's Spirit in the world in a particular manner, and that the events need not have been always quite normal.

The names of Elijah and Elisha again are associated with another great crisis in the religious history of the nation. They represent the prophetic activity in its highest stage before the creation of written prophecy ; they guarded the belief in the God of Israel against the insidious attacks of nature-worship ; they represented the beginnings of the movement which created the sublime monotheism of later Israel. Then, too, I can believe that there was a great outpouring of God's Spirit in Israel.

For if we doubt the evidence for the particular miraculous manifestations of the history of Israel, there can be no doubt of the miraculous character of the history as a whole. The selection of one nation to be the vehicle of God's revelation to mankind, the teaching through it of a lofty ethical monotheism, the building up of an elaborate cult which would enshrine and teach these ideals, the creation of a strong moral rule of life, the preparation for the coming of the Messiah, all would seem to imply the divine purpose running through the history of Israel and working on the principles of selection. God's Spirit was teaching mankind in the history of Israel.

And our position would be somewhat similar with regard to the miracles of the Christian Church. The Holy Spirit has always worked in the Church. His power has been shewn in the moral, the spiritual, and the religious sphere, in the sanctity, the purity, the self-sacrifice, and the devotion of countless numbers of Christians. It has been shewn also in the silent spiritual life of many. It has enabled them to overpower the weakness of their bodies. It was shewn undoubtedly in the days of the Early Church in spiritual power over those possessed with diseases; it has probably been shewn in all ages to a greater or lesser degree by the power of the sanctified human mind over the body. To what further degree miracles may have happened must be a question of evidence. What I would put before you is that on no grounds is it necessary for us to bar out miracles or to make a sharp distinction between the time of our Lord and other periods in the

Christian Church, or to say that miracles in the Church could not happen. In a very large number of cases undoubtedly the evidence is poor and unsatisfactory; in some cases it is obviously legendary. There are many cases in which we should feel inclined to exercise some sort of suspension of judgement. What I would ask is that the possibility of miracles should not be ruled out. Nor even at the present day should we doubt that the human mind strengthened and inspired by God's Spirit has great power over the human body and over other minds. We know that faith must play a large part in life, that it plays a large part, too, in recovery from sickness. Because undoubtedly there is a good deal of superstition and even fraud connected with theories of faith-healing and so on, that is no reason for doubting either the power of the mind over the body, or still less the power of the sanctified mind over the body.

IV

It remains to consider the evidential value of miracles. This is a subject on which the most varied opinions have been held. While Spinoza thought that miracles could not give any evidence of the nature of God, Paley, and to a certain extent Butler, were prepared to rest the evidence for revelation upon them ; and Mozley argues that they are necessary. A less trenchant position is occupied by Dr Illingworth. He insists on the fact that miracles never are, nor were, a primary proof of the Incarnation. That is a spiritual fact, and therefore must be spiritually discerned. "No conceivable amount of evidence that was merely material could prove it." But although miracles are not proof of the Incarnation, the Incarnation makes miracles credible, and the miracles strengthen the evidence.

"This then was the original evidence on which the Incarnation was received. It was the gradual self-revelation of a Person to spiritually minded persons. But among the attributes of this Person was included the power of working miracles : and there cannot be a shadow of doubt that this was an integral element in the total impression which He produced. His miracles do not prove His character, but they essentially confirmed the claim which His character meanwhile predisposed men to accept."[1]

In dealing with the evidential value of miracles we must distinguish between their value in the first days of Christianity and that at the present time. As regards the beginnings

[1] *Divine Immanence*, by J. R. Illingworth, chapter iv., p. 90. Ed. 1900.

of Christianity, it is a question of fact. How
did the disciples come to believe in their Master ?
To believe was, we must remember, something
that made great claims on their insight and
imagination. Here was one quite unlike
prophet or sage such as Israel had known, one
quite unlike the Christ that they expected.
How did they come to believe on Him ? The
answer is that His personality gradually
impressed itself upon them, and by miracles was
the true nature of His personality revealed. It is
quite true that it was not the miracles alone that
attracted men to Him. It is quite true that
alone they might not have been effective, that
they were able to repel as well as to attract.
His authority, His power, the dignity of His
claims, the beauty of His nature, the truth of
His teaching, all these joined in the general
impression created. We may recognize to the
full other influences, but we shall always have to
recognize that miracles were an essential
element in this impression, and we may well
ask whether His followers could have come to
Him first if He had not worked miracles.
That is one of the questions which we naturally
ask, and cannot answer. Yet the fact remains
that the only account we have of how men
came to Him puts miracles in the forefront
of His credentials.

And equally is it the case with the miracle

of the Resurrection. We have simply to ask the question: What, as a matter of fact, was it which gave the disciples courage to believe in Jesus in spite of His death on the cross? The answer must be definite and decisive. They believed in Him because they believed in a miracle, namely, the Resurrection, and that they had good grounds for their belief. We may recognize, of course, that this was not the only cause: there were the memories of the Master, there were their own spiritual experiences, there was the gift of the Spirit, there was the testimony of the Old Testament studied in the light of newer revelation. All these elements helped to strengthen their belief, but the fact remains that only by a miracle, and because of a miracle, had they courage to believe.

Statements, then, such as that miracles cannot prove anything do not really count; they are contradicted by fact. The first disciples preached Christianity because they believed that miracles had taken place.

Nor can I quite subscribe to the remark of Dr Illingworth that a miracle is something material. It is something, of course, that comes to us through a material environment, as in fact everything which appeals to our senses and all, or almost all, our knowledge must come. But the whole essence of a miracle is that it is spiritual:

it is a sign of the working of God's Spirit, and therefore takes its place with all the other spiritual evidence. So it is able to appeal to us in relation to spiritual things. Our answer then to the first question as to the evidential value of miracles at the beginning of Christianity must be that they were, as a matter of fact, a part, and a very important part, of what made people believe in Christianity.

But now what of our own time ? We are clearly in a very different position. On the one hand, we can only have second-hand evidence of the miracles of the past; on the other hand, we are able to know what Christianity is very much better than those to whom it was first preached. They had nothing to go on : Christianity had no authority, no prestige, no apparent power or position. It seemed to contradict many of the religious prejudices and habits of the time. Now it comes to us with the authority, the history, the experience of nearly nineteen centuries. Most people accept Christianity nowadays because of the fact of its existence, because of the authority of the Church (however people may define that term), through which it comes. And then secondly, because it responds to their spiritual needs and experience. It is only later that they investigate its claims, and then, of course, only some people do so. And when we come

to the investigation of claims, the number of
lines of study are many. There is the connexion
of the Old and New Testament, there is the
transformation of the human mind in Christianity,
there is the growth and power of the Church,
there is the work that Christianity has done.
But all the same ultimately we come to the
fact of a revelation, and in relation to that
miracles seem to take a natural place.

Here are events certainly very remarkable
in their character, and in what was accomplished.
From small, apparently insignificant beginnings,
there came a new departure in the history of
the world. How great was the change may
be seen by comparing any typical Christian
literature with anything that had preceded it.
The transformation of the possibilities of human
nature is enormous. How great the change
is we can see from the different points of view
from which we approach Christian history. No
doubt there was failure, disappointment, dis-
illusionment. It is not what we might look
for as an ideal ; but consider what it is compared
with any other history in its hopes, its ideals,
and aspirations.

Now what was the cause of this change in
history ? The answer that Christianity gives is
first of all the Incarnation, the coming to earth
of God in human form. Here we have a great
miracle—an event abnormal from the point

of view of human experience, although not from the point of view of divine wisdom, for it was part of the purpose and fore-knowledge of God. The Incarnation itself is what Butler calls 'a secret miracle'—one that took place without any knowledge of it being possible ; but it was witnessed to by a series of events which in their totality are quite unprecedented : the appearance of a unique personality, a new and inspired teacher, a great outpouring of spiritual power, shewn in an abnormal and miraculous supremacy of the spiritual over the natural, and the intensification of the spiritual experience of human life : all these form part of one self-consistent series of phenomena. They seem to corroborate one another, to witness to the unique event of which they tell us, and to be in harmony with it.

Now here, surely, we have an adequate cause for all that comes afterwards. And I would ask you in conclusion quietly to think of all these phenomena, and ponder over them, to consider whether they do not harmonize together and form in their harmony very strong evidence. The marvellous manifestation of spiritual life is witnessed to by its effect in the world, and is the natural result of the life of Him who came amongst men. Clearly there was something that happened, something which had an immense influence on the history of mankind. The answer which Christian history gives to the question, What was it? is: 'The Manifestation of Jesus Christ the Son of God, and the new power that He brought into the world.'

INDEX

N.B.—*References in thick type* (159) *refer to passages where the subject mentioned is fully discussed.*

P

Palestine, extent of education in, 193
Paley, Archdeacon William, 43, **45**, 68, 344
Panama Canal, the, 102
Pantheism, 21, 30, 120, **121** *et seq.*
Panthera, 288
Papias of Hierapolis, 179, 190, 195
Paralytic man, healing of the, 199
Paul, S. : Epistles of, 181
    character and temperament, 235
    evidence on the Resurrection, 247
    his witness to miracles, 230
Paulus, H. E. S., **47**, 63, 69, 132, 323, 337
Pearson, Karl, 81, 119
Personal God, belief in, 59
Peter, S., 190, 191, 193, 320, 322
    rebuke of, 214
Petrine tradition, the, 229
Philostratus, 15
Physiology, 102
Pilgrims' Way, the, 317
Presuppositions, theological, 57
Prophecy in S. Matthew's Gospel, 291
Protevangelium of James, 296
Purpose in the world, 138

Q

" Q," 100, **168**, **169**, **183** *et seq.*
Quadratus, 11
Quirinius, 276

R

Rabbis, 194
Rachel, 292
Rackham, Rev. R. B., 168
Raising the dead, 228
Ramsay, Sir William, 167, 169
Rashdall, Dr, 258
Rationalism, 132
Relativism, 128
Renan, Ernest, 54, 310
Resurrection, the, 53, 60, 106, 145, **244** *et seq.*, 332, 347
    apostolic witness to, 191
    belief of Church universal, 244
    character of the evidence, 247
    evidence of S. Paul, 247
    evidence of the Gospels, 252
    influence on the disciples, 262
    Jewish reports concerning the, 255
    possibility of imposture, 267
    the appearances of our Lord, 260
    the empty tomb, 249, **253**
    explanations of the, 49, 263
    the Resurrection body, 251
Revelation, 35, 139
    miracles as evidence for, 59, 332
    signs of a, 141
Revolution, the French, 46, 154
Rickaby, Rev. J., 22
Röntgen rays, 90

S

Samaria, woman of, 320, 321
Sanday, Dr William, 173
Schechter, Dr, 174

PRINTED BY
OLIVER AND BOYD
EDINBURGH

BY THE SAME AUTHOR

St Paul and Christianity

Crown 8vo.   5s. net.

THE purpose of this book is to examine the writings of St Paul as a whole in the light of other early Christian teaching, and to show, as the writer maintains, that Paulinism does not represent any new departure in Christian thought, but the natural development of fundamental Christian principles, the germs of which are to be found in the teaching of Christ, and of the Primitive Church.

"We have pleasure in recommending this study of St Paul as an independent analysis of his writings, giving a valuable estimate of their teaching as it appears to a scholar of recognised standing among ourselves. It will help to correct the extravagances of some of the theories that have appeared on the Continent."— *Church Family Newspaper.*

History, Authority, and Theology

Large Crown 8vo.   6s. net.

I. The Sources and Authority of Dogmatic Theology.
II. The New Theology.
III. The Athanasian Creed.
IV. The Church of England and the Eastern Churches.
V. The Teaching of the Russian Church.
VI. Methods of the Early Church.
VII. The Church of the Apostolic Fathers.

"There is a calm frankness, an obviously deep sincerity, and a width of view about the writer's method which is eminently reassuring. His wide and deep learning gives a sound foundation, and on that foundation he builds with a combination of enthusiasm and common sense which is too rare among the theologians of to-day."—*Guardian.*

LONDON: JOHN MURRAY.

SOME PRINCIPLES OF LITURGICAL REFORM.
A Contribution towards the Revision of the Book of Common Prayer. By the Rev. W. H. FRERE, D.D., of the Community of the Resurrection. New and Cheaper Edition. Crown 8vo. 2s. 6d. net.

ENGLISH CHURCH WAYS. Described to Russian
Friends in Four Lectures delivered at St Petersburg in 1914. By W. H. FRERE, D.D., of the Community of the Resurrection. Crown 8vo, 2s. 6d. net.

A CHAIN OF PRAYER ACROSS THE AGES. Forty
Centuries of Prayer, B.C. 2000—A.D. 1912. Compiled and Arranged for Daily Use by SELINA FITZHERBERT FOX, M.D., B.S. Square Demy 8vo, 5s. net.

ROME, ST PAUL AND THE EARLY CHURCH,
showing the Influence of Roman Law on St Paul's Teaching and Phraseology, and on the Development of the Church. By the Rev. W. STEPHENS MUNTZ, D.D., Vicar of St John's, Upper Holloway. Large Crown 8vo. 5s. net.

THE MOVEMENT TOWARDS CATHOLIC REFORM
IN THE EARLY SIXTEENTH CENTURY. By G. V. JOURDAN, D.D., Rector of Rathbarry Castlefreke. Large Crown 8vo. 7s. 6d. net.

THE CANON LAW IN MEDIAEVAL ENGLAND. An
Examination of William Lyndwood's "Provinciale," in Reply to the late Professor F. W. Maitland. By the Rev. ARTHUR OGLE, M.A., Rector of Otham, Maidstone. Large Crown 8vo. 6s. net.

LANDMARKS IN THE HISTORY OF THE WELSH
CHURCH. By the Right Rev. the Lord Bishop of St Asaph. With Illustrations. Large Crown 8vo. 6s. net.

THE INFALLIBILITY OF THE CHURCH. By
GEORGE SALMON, D.D., sometime Provost of Trinity College, Dublin. New and Cheaper Edition. Large Crown 8vo. 2s. 6d. net.

LONDON: JOHN MURRAY.

THE BIBLE TO-DAY. The Second Part of a Charge
Delivered at his Primary Visitation, 1912. By the Rt. Rev.
BERTRAM POLLOCK, C.V.O., D.D., Bishop of Norwich. Demy 8vo.
2s. 6d. net.

The BISHOP OF LONDON in a letter says:—"I have read this book
with great delight. It will do much good."

HOURS OF INSIGHT and other Sermons. By the late
WILLIAM EDWARD COLLINS, D.D., Lord Bishop of Gibraltar.
Crown 8vo. 3s. 6d. net.

A CAMERA CRUSADE THROUGH THE HOLY
LAND. By DWIGHT L. ELMENDORF. With 100 Illustrations
from Photographs by the Author. 4to. 10s. 6d. net.

SOME FRENCH CATHEDRALS on French Gothic,
Bourges, Chartres, Amiens, Beauvais. The Times Series of Reprints.
1s. net.

"Five admirable articles which appeared in The Times are now
gathered into a dainty little volume."—Church Times.

MURRAY'S DICTIONARY OF CHRISTIAN BIO-
GRAPHY AND LITERATURE to the End of the Sixth Century.
With an Account of the Principal Sects and Heresies. Edited by the
Very Rev. HENRY WACE, D.D., Dean of Canterbury, and the Rev.
WILLIAM C. PIERCY, Dean and Chaplain of Whitelands College.
In 1 Vol. 1040 pages. Medium 8vo. 21s. net.

MURRAY'S ILLUSTRATED BIBLE DICTIONARY.
Combining Modern Research with Ancient Faith. Written by
Leading Scholars of To-day, and including the Results of Modern
Research. Edited by the Rev. WM. C. PIERCY, M.A. With
numerous Illustrations and Maps. 21s.; leather, 25s.

A SMALLER DICTIONARY OF THE BIBLE. By
Sir WM. SMITH, D.C.L., LL.D. With Maps and Illustrations.
Large crown 8vo. 2s. 6d. net.

LONDON: JOHN MURRAY.

THREE WORKS ON THE BIRTH OF THE ENGLISH CHURCH

By Sir HENRY H. HOWORTH, K.C.I.E.

With Illustrations. Demy 8vo, 12s. net each volume.

SAINT GREGORY THE GREAT.

"Sir Henry Howorth has written a life of 'Gregory the Great' which is marked with all the qualities of breadth of view, calm impartiality, soundness of judgment, accuracy of statement, and unfailing discrimination of outstanding facts and principles. No students of the beginnings of the Church of England can afford to neglect such a book, and much may be learned from it."—*Church of Ireland Gazette.*

SAINT AUGUSTINE OF CANTER-BURY.

"Learned, lucid, and always interesting."—*Athenæum.*

"The book is doubly valuable in that it not only throws light upon the work of the Augustine Mission, but also gives us an excellent and learned account of contemporary Christendom."—*Outlook.*

THE GOLDEN DAYS OF THE EARLY ENGLISH CHURCH.

Two volumes.

These volumes will complete the series on the Birth of the English Church, of which "St. Gregory the Great" and "St. Augustine of Canterbury" were the first parts. The authority with which these works have been written has been acknowledged by the leading and best-qualified scholars.

THE PSALMS IN HUMAN LIFE. New and Enlarged Edition. By ROWLAND E. PROTHERO, M.V.O. 2s. 6d. net.

THE TRUTH AND ERROR OF CHRISTIAN SCIENCE. By M. CARTA STURGE, Moral Science Tripos (Cambridge). 2s. 6d. net.

THE EARLY HISTORY OF THE CHURCH. From its Foundation to the End of the Fifth Century. Rendered into English from the Fourth Edition. By Monsignor L. DUCHESNE.

Vol. I. 9s. net.   Vol. II. 9s. net.

LONDON : JOHN MURRAY.